MAY
MODI
AZAD

Celebrating
30 Years of Publishing
in India

Praise for the Book

'The profound social shifts in the post-Modi BJP have been observed but rarely dissected minutely. Sudha Pai and Sajjan Kumar have filled this gap substantially in this study of Dalit politics in Uttar Pradesh following the decline of the BSP. The book has added immensely to our understanding of the political churning in India.'

—Swapan Dasgupta

'In *Maya, Modi, Azad*, Sudha Pai and Sajjan Kumar investigate the place of Dalits in Indian politics at a time when it is dominated by Hindutva nationalism. Reviewing the rise of Dalit politicians from the effort to form a "rainbow party with a Dalit core" to an era where fragmentation and sub-regionalization seem to be increasing, the book covers considerable ground with lucidity and thoroughness. A richly researched and insightful work on a crucial subject.'

—Shashi Tharoor

'Attempts to create an independent political party of, for and by Dalits were begun by Dr B.R. Ambedkar himself. The Scheduled Castes Federation established by him soon became the Republican Party of India. Subsequent history has shown the severe limits of such endeavours. Dalit political formations have not only suffered many splits, but their limited electoral success has required alliances with mainstream political parties, especially the BJP. A significant section of the Dalit community has indeed been influenced by the social, political, cultural and religious activities of Hindutva organizations. *Maya, Modi, Azad* examines this journey with admirable research. It will benefit all those interested in knowing the inherent contradictions, compromises and complexities in Dalit sociology-political movements in contemporary India.'

—Sudheendra Kulkarni

'How do we explain the simultaneity of Dalits' political outrage against atrocities and their electoral preference for the BJP? Sudha Pai and Sajjan Kumar offer a wide-ranging and nuanced engagement with the intriguing puzzle of Dalit politics in Uttar Pradesh today. This is the first comprehensive treatment of what the fragmentation of the Dalit movement and the fracturing of the Dalit vote portend for the future of Mayawati's BSP.'

—Niraja Gopal Jayal

'The analysis of Dalit politics by Professors Sudha Pai and Sajjan Kumar is an indispensable addition to the literature on Indian politics. They rightly focus on India's largest state, Uttar Pradesh, where Dalit politics took on its most explicitly institutional form, though there has been a significant drift of the Dalit vote recently towards the Hindu nationalist Bharatiya Janata Party (BJP), which controls the government in the state and at the center. Support from Dalits, at the bottom of the traditional Hindu caste hierarchy, is critically important to the BJP beyond their vote; it strengthens its case that Hindutva encompasses all Indians and rejects caste hierarchy. This drift of support also suggests the BJP is doing a better job at appealing to the current aspirations of many Dalits than the so-called secular parties. It also seems to confirm the argument of the late Susanne and Lloyd Rudolph that class plays a marginal role in Indian politics.'

—Walter Andersen

'In this timely and insightful book, Pai and Kumar analyse the reasons for the BSP's decline, whether and why Dalit voters are attracted to the BJP, and what the future politics of the state may hold. They outline the BSP's internal problems, detail the rise of smaller and more assertive Dalit organizations, and document the economic and cultural strategies successfully employed by the BJP to secure Dalit support. Their prognosis for autonomous Dalit politics in UP is bleak, but this book could contribute to debates about future directions. Drawing on decades of research and observation, *Maya, Modi, Azad* offers an engaging, accessible and illuminating account that helps readers navigate the tumultuous shifts in political alignments in Uttar Pradesh, and is essential reading for those interested in Dalit mobilization and its possibilities in India.'

—Hugo Gorringe

MAYA MODI AZAD

DALIT POLITICS IN THE TIME OF HINDUTVA

SUDHA PAI
SAJJAN KUMAR

HarperCollins *Publishers* India

First published in India by HarperCollins *Publishers* 2023
4th Floor, Tower A, Building No. 10, DLF Cyber City,
DLF Phase II, Gurugram, Haryana – 122002
www.harpercollins.co.in

2 4 6 8 10 9 7 5 3 1

Typeset in 11.5/115 Sabon LT Std at
Manipal Technologies Limited, Manipal

Printed and bound at
Replika Press Pvt. Ltd.

For Aisha, Amyra and Avyan

—Sudha Pai

For my parents

—Sajjan Kumar

Contents

Part III
New Stirrings: Emerging Dalit Organizations

8. Fragmentation of the Dalit Movement in UP   173

    Epilogue   191
    Acknowledgements   215
    Appendix   217
    Notes   229
    Bibliography   279
    Index   291

Prologue
Dalit Politics in the New Millennium

———∽∾———

Back in May 2017, in Jatav Nagar, a Dalit locality in Saharanpur town in western Uttar Pradesh, there was an animated discussion among community members on the shrinking base of the Bahujan Samaj Party (BSP) in the state because a significant section had embraced the BJP.[1] Saharanpur district with a high percentage of Dalits (21.3 per cent)[2] has long been a stronghold of the Dalit movement, including, many leaders who had worked with BSP founder Kanshi Ram in the 1990s. While some speakers were dismayed at this development, Nepal Singh, a relatively better-off businessman who had joined the BJP along with other BSP members in the town, while asserting that the BJP was more accommodative and inclusive of the Dalits culturally and socially, pointed to the inherent anti-Dalit approach of other parties, and the BSP's silence on the issue. When confronted with BJP leader Daya Singh's use of objectionable language against Mayawati that showed the anti-Dalit mindset among BJP leaders, Nepal Singh passionately argued that the saffron party took immediate action by suspending Daya Singh. He drew attention to what Samajwadi party (SP) leader Azad Khan had said just before the 2017 assembly elections that *Babasaheb ki uthee unglee ka matlab hai, samne jitni zameen hai, wo Dalit hadap le.*[3] His inference was that the insult to Dr Ambedkar was bigger than to Mayawati, but BSP cadres did not react. Did this place Mayawati, he argued, above Babasaheb?

The narrative mentioned above highlights how the changed Dalit landscape in India, during a short period of five years since the defeat of the BSP in 2012, offers a difficult analytical puzzle. Three rapidly shifting scenarios have emerged: the decline of the BSP and identity politics that once drove both electoral and mass politics in the Hindi heartland and shaped national politics; the shift of a considerable section of the Dalits towards the BJP and its redefined subaltern-Hindutva under Prime Minister Narendra Modi; and the protests against recurring atrocities and right-wing hegemony led by new Dalit organizations such as the Una Aytachar Ladat Samiti in Gujarat under Jignesh Mevani, the Vanchit Bahujan Aghadi in Maharashtra led by Prakash Ambedkar, and the Bhim Army/Azad Samaj Party by Chandrashekhar Azad in UP. In this scenario, two contrasting trends are visible in Dalit politics today, *political protest* against atrocities and *electoral preference* during elections for the BJP. Why does the political outrage of Dalits fail to translate into anger, electorally, against the BJP?

In the backdrop of this contradictory trend between the political and the electoral, we would like to tell the story of how and why the Dalit discourse has unfolded and responded to the changing socio-political contexts in the last one decade in general, and in the context of right-wing hegemony, in particular. The significance of our work is that it provides a narrative of the Dalit movement, and its representative party the BSP, from its dominant position in the 1990s. But more particularly from its high point of 2007—when after much struggle Mayawati was able to obtain an absolute majority—to the existential crisis the BSP is facing today, internally and due to the shift of a substantial number of Dalits towards the BJP, a right-wing, Hindutva-centric party. While detailing the rapid decline of the BSP, we discuss how Dalits, particularly a younger generation with new ideas and aspirations, have reacted to changes in UP politics in the new millennium.

While Dalit parties and organizations exist in a number of states, our focus is on the state of UP which provides a useful site for understanding this phenomenon. UP is the key state where Dalit politics has shaped democratic politics in the Hindi heartland and the country since the mid-1980s; as it sends eighty members to Parliament, it is often said that the road to New Delhi passes through Lucknow. Today, it is the state where the threefold nature of the Dalit crisis is clearly reflected: the existential predicament facing the BSP, simultaneously, the revival and reconstruction of the BJP from being an upper-caste-centric party to adopting a new subaltern approach of Dalit inclusion, and the emergence of sub-regional Dalit organizations that signal both the collapse of a pan-UP movement and the hope of rejuvenation in the future.

Equally important, it is the state where two strong leaders—Mayawati, using her sarvajan agenda attempted, though unsuccessfully, to create a new 'umbrella party' like the erstwhile Congress party with a Dalit core, and Narendra Modi, whose success in attracting a section of Dalits into the

saffron fold—have shaped Dalit politics in the 2000s. It is also
the state where a new Dalit leader, Chandrashekhar Azad,
poses a challenge to Hindutva hegemony and is attempting to
revive the Dalit movement based on the ideology of Kanshi
Ram and Dr Ambedkar in a more assertive way. It is this
triangular contestation and intersectionalities between Maya,
Modi and Azad, and the possibilities this presents that makes
our narrative interesting and of great significance for the future
of not only Dalit, but democratic politics in India.

Our work also assumes importance as little attention has
been paid to the BSP and the Dalit movement in the Hindi
heartland in recent years. There is proliferating literature on
the BJP since its revival under Narendra Modi. Attempts have
been made to address the construction of Hindu nationalism,
the 'Deep' majoritarian state, right-wing hegemony and its
impact on disadvantaged sections and minorities.[4] A number
of eminent scholars have collectively analysed the reasons
for the victory of the BJP in 2014, its core ideological
beliefs, economic policy and impact on secularism.[5] Others
have examined the reasons underlying the rise of Hindu
majoritarianism and the establishment of hegemonic power.[6]
Another genre, consisting of books and articles on the reasons
underlying the victory of the BJP in 2014 and 2019,[7] explains
the BJP machine and how it wins elections[8] and why the poor
and lower castes voted BJP.[9]

Most of the existing literature on the Dalit movement in the
Hindi heartland is about the BSP's poor electoral performance[10]
and decline since 2012,[11] the poor economic condition of
Dalits,[12] and the problems of reservation, rising caste atrocities,
protests and unemployment.[13] The rise of an educated class of
Dalits in neo-liberal India, who aspire for well-paying jobs in
the new private economy, has been documented.[14] Attention

has been given to the shift by a section of Dalits towards the
BJP following the Muzaffarnagar riots of 2013,[15] and how the
BJP has been able to obtain the support of other backward
classes (OBCs) and Dalits, though much of it is in the period
before the rise of Modi.[16] A recent volume explains the
'strategies' used by the Rashtriya Swayamsevak Sangh (RSS)
to absorb all social groups, including Dalits, reinterpret and
incorporate Dr Ambedkar, the political appeal of Hindutva
and how these strategies are reshaping Indian democracy.[17]
But there has been little sustained and comprehensive effort
to trace the trajectory of the Dalit movement in the Hindi
heartland, and the direction it is taking in the second and third
decade of the twenty-first century.

We fill this vacuum by tracing the trajectory of the Dalit
movement in UP, from the direction it has taken following the
decline of the Congress party that once drew Dalit support to
the rise of right-wing forces, the fragmentation of Dalits into a
number of groups and the decline of the BSP.[18] With the Dalit
movement under Mayawati facing an existential crisis and
entering a post-BSP phase, our book brings to the fore some
critical questions: What is the future of the BSP and Mayawati?
What is the significance of the rise of new Dalit organizations in
UP such as the Bhim Army? Why does a section of Dalits today
support the BJP electorally and culturally? Will the BJP be able
to sustain its subaltern reach and bring all Dalits into a 'Maha
Hindu' identity to realize its ideological vision? What are the
changes within a considerable section of the Dalit community
that have led to it supporting the BJP? Are they merely tactical
or longer-term cultural changes? Or, as well-known academic
and social activist Gail Omvedt once famously argued, there
has never been a 'full-blown, anti-caste movement' on the
Indian sub-continent.[19] In this prologue, we map some of the

major contours of our narrative, on the basis of which we will answer these questions.

I

The new millennium brought important changes which were to have a far-reaching impact on UP politics, particularly Dalit politics. The impact of globalization was 'late' in UP compared to the states of southern and western India due to a decade of hung assemblies and short-lived governments unable to take advantage of liberalization. The weakening of identity politics based on caste and religion created a feeling of being left behind and fuelled a yearning for economic development of the state and personal material advancement. Among Dalits specifically, with their having achieved a modicum of self-respect and dignity, there was a shift from the desire for social justice to economic aspiration for material advancement, impacted by both globalization and cultural modernization.[20] Consequently, in the first two decades of the twenty-first century, a new relationship between *caste, development, and electoral politics* emerged, that helps explain the decline of the BSP, the BJP's successful outreach to Dalits in a new form of inclusionary politics, as well as new stirrings leading to the emergence of Dalit organizations-cum-parties such as the Bhim Army/Azad Samaj Party and other emerging smaller Dalit organizations. While caste has not lost importance, there is a new relationship with the idea of development. Caste and identity alignments based on it had, in fact, been weakening since the late 1990s and, as a study argues, it alone was no longer a 'predictor of vote choice' and 'probably at its weakest for thirty years in 2012'.[21]

Closely linked to these transformative changes in UP society and polity are the tremendous changes witnessed in Dalit politics during the decade of the 2000s, and its representative party—the BSP. On the one hand are the successive defeats the BSP faced due to poor performance in the 2014 and 2019 general elections, and the 2017 and the recent 2022 assembly elections in UP. And on the other hand is the breakdown of its once-strong organizational structure at the district and zonal levels, and the exit of a number of trusted leaders owing to either expulsion or attraction towards the Hindu right, due to which the party is in decline. Is it the end of the road for the BSP and Mayawati?

II

In our story of the rapid decline of a once-dominant party, a central feature is the unravelling of the BSP and a caste–class dispersion of the Dalit movement due to inherent, long-term weaknesses that have come to the fore, and the more immediate failures of the party leadership in the 2000s that we document in detail. While there was consolidation of all Dalit sub-castes within the BSP in the 1990s, it was only insofar as voting was concerned; social and cultural differences, and even hostility between sub-castes, remained. Bahujan identity and consciousness formulated by Kanshi Ram did not reach all Dalit sub-castes in the Hindi heartland; it remained an elite and not a mass phenomenon. It was the numerically larger, dominant and better-off Chamar–Jatavs[22] (henceforth Jatavs) located mainly in the western region of UP, who were deeply influenced and united by it, and who have historically formed the 'vanguard' in all movements. As a result, most still remain loyal to the BSP and to Mayawati, who also belongs to the same sub-caste. The smaller, poorer and marginalized sub-castes, living in the more backward regions and who have been subjected to Hinduization since the colonial period, have retained their specific sub-caste identities, customs and local cultures. Rather than identity, important in defining and cementing socio-political relations among various Dalit groups earlier, social jealousies, cultural aspirations and economic anxieties are the driving forces in the twenty-first century.[23] Consequently, the Dalit movement today is characterized by fragmentation into the pro-BSP or Ambedkarite and the pro-BJP or Hindutvawadi Dalits; the groupings are more complex and each of these groups is further divided on the ground.

An equally important contributing factor was the shift of the BSP from a radical movement to a competitive party in the mid-1990s, and the strategies used to capture power, which help explain the predicament the BSP finds itself in today. The Dalit movement almost everywhere in India has shifted from 'successful social mobilization to political institutionalization' in the form of parties.[24] While this transition is made to capture power and obtain justice, party politics deprives social movements of their radicalism as success in electoral politics demands compromise with competing castes or communities. Dalit parties achieve only partial success and that too when they join electoral alliances or coalitions, and they seldom return to the politics of protest. This is clearly visible among the Dalit Panthers in Maharashtra and the Dalit Panther Iyakkam (DPI) and the Puthiya Tamizhagam (PT) in Tamil Nadu.[25] The BSP was initially more successful as it headed coalition governments in the 1990s and obtained a majority based on the sarvajan experiment in 2007, but eventually these strategies created divisions and weakened the Dalit identity and the unity of the movement. Despite these differences, the coalition under the leadership of Mayawati survived until 2012 when an ignominious defeat triggered a downward spiral.

A significant feature that has impacted the BSP in the 2000s is that it was formed as a party primarily meant to provide Dalits dignity, self-confidence and political empowerment. It was not meant to be, and is not a party equipped for, or whose main aim was, providing an alternative economic agenda to deal with the problems of economic deprivation, in the conventional sense, for Dalits.[26] By the time Mayawati attempted her sarvajan experiment, in which an effort was made to provide economic development to all castes and classes in 2007 when the party gained a majority, the material expectations of Dalits were much too high to be met within a short span of five years. As our narrative shows, the sarvajan experiment created differences within the BSP, a return to the ideology of social justice has not been possible, nor has the leadership thrown up any new ideas in keeping with the changing political situation. Consequently, in the popular perception, including among Dalits, the party is on a downward spiral and is difficult to revive.

Does this mean that the BSP has outlived its *foundational* purpose and thereby its usefulness for Dalits? It is important to underline that the BSP has, in great measure, fulfilled its original promise of providing Dalits identity and self-respect, and contributed to the social deepening of democracy in India. Having obtained a measure of political consciousness and self-confidence to challenge the upper castes, a significant section of Dalits, mostly the non-Jatavs, are in search of a political party/movement that can offer them economic betterment and are also attracted to the idea of inclusion within the larger Hindu identity.

We believe that the Dalit movement in UP has entered into a post-BSP phase, a development, which we argue, need not be seen in a negative light, as much has been achieved. Two features make this clear. First, we are witnessing the maturing

of the Dalit movement in north India, with Dalits confident of
making their own social, political, and electoral choices, and
moving towards different parties, depending on the situation.
Other caste groups—the upper-castes and backwards—have
exercised their political preferences; Dalits, too, are now
exercising their options. The upper-castes, particularly, have
been quick to move to different parties if it benefited them:
from the Congress to the BJP, to lower-caste parties such as the
SP and the BSP. Why are only Dalits criticized for shifting their
loyalties? Second, despite the decline of the BSP, Dalit assertion
on the ground remains strong and, as our narrative shows, we
are witnessing multiple forms of assertion in UP, the Bhim Army
being one of the best known.

III

A key puzzle that our narrative addresses is why have Dalits—
given their long struggle against upper-caste domination—
embraced a right-wing Hindutva party, the BJP, they once
derided as 'Manuvadi'. Since 2014, the BJP under the leadership
of Narendra Modi has obtained massive majorities in both
national and UP assembly elections. More important, there has
been a steady rise in the percentage of Dalits, particularly the
smaller sub-castes supporting the BJP.[27] In fact, in the recent
2022 assembly election, despite gaining fewer seats, the BJP
gained the support of 41 per cent of the other scheduled castes
(SCs), and as much as 21 per cent of the Jatavs, signalling
perhaps for the first time, the move of a larger section of the
latter towards it.

   While the collapse of the BSP provides an explanation,
a recent study of Dalit movements across India provides
an interesting explanation by highlighting the more

enduring legacy of strong identity-based movements than of Dalit parties more interested in the immediate capture of power.[28] Making a distinction between 'movement' and 'non-movement' states, it illustrates that where, historically, strong social mobilization of Dalits precedes the formation of a Dalit political party, as in the case of Tamil Nadu by radical organizations, Dalit parties have not been electorally successful. But, due to the long period of social mobilization, Dalits have retained their pride in low-caste identity and not shown a proclivity to move towards upper-caste parties such as the BJP; they are, in fact, hostile to it.[29] In contrast, in UP, the BSP was not the end-product of a long social movement but was consciously formed by Kanshi Ram as a movement-party to introduce social transformation 'from above' using state power rather than from below, which, he argued, would take a long time. Consequently, once the party lost power and began to decline, Dalits started to move towards the BJP.

More immediately, under the new generational leadership of Modi, the BJP has been successful in taking advantage of the growing weakness of the Dalit movement and the disillusionment of the smaller sub-castes with the BSP, as well as addressing their rising aspirations. It is also because the objective has been two-fold: to obtain the electoral support required in a key state like UP and include them within the saffron fold in order to build a Hindu Rashtra. Feeling neglected within the BSP vis-à-vis the dominant Jatavs, the smaller Dalit sub-castes have been attracted to the BJP and thus been rendered vulnerable to its mobilizational strategies.

A variety of creative strategies and tactics have been employed by the BJP, ranging from promises of development, welfare programmes, cultural inclusion and nationalism to religiosity. Interestingly, each of these strategies has been used in different elections, regions and contexts, where it was believed that the BJP would benefit. The BJP has been the first party to use market mechanisms like employing agencies to manage elections, run highly personalized and plebiscite-like campaigns using social media and charismatic speeches by Modi, which have appealed to the poor. The party has been described as a 'corporate behemoth' which has assembled a huge team that is in 'constant election mode', maintaining and widening its Hindu vote bank.[30] It is a party of leaders involved in the 'relentless pursuit of power' and one that has the 'right balance' between an individual and an 'organized party'.[31]

Equally important in the BJP's success story of mobilizing Dalits has been its strategy of 'new welfarism', which has been skilfully marketed as being based on a well-organized, huge welfare state, with Modi projected as the 'messiah' of the poor.[32] It has provided a range of goods and services to the poorer sections, many of whom are Dalits, such as bank accounts, cooking gas, toilets, electricity, housing, water and, more recently, free rations and cash. All these give immediate electoral returns as against services such as health and education that would deliver benefits in the distant future. Thus, through a series of multifaceted strategies, the BJP has deftly obtained the support of the smaller sub-castes in UP by bringing together a new politics of 'recognition' of the distinct historical, social and cultural identity of each sub-caste and 'redistribution' through the employment of massive welfare schemes and their efficient delivery on the ground.

But the story of Modi's success in mobilizing Dalits contains two complex questions that we took up through interviews and field studies. First, why do Dalits exhibit both *political protest* against rising atrocities and *political preference* of supporting/ voting for the BJP? Our narrative points to a disjuncture between the political and the electoral; the former is full of contradictions but it is insulated from the latter. Fieldwork indicates that the smaller Dalit sub-castes prefer to vote for a party that can provide them protection against the locally dominant Yadavs, who rose to positions of dominance in the 1990s and 2000s when the SP was in power and was viewed as a goonda or mafia party. With the decline of the BSP, they view the BJP as the only party that can protect their interests.

Second, does the move by Dalits towards the BJP signify tactical or instrumental support due to the decline of the BSP or conversion to the party's ideology? Our study suggests that the tactical and the ideological are not separate; they need not be viewed in a contradictory position. While the initial decision was tactical, the chances of ideological conversion increase if the trend continues over a number of elections. Since 2014, the BJP–RSS have attempted to take the cultural mobilization of Dalits further by providing greater space within the Hindu identity by catering to their feelings of marginalization, acknowledging their specific sub-caste identity, giving space to practise rituals and building small temples to their local deities, thereby according them dignity and respect. These are some aspects that Dalits feel have been ignored by the BSP in recent years.

Our discussion throws up a number of questions of significance for the future of the Dalit movement. If the BJP were to lose power in the future, or if the BSP were to revive itself, will the Dalits still move towards the BJP, or towards other parties? Or do the successive BJP victories since 2014, including in 2022, mean that the saffronization project has run deep and Dalits will remain with it? Does this mean that Hinduization of Indian society is now irreversible, and what does this mean for the Dalit movement?

IV

A feature of Dalit politics in UP, to which adequate attention has not been paid, is the rise of new Dalit organizations in the vacuum created by the decline of the BSP, in a situation where Dalit political consciousness and assertion on the ground remains strong. Our fieldwork and interviews with Dalit activists indicate that with the decline of the BSP, rather than a new, pan-UP Dalit party, many organizations in different sub-regions have sprung up across the state. The pattern of the future seems to be the BSP co-existing as a diminished party with a number of smaller Ambedkarite initiatives on the ground. Based on our interviews with leaders of a number of small and largely unknown organizations, we tell the story of the rise of three new organizations that came into existence in 2016, 2019 and 2020.

What is interesting is that these formations describe themselves as Ambedkarite organizations; they invoke Kanshi Ram and claim to be the legacy of the BSP. Yet they are also competing with each other, and each hopes to fill the space vacated by the BSP. Since these are small organizations based on individual initiatives and governed by logistical and resource constraints, they are largely involved in the politics of agitation around issues concerning Dalits. In fact, the realm of electoral politics is used by them to accentuate their public relevance in the eyes of the Dalit community and the government.

A key question we explore is whether the new leaders have the potential to fill the void created by Mayawati's diminishing popularity and regenerate the Dalit movement overcoming fragmentation, unfulfilled aspirations and the challenge of Hindutva politics.

V

In conclusion, we bring together the threads of our narrative to discuss the longer-term prospects of Dalit politics in UP and the Hindi heartland. The future of the BSP is of significance as it is the leading Dalit party in the country, and its survival and strength carry great meaning for our democracy. Has it run aground with no new ideas or strategies to proffer or is it merely in decline with hope of revival? Has it lost relevance with little to offer to Dalit millennials aspiring for rapid economic advancement? Is its decline a systemic problem affecting most of the parties that emerge from a movement, or is it primarily on account of the failures of individual leaders?

Today, the BSP faces a growing crisis which is both *normative* and *political*. Normative, as Dalits reject partially or review earlier norms and ideas that held the Dalit movement together and provided moral meaning to their existence and identity. Political, as sub-caste divisions have regained importance following the collapse of the BSP and class divisions assumed significance due to a desire for upward mobility. Simultaneous is the rise of new Dalit organizations on the ground and their growing popularity among the younger generation, which point to the emergence of a post-BSP phase in UP.

The political arena within which Dalit politics operated earlier in the country has significantly altered. Besides increasing caste oppression, there is also the ascendency of a hegemonic Hindutva party both at the Centre and in UP. In this situation, the space for revival of older Dalit parties or for organizations to build a new movement seems severely limited and challenging. If the new socio-political coalition of the upper, backward, and lower-castes formed by Modi continues for long as the dominant ruling dispensation, the higher the possibility of greater absorption and incorporation of Dalits into the Hindutva-fold. However, if the new generation Dalit leaders espousing an anti-Hindutva agenda succeeds in shifting the community's anger into the electoral arena, we may witness a new wave of Dalit assertion.

Our narrative of the present-day decline of Dalit politics and the enormous challenges it faces, both from internal weaknesses and the electoral and cultural *assimilation* and social *hegemony* of the BJP, provide the backdrop to the electoral battle between these two contending forces in the 2022 UP assembly elections. With the renewed dominance of the BJP and poor performance of the BSP in the assembly elections, in the concluding section we discuss which way Dalit politics in UP is headed.

PART I

Building a 'Rainbow' Party with a
Dalit Core

1

The Sarvajan Experiment

—∞—

From, *Tilak, tarazu aur talwar, inko maro joote char'* to
'*Sarva samaj ke samman mein, Behenji maidan mein*'.[1]

No one could predict that in just over two decades the Bahujan Samaj Party (BSP), formed in 1985 with primarily a Dalit base, would obtain an absolute majority in 2007 in Uttar Pradesh (UP) one of the largest states in India, and form a government on its own. The victory of the BSP under Mayawati's leadership, based on her sarvajan strategy, was greeted with surprise by the media and sections of the scholarly community. During the electoral campaign, the idea of working for *sarva samaj* (all sections of society) had generated great interest. Most commentators had argued that it would not work as Brahmins would not vote for a lower-caste party.

Others held that it would divide Dalits, making the BSP lose its hard-won values of identity and social justice which had united them and posed a challenge to upper-caste domination in UP.[2]

However, Mayawati went on to gain a majority and, as Kanshi Ram, the founder of the BSP and her mentor, had envisioned, form a Dalit government though the experiment did not last beyond a single term.[3] It was the first single-party majority government formed in seventeen years since the Bharatiya Janata Party (BJP) gained power at the height of the Ram Janmabhoomi movement. Already recognized as the tallest Dalit leader in the country, achieving a majority in the assembly election of 2007 provided Mayawati greater stature. Her success was possible not because she was an opportunistic leader, as is often made out in the popular media, but because she was a good strategist who often outpaced her rivals with speed, stamina, perseverance and tenacity.

Once the results were known, Mayawati's success was the cover story in most magazines and newspapers. *India Today* commented that 'by wooing the upper castes, Mayawati has shown her acumen as a master strategist, perhaps even better than mentor Kanshi Ram'.[4] The magazine further pointed out what many were saying, that this was a different party from the one Kanshi Ram had founded in 1984 to create a political identity for Dalits, with the abusive slogan, *'tilak, tarazu aur talwar, inko maro joote chaar'*,[5] pitched against the upper-castes. Another popular magazine described her as 'King Mayawati' for her unique and innovative strategy and argued that she would play a critical role in national politics.[6] *The Times of India* on its front page reported that UP awoke to a 'blue sunrise' on 12 May 2007. It also commented that 'Jatavs, who are the engine of this social alliance, now have the upper castes playing a supportive role'.[7] While the BSP had been a significant player since its inception in UP, this victory made it a mainstream party that broke all rules to reach its goal.

What exactly was the strategy Mayawati put forward to her Dalit constituency? A scholar neatly put forward her calculus, much before her victory in May 2007.

The upper castes will not cast their votes in favour of the Bahujan candidate. But Bahujan caste voters should transfer their votes totally in favour of the upper-caste candidates in every constituency where they are contesting on the BSP ticket, though in such constituencies the upper castes will not vote en masse for the upper-caste candidate contesting on the BSP ticket. But in the process, even if the upper-caste BSP candidate gets 2 to 3 per cent of the upper-caste votes, the BSP as a party can enhance its tally from the present by 50 to 60 seats. This will give the BSP a chance to form a majority government for the full five-year term in the state.[8]

The reasons for the adoption of the sarvajan strategy, and subsequent victory of the BSP, constitutes an interesting story as the party attempted to redefine itself from being avowedly Dalit to savarna. The massive victory fuelled talk of Mayawati being considered as the prime minister in 2009. However, more importantly for our narrative, it represents the high watermark of the party's success after which, following the defeat in the 2012 assembly elections, it began to decline rapidly. The BSP performed badly in both the assembly and general elections in UP, culminating in a humiliating showing in 2022 when it obtained just one seat and garnered only 12.9 per cent of the votes.

Mayawati's search for a *new social constituency* surprised most observers as it went against the basic tenets of a Dalit party. The question is significant because it was a unique experiment. We go back fifteen years to provide a narrative of the formation of this strategy, what made it possible, the actors involved, and its smooth operationalization in the campaign for the 2007 elections. The story remains relevant as Mayawati once again attempted to woo the Brahmins prior to the UP assembly elections of 2022, as they were viewed as being unhappy with the Yogi Adityanath government.[9]

Genesis of Sarvajan

The seeds of what later came to be called the sarvajan strategy can be traced, as claimed by Nasimuddin Siddiqui, a close confidant of Mayawati, to events in the mid-1990s. The BSP began as a radical, anti-upper-caste movement, with a strident demand for social equality for Dalits. It was a phase of militant hostility towards the upper-castes, mobilization of the poor and underprivileged, criticism of mainstream parties as Manuvadi,[10] highlighting the failures of the Congress regimes, and opposition to Hindutva and caste-based atrocities. Provocative epithets were used through which the party's anti-Manuvadi message was put forward. Slogans such as '*Brahmin, Bania, Thakur chor, baki sab hein DS-four*' and '*Tilak, tarazu aur talwar, inko maro joote char*' were popular.[11] At this stage, Kanshi Ram was categorical about not including the *savarnas*: 'There are lots of other parties which accommodate upper-caste people, but they should avoid us.'[12]

But in the early 1990s, the BSP leadership realized that capturing state power and bringing in change 'from above' was required as grassroots mobilization and social transformation was difficult and would take a long time given the hostility and dominant position of the upper castes in UP. Moreover, its electoral reach was limited to a narrow segment of the population as Dalits in UP formed only 22 per cent[13] of the population. After they managed to gain the electoral support of this segment; the party reached a plateau, and was unable to move beyond it and capture power on its own. Hence, prior to the 1993 assembly elections, Kanshi Ram decided to form an alliance with a like-minded party, the Samajwadi Party (SP), representing another lower caste, the backwards.

Kanshi Ram's idea was to form a society for the low born or a society of the lower castes 'bahujan samaj' and thereby, as he had envisaged while forming the BSP, a 'bahujan party' or alliance of the lower castes. The word 'bahujan', meaning the majority, was borrowed from the nineteenth-century social reformer Jyotiba Phule. But in UP politics it meant the coming together of Dalits and backward castes who together constituted about 50 per cent of the population, which would allow them to jointly win power and prevent upper-caste domination. Politically, in 1993, this was a correct strategy, as the confrontation between the forces of Hindutva and the backward castes and Dalits had sharpened, creating communal tension, leading to the demolition of the Babri Masjid on 6 December 1992. In the 1993 assembly elections, the Dalits, backward castes and Muslims were able to 'contain' the BJP. The SP won 106 seats, the BSP 66, while the BJP managed only 177 seats against its earlier tally of 221 in the 1991 elections.

The air of optimism among the Dalits and BCs, and opposition to the BJP following the victory in 1993 was apparent in the popular slogan of the time: *Mile Mulayam–Kanshi Ram, hava me udh gaye Jai Shri Ram* (Mulayam and Kanshi Ram joining hands has led to the Jai Shri Ram party being blown away).[14] The slogan was created impromptu by Khadim Abbas, a BSP leader from Etawah who was close to Kanshi Ram, at a gathering in Mainpuri in 1992. While the crowd awaited the arrival of

Mulayam and Kanshi Ram, Abbas was requested to speak. He came up with this slogan which was received enthusiastically by the audience, and he was made to repeat it several times. The slogan changed the political atmosphere as it reverberated across the state and contributed to the creation of a favourable political atmosphere for the SP and BSP.

The SP–BSP coalition headed by Mulayam Singh Yadav, formed after the 1993 assembly elections, lasted only from November 1993 to June 1995; the two parties have not joined hands again except briefly against the BJP, much later in a different political scenario, in the by-elections of 2018 for two seats in eastern and one in western UP.[15] The 1993 coalition fell apart due to strident class differences between the two groups. The cadres of the two parties remained separate and hostile on the ground, as seen in violent disputes over land, wages and tenancy; the backwards as landowners constituted the direct oppressors of the landless Dalits in the countryside. In urban areas, the two remained in sharp competition over reservations in educational institutions and government jobs.

Equally, if not more, important was a tragic incident that created bad blood and lasting enmity between the leadership of the two parties. On 2 June 1995, the BSP's announcement to withdraw from the coalition resulted in an angry and unruly mob of SP workers entering the Meerabai Guest House in Lucknow, where Mayawati was in a meeting with her MLAs. As Naseemuddin Siddiqui disclosed to us,[16] her room was vandalized, casteist and sexual slurs were made, and she was allegedly beaten up. The MLAs failed to protect her. Only two persons intervened: Siddiqui, who was outside the room in which Mayawati was locked up, and BJP MLA Brahm Dutt Dwivedi,[17] who lived close by and whom Mayawati phoned for help. While the former prevented the SP workers from breaking down the door, the latter arrived and escorted Mayawati to safety. This incident is considered one of the biggest deal-breakers between Mayawati and Mulayam and has been picturized in the film, *Madam Chief Minister*,[18] which shows how Mayawati does not trust anyone ever since then and remains suspicious of Mulayam Singh and his party.

After this, Kanshi Ram and Mayawati decided to form a coalition government with the help of BJP in 1995, 1997 and 2002. Underlying these moves was not ideology but 'technological rationality', that is, a desire to increase votes by means of vote arithmetic.[19] Kanshi Ram justified the formation of a coalition with an upper-caste party as a 'temporary and tactical method' to gain power, itself a form of mobilization, encouraging Dalits to stand up for their rights.[20] Considering the oppressive practices used by upper-castes, he argued that the use of *any* method to capture power was justified. He pointed out that 'political power is the guru *killi* (master key) which enables its wielders to open every lock, whether social, political, economic or cultural'.[21]

Kanshi Ram was proved right. The assumption of Mayawati, a *Dalit ki beti* (a Dalit's daughter, as she was known popularly), as the chief minister of UP, one of the most conservative and caste-ridden states, proved to be highly symbolic and encouraging for Dalits, especially Dalit women. During fieldwork in 1997, we asked newly elected Dalit women pradhanis—panchayat heads—how they felt about this. The impact was apparent in the immediate reply from one of them: '*Maine apne admi ko bola, agar wo mukhya mantri ban sakti hai, to meri beti school ja sakti hai.*' (I told my husband, if she [Mayawati] can become the chief minister, then my daughter can go to school.)[22] However, upper-/backward-caste landowners in UP felt differently. The *Times of India* on its masthead carried the message they gave to their landless labour: 'Wo *mukhya mantri bani hai waha, par tum yaha mere khet me begar karoge.'* (She may have become the chief minister there, but you will continue to do unpaid labour in my fields.) The coalition governments formed by the BSP with the support of the BJP in the 1990s lasted for only short periods, as once in power Mayawati used her term as chief minister to implement a number of socio-economic and cultural policies exclusively for the Dalits, and, to a lesser extent, the backwards and the Muslims, which angered the BJP.[23]

Simultaneously, Kanshi Ram implemented a strategy in the 1996 assembly elections and the 1998 and 1999 Lok Sabha elections of giving tickets to non-Dalits in the hope of widening the party's base. But the number of tickets given to the upper castes remained lower than those given to Dalits, OBCs and Muslims; hence the outreach to upper castes remained limited. While the upper castes were given about 16.6 per cent in the 1996 and 1998 elections, Dalits were given the greatest share in 1996, while in 1998, the backwards, in cognizance of the rising demands by the most backward castes, received the largest share.[24] A similar distribution pattern is seen in the 1999 Lok Sabha elections.[25]

Still, the importance of this strategy cannot be ignored. Naseemuddin Siddiqui, closely associated with Kanshi Ram in the formulation of this idea, argues that the evolution of the sarvajan strategy of the 2000s can be directly traced to this move. He mentions that one of the first upper-caste leaders to be given a berth in the Rajya Sabha under this strategy was Jayant Malhotra in 1996; later H. Dixit, Ram Upadhyaya and others were included. Many were close to Kanshi Ram and supporters of the BSP. An interesting story doing the rounds in November 1993 was how Jayant Malhotra, an industrialist and supporter of Kanshi Ram, over a dinner with Prime Minister Narasimha

Rao, was able to persuade him to release the BSP's MP unit president who had been arrested by the Congress government of the state. The Congress obliged, and significantly, talks on seat adjustments in UP started soon after between Kanshi Ram and Rao's political adviser, Jitendra Prasad, in the hope of rejuvenating the fortunes of the Congress party in the Hindi heartland. Though the talks did not succeed, Jayant Malhotra was given a Rajya Sabha berth by Kanshi Ram.[26]

At the same time, though Dalits were given a larger share of the tickets, the BSP *ignored the smaller Dalit sub-castes*.[27] In UP, there are sixty-six Dalit castes, constituting 21 per cent of the population of the state. According to the 2011 Census, the Jatav community comprised 54 per cent of UP's total 22,496,047 scheduled caste (SC) population. The Pasi community occupied second position with 65.22 lakh persons and 15.9 per cent share. The Dhobi community occupied third spot with a population of 24.32 lakh, Koris constitute 22.93 lakh, Balmikis 13.19 lakh and Khatiks 9.3 lakh persons. The fourth rung comprising Gonds, Dhanuks and Khatiks, constitute about 5 per cent. The BSP has generally distributed its reserved seats in the state legislative assembly and Lok Sabha among the Chamars and Pasis.[28] The BSP did develop leadership across the state among the smaller castes neglected by other political parties, such as the Pal, Shakya, Baghel, Maurya, Pushkar and Saini among the backwards, and the Sankhawar, Pasi, Dhobi, Valmiki and Khatik among the Dalits, but it did not give them tickets. This limited the spread of the party among Dalits as there was hardly any representation for Gonds, Dhanuks and Khatiks. In more recent years, the BJP has taken advantage of the unhappiness of these groups by giving them tickets, addressing their needs and trying to bring them under the umbrella of a larger Hindu identity.[29]

Despite this, however, the performance of the BSP in the 1998 Lok Sabha elections was disappointing; instead, the BJP performed well. The BSP managed to retain its vote share of 20.90 per cent, but gained only four seats, and was pushed back to its original base in the eastern districts, gaining no seat in any other region. But in the 1999 Lok Sabha elections, the BSP increased its vote share to about 22 per cent, which for the first time was higher than the percentage of SCs in the population (21 per cent) and obtained fourteen seats. Two upper-caste, two Muslim, two backward and eight Dalit candidates won on the BSP ticket; the BSP also occupied second place in another fifteen constituencies, in four of which it lost by very narrow margins.

It was the limited success of the BSP's strategies of compromise with the upper castes, followed by splits and desertions by BC leaders that encouraged Mayawati to adopt the sarvajan ideology. Rising political consciousness among the backwards by the end of the decade led to the more assertive and better-off BC leaders deserting the BSP. Raj Bahadur and Jung Bahadur—two Kurmi leaders—created a split and formed the BSP (R) and the Bahujan Samaj Dal, respectively. More importantly, at the same time, Sone Lal Patel, an important Kurmi leader from Kannauj, unhappy with the importance given to Mayawati as against other hardworking leaders, left the party and decided to float his own party, Apna Dal, on 4 November 1995. This party, unlike the others, has survived and, as our narrative shows, has been a key ally of the BJP in the 2000s. An educated leader who had started his career with Charan Singh's backward caste movement, he was attracted by Kanshi Ram's idea of social justice and was one of the founder-members of the BSP.[30]

In this situation of competition within the party, by the end of the 1990s the question of who would succeed Kanshi Ram as leader of the BSP began to be asked. Two prominent leaders, R.K. Chaudhary (founder member of the BSP and former minister in the SP–BSP coalition government of 1993 in UP) and Barkhoo Ram Verma (former assembly speaker from 1995 to 1997 during the BSP–BJP coalition government) had been trying to impress upon the party rank and file that they were the favourites of Kanshi Ram, despite their strong differences with Mayawati. Scotching all rumours about a rift between the two, Kanshi Ram on 15 December 2001 formally declared senior leader Mayawati as his successor, ending what he termed as the 'struggle for rule by the bahujan samaj'.[31] Addressing a massive rally in Lucknow attended by an attentive and responsive crowd, his declaration appointing Mayawati as his 'heir' drew thunderous applause. The announcement was meant to give a blow to Mayawati's detractors, some of whom had been recently shown the door by her. This helped Mayawati make the decision to adopt the strategy of sarvajan with the help of selected advisors much easier in the 2000s.

Sarvajan in the 2000s

Significant developments in the early 2000s pushed Mayawati to experiment with the strategy of transforming the BSP into a savarna party. At the time, UP witnessed the rapid decline of the BJP—which many attributed to the moderate leadership of Atal Behari Vajpayee who shelved the Ram temple issue[32] and concentrated on economic reform and governance—and the failure of the Congress to rebuild itself. This was evident from the poor performance of these parties in the February 2002 state assembly elections which resulted in a hung assembly, and particularly in the by-elections to two Lok Sabha and sixteen assembly seats that followed in June 2005.[33] This created polarization, leaving the BSP and the SP as the two strongest contenders for political power. The SP emerged as the largest party with 143 seats in 2002, but the BSP and BJP formed a coalition.

In August 2003, the SP split the BSP, leading to thirty-seven MLAs forming their own group, thus bringing down the BSP–BJP coalition, leading to the formation of a new government with the defectors, with Mulayam Singh Yadav as chief minister.[34] The move was illegal, but was permitted by the then speaker of the UP legislative assembly because of a secret collaboration between the BJP and the SP.[35] This heightened competition between the BSP and the SP set the stage for an anti-Yadav consolidation by the BSP, which later became a part of the sarvajan campaign for the 2007 elections.

The death of Kanshi Ram in 2006 was described as the final 'sarvajan moment' for the party by Naseemuddin Siddiqui.[36] It meant that advisors such as Satish Chandra Mishra and Siddiqui himself, who had both earlier supported the move to give tickets to non-Dalits, became important. While Siddiqui remained Mayawati's close confidant, Satish Mishra was made a Rajya Sabha member. He rose in the party and took up the job of fighting cases against Mayawati in court. While the BSP's vote percentage had grown due to their persuasive power, there was a realization by Mayawati that the BSP had reached a plateau in the second half of the 1990s, the party had not been able to increase its seats despite giving tickets to non-Dalits. It was then that the sarvajan strategy, which was conceptualized and launched in 2005, was taken up more seriously.

Finally, the gradual waning of identity politics from the late 1990s led to broad and aggregative 'social rainbow' identities, and based on them, new alignments began to be constructed by all political parties. The BSP was the first to recognize this shift. The rise of a desire for economic advancement among Dalits meant that it was possible to experiment with moving away from a highly exclusionary and Dalit-oriented strategy to a broader, electoral one that could also appeal to a larger cross-section of the UP electorate.

These developments led Mayawati to redefine the identity of the BSP, reassess its strategies of electoral mobilization vis-à-vis other parties and social groups, and gravitate towards more inclusionary politics. She attempted a shift from 'bahujan samaj' (majoritarianism for the lower castes) to 'sarvajan samaj' (entire society), a move that would involve a departure from the party's earlier ideology. While the BSP had given tickets to non-Dalits earlier, it now decided to try and gain the support of the upper castes by approaching and mobilizing them directly, a difficult task for a Dalit party.

Operationalizing Sarvajan: Ideology and Structure

A recent study has argued that sarvajan was *not a major shift*. It was in keeping with the BSP's notion of democratization of the undemocratic order, evident in its political slogan: *Jiski jitni sankhya bhari, uski utni bhagedari* (Political representation and share in power will correspond to the support of the particular caste in terms of number of votes).[37] The BSP's goal had been 'equalization of caste, rather than its annihilation', which it believed could be achieved through 'democratization of the undemocratic order'. The sarvajan strategy was a step forward in this direction—through it there could be both capture of power and equalization of representation.

As Gaya Charan Dinakar, a BSP MLA from Banda and close confidant of Mayawati, pointed out, 'the BSP's idea of equalization of castes' should not be treated as the party's shift from the Ambedkar ideology; rather it gels with Ambedkar's vision. As he said, 'If individuals are part of castes and if castes are part of a hierarchically organized social order, then the first step towards the realization of an individual-based society would be equalization of castes rather than annihilation of castes.' Dinakar's argument is that to realize Ambedkar's vision of equality of individuals, one must work from within the caste structure, rather than try to annihilate it because caste is a reality. We should face the fact that a Dalit is discriminated against and humiliated by the caste Hindu society because of his caste and not because of his personality or behaviour. 'And we are using caste to weaken the caste mindset,' claimed Dinakar.[38]

The move towards sarvajan is significant for our story. While the strategy was meant to capture power in 2007, the larger aim of the BSP was to build a system similar to the erstwhile combine of the upper castes—Dalits–Muslims that had enabled the Congress party to rule UP for a long period. This would allow the party to overcome its inability to capture power alone and also build a social combine in which the Dalits are in a core commanding position.

In 2005 a structure to operationalize the sarvajan campaign was setup.[39] It points to a clear-cut strategy and a strong, well-organized party able to campaign effectively, compared to the post-2014 period when this structure broke down. While in the media sarvajan was identified with mobilizing the Brahmins, it was a euphemism for a much larger attempt at consolidation. Siddiqui pointed out that Brahmin 'bhaichara' committees were widely reported. As many as thirty-two kinds of bhaichara committees[40] were created in a bid to throw the net wide and capture many castes. Made prabhari or in-charge of the system overall, some of the bhaichara committees, he mentioned, included Brahmins, Muslims, Vaishyas, Kurmis and Christians. Such committees were formed in every assembly constituency, and where polling booths were located. He claimed that the BSP was the first to set up panna pramukhs[41] and argued that '*BJP ne hamari nakal kiya hai*' (The BJP has copied us).[42]

The head of each bhaichara committee was expected to give a written monthly report of the number of meetings or programmes held, speeches given and those who attended. Siddiqui travelled to each village and zilla to supervise these functions, holding six to seven hours of meetings with the committee heads, thereby putting moral and supervisory pressure on them. He claimed to have interacted with Hindu, Dalit and Muslim workers and voters, without making any differentiation, gaining the respect of party cadres and Mayawati: 'I have always respected all religions and this underlay my success.'

Prior to the 2007 elections, the BSP had not attempted to woo Muslims directly. But during the campaign, Mayawati decided to give sixty-one Muslims tickets and 'Mission Muslim' was launched with Muslim bhaichara committees in Agra, Meerut and Devipatan divisions, followed by many others later. The committees consisted of Dalit–Muslim members at the division, assembly and booth levels; they highlighted the social marginalization and exploitation by political parties of both communities to forge a bond. While the BSP lost in some densely populated Muslim constituencies (such as Baharaich,

Muzaffarnagar and Moradabad), it won in some others (such as Bareilly, Kaiserganj, Domariaganj and Balrampur).[43]

However, equally important was an attempted, strident anti-Yadav consolidation. Mayawati had not forgotten the guest house incident of 1995, nor Mulayam breaking her 2002 coalition government by poaching BSP MLAs with the BJP's connivance. The SP was portrayed as a Yadav party full of goons, a popular slogan being: *Chadh gundon ke chhati par, laga mohar hathi par* (Climb the chest of goondas and stamp your vote on the elephant). It led to intense competition between the BSP and SP, leading certain sections of non-Yadav caste groups to support the former.

The Brahmin–Dalit–Muslim alliance was the responsibility of Mayawati's close advisor Satish Chandra Mishra and the well-known 'Banda trio' consisting of Naseemuddin Siddiqui, Babu Singh Kushwaha and Gaya Charan Dinkar.[44] But the star campaigners were Mishra and Siddiqui who constituted the Brahmin and Muslim faces of the party. Mishra, the first Brahmin national general secretary of the BSP, is one of Mayawati's most trusted lieutenants.[45] A lawyer by profession, he was chairman of the Bar Council of Uttar Pradesh in 1998–99, advocate general of UP in 2002–03, has been a member of the Rajya Sabha 2004 and is currently serving his third term in the house.[46] He has successfully defended Mayawati in several cases including the Taj Heritage Corridor scam. He played a leading role in the reconfiguration of the BSP's identity and bringing Brahmins closer to Mayawati during the 2007 campaign.

Supporting the idea of sarvajan, of which he was one of the main architects, Mishra told us that despite being a Dalit party, the aim of the BSP since its formation has been achieving 'Sarvajan *sukhay,* sarvajan *hitay*' (The well-being of entire society, the benefit of entire society). Criticism of the upper castes and classes by the BSP was aimed at demanding equality and social inclusion in society, but the party stood for the welfare of society as a whole. He pointed out that prior to 2007, whenever Mayawati became chief minister, it was for a very short time, and since she was dependent on other parties for her position, she worked largely for the very poor and disadvantaged sections of society. For example, in 1995, when she became chief minister for the first time, she established the SC/ST Welfare Department which was tasked to look after the welfare of these groups. But prior to the 2007 elections, using a new strategy, Mayawati directed her party to set up bhaichara committees across the state that propagated and promised programmes for the betterment of each section of society. Once in power, she kept her promise and this, according to Mishra, validates the claim that the party has always worked for the advancement and uplift of every social group.

Siddiqui, a former contractor for Indian Railways, was Mayawati's closest confidant for three decades until his fallout with her in 2017. Hailing from Banda, he joined the BSP in 1990. Following his defeat as an independent candidate in a local election in 1988, Siddiqui left Banda for Lucknow and gradually managed to become close with Behenji. As there were few Muslims in the party, his stature grew; he invested time and effort, and later some of his family members too joined or worked for the BSP. Though he lost the 1993 assembly election, Mayawati sent him to the legislative council and made him minister in her coalitions with the BJP in 1995, 1997 and again in 2002, when he was given the important ministries of environment, transport and excise.[47]

Similarly, Babu Singh Kushwaha joined the BSP in 1995, and rose from being a telephone attendant in Mayawati's office to becoming one of her trusted lieutenants; he was responsible for attracting the backward castes to the party. He rose to be one of her powerful cabinet ministers after the 2007 victory. Gaya Charan Dinkar, a Dalit, had worked extensively with Kanshi Ram and was one of Mayawati's trusted aides. After winning in 1991, 1993 and 2002, Dinkar became a part of Mayawati's cabinet between 2002 and 2003. He was elected to the assembly for a fourth term in 2012. Deemed an expert in parliamentary affairs, he was appointed the leader of opposition in the UP assembly in 2016.[48]

During the campaign, only Siddiqui and Mishra were allowed the use of expensive helicopters. When the BSP formed its first majority government in 2007, Siddiqui became the second most powerful minister, often referred to as the 'mini-CM', with about ten departments under him, including public works and excise. In 2010, his wife Husna became a Member of the Legislative Council from the BSP, joining him in the Upper House. Siddiqui's family members, including his brother, brother-in-law and son, also became active in the party. Mishra, too, was given important cabinet positions in 2007. Mayawati acknowledged that she owed her 2007 victory to these two.

The Campaign

The methods and tactics used by the BSP during the 2007 election campaign to gain the support of the upper castes captured media headlines. Starting in 2005, the BSP held about sixty 'Brahmin-jodo sammelan' (or enrolment conferences for Brahmins) spread across twenty-one districts in UP. Brahmin leader Satish Chandra organized a series of rallies projecting BSP's poll symbol, an elephant, as Lord Ganesh. Large meetings were held for Brahmins alone in cities such as Gorakhpur in eastern UP; Pratapgarh, Sultanpur and Gonda in Awadh; Allahabad, Kannauj and Sitapur in the upper Doab; and Saharanpur in western UP. Dalits were not invited. These congregations culminated in a state-level meeting held in Lucknow on 9 June 2005, addressed by Mayawati and attended by about one lakh Brahmins from across the state.[49] Similar conferences were held for the Vaishya, Thakur and Muslim communities.

At these meetings, Mayawati was greeted with Brahmanical rituals, such as the chanting of Vedic hymns and the blowing of conches, while Brahmin leaders presented gifts to her. The BSP employed new icons and symbols to create a savarna identity for itself, such as Lord Parashuram and his mythical weapon, a silver axe. There were slogans too, such as '*Haathi nahin, Ganesh hai, Brahma, Vishnu, Mahadev hai; Haathi badhta jayega, Brahmin shankh bajaega*; and *Sarva samaj ke samman mein, Behenji maidan mein*'.[50] (It is not an elephant, it represents Ganesh, Brahma, Vishnu, Mahesh; The elephant will keep moving ahead, the Brahmin will blow the conch; and For the good of the community as a whole, Behenji will step out and contest.)

It was not easy for Brahmins to join a party that once abused them as Manuvadi, but they were attracted by the importance that this mass-contact programme gave the community, with Mayawati promising them tickets and cabinet positions. As Deep Shukla, a Brahmin resident of Kalyanpur, a town close to Kanpur, argued, Mayawati had recognized that *atma-samman* (self-respect) given their high position in society was very important for Brahmins. He pointed out that chairs were arranged for all at the Lucknow Brahmin conference—at BSP gatherings, cadres sat on the floor—and the pandal looked like a temple.[51]

In contrast to her earlier rhetoric, Mayawati, like her chief adviser Mishra, argued at rallies that her party had never been against upper-caste communities or Hindu religion, but against discriminatory practices such as caste oppression. The BSP's main aim had been to build a society free of caste divisions but it had been misrepresented as an anti-upper-caste party. The party had been trying to propagate a true understanding of its mission and had made much progress among Brahmins during the campaign.[52] Arguing that Dalits and Brahmins could together rule the state, she reminded them that Ambedkar 'not only accepted a Brahmin surname given by a Brahmin teacher but also married a Brahmin'.[53]

There were media reports in some parts of the state that a change was visible on the ground. In the Unnao constituency which had a Brahmin Lok Sabha representative from the BSP, a membership drive was launched in 2005—from each of its seven assembly segments, workers were asked to bring in 7,500 Brahmin members. The membership fee was fixed at ₹20 per head, which meant that the party hoped to collect ₹1,50,000 from each unit. By June, the district convener, Brijbhushan Pandey, a member of the party since 1995, claimed that 90 per cent of this amount had already been collected.[54]

Why did a section of the twice-born, particularly Brahmins, take the political decision to move towards the BSP? In UP, Brahmins constitute about 8 per cent of the population and account for 10 to 20 per cent of the votes in as many as forty of the eighty Lok Sabha constituencies.[55] A conservative group, they have preferred the Congress and the BJP, and have traditionally not voted for lower-caste parties. Considering themselves the elite, with control over politics and particularly the economy, they have been quick to move to parties that would ensure their position remained intact.

For Brahmins, the 1990s had been a trying period. The decline of the Congress, the rise of the SP with its Yadav–Muslim axis and the emergence of the overtly anti-Brahmin BSP had pushed them towards the BJP. By 1999, and increasingly over the 2002 assembly and 2004 Lok Sabha elections, disillusionment with the BJP had begun to spread rapidly among them.[56] From 1999 onwards, their preference was for the Congress. For example, in Mirzapur, the sitting BJP MP, Virendra Singh, who had defeated SP's Phoolan Devi by 52,777 votes in 1998, lost in 1999 by a margin of 84,476 votes. This was possible as Brahmins decided to vote for Congress's Shyamdhar Mishra, a wealthy carpet manufacturer who had been a state minister earlier.

The Brahmins found that the BJP–BSP coalitions did not provide stability, and Mayawati, once in power, favoured her own constituency, which hurt their economic interests. Also, the Mandal Commission in the early 1990s had given 27 per cent quota to OBCs, and made the Brahmins compete for government jobs. Many of them supported reservation for scheduled castes and scheduled tribes, but opposed it when it came to the other backward castes. Moreover, they found that the backward castes were given more importance in the BJP, as seen from the fact that no Brahmin had been made chief minister of UP or Madhya Pradesh. Hence, in May 1999 the Brahmins organized a virat Brahmin mahasammelan, a massive state-wide congregation for their community, at Bithauli village in Sitapur district, to discuss their future political strategies. Newspaper reports showed they openly expressed their dissatisfaction with the BJP.[57]

By the 2002 elections, Brahmins had begun to actively rethink their options. Their strategy of getting as many Brahmins as possible into the assembly regardless of the party symbol was not easy to implement, especially following the victory of the Congress-led UPA at the Centre. The Congress party was trying hard to get back its upper-caste base in UP. By 2004, the magic of Atal Behari Vajpayee, the Brahmin icon, began to wane for the first time since the 1991 elections. Brahmins were heard openly criticizing him. Senior BJP leader Murli Manohar Joshi found himself in a difficult position during the campaign for the Allahabad seat in the 2004 Lok Sabha election, despite having won a record three times in 1996, 1998 and 1999; this time he lost. Neither his being a Brahmin nor his close identification with the Ram Janmabhoomi movement helped. Finally, when the BJP began to give an increasing number of tickets to the OBCs and SCs to counter the SP and the BSP, the Brahmins felt that their share in power had begun to shrink.[58]

The Brahmins preferred the BSP to the SP as most held the latter responsible for the establishment of the Mandal Commission. Regarding it as a party dominated by the aggressive Yadavs and Thakurs, they felt that the Brahmin–Dalit combination could meet the challenge posed by them. Moreover, along with the Dalits, they had voted for the Congress party for many years.

The long-drawn-out campaign also witnessed a keen contest between the BSP and the SP for the support of Brahmins. The SP held conferences to attract Brahmins in districts where they had a sizeable presence and declared Parshuram Jayanti (11 May) as a public holiday. Some media reports said that a small section of Brahmins preferred joining the SP because they argued that it did not abuse them like the BSP had done in the past. The SP also employed various methods to attract the Vaishya community, such as welcoming important leaders like Naresh Agarwal who had defected from the Congress and Banwarilal Kanchhal from the BJP, and deciding not to implement value-added tax in the state. This resulted in important victories including that of Shyamcharan Gupta from Banda on an SP ticket.[59] Mayawati, in turn, argued that the deterioration in law and order in UP during the rule of the SP had instilled a sense of insecurity among traders, who were now tilting towards the BSP. Pointing to the drive against criminals during their rule on the slogan of 'Bahujan–Mahajan bhai-bhai', the BSP pointed out that both Dalits and traders were the victims of social violence and crime.

Neither the SP nor the BJP took Mayawati's campaign seriously. The former believed that the Brahmins were interested only in tactical caste voting across parties, and their turnout at Mayawati's conferences was not an accurate indication of their intentions. The BJP leadership felt that the Brahmins would soon be disillusioned with Mayawati and return to their party. Nevertheless, Mayawati's tactics added a new dimension to caste politics in UP, and Brahmins began 'feeling wanted' after a long time.

Electoral Results: BSP still a Dalit Party

In the 2007 assembly elections, contrary to expectations, the BSP obtained an absolute majority for the first time, gaining 206 seats and 30.43 per cent of the votes,[60] a massive gain of 108 seats and 7.31 per cent over the 2002 elections. While the SP marginally increased its vote share, the BJP and Congress obtained fewer seats and votes than in 2002. The BSP was the only party that gained seats and votes from all classes and regions in UP.[61] Cutting across age, gender, education, locality and economic status, its highest gains were among the educated and middle-class voters. The party's highest seat gains were in east UP and Doab, the highest number of votes in Doab and

Avadh. There were twenty-one districts where its vote share rose by more than 10 percentage points.[62]

A study argued that while caste was certainly an important variable in the BSP victory, it was one among several that voters took into account.[63] Using a disaggregated analysis, by assembly seats and by region, it pointed to no simple correlation between caste and outcome. The BSP did use caste but only as 'a metaphor to build innovative grassroots alliances,' which demonstrated that the concerns of other communities mattered as much as those of the Dalits. Further, on a rough count, the BSP's 206 victors were from a wide selection of castes: about sixty-two SCs, fifty-seven Muslims, thirty-four Brahmins, nineteen Thakurs and about fifty from the OBC communities, represented largely, but not exclusively, by Yadavs. The BSP won sixty-two of the eighty-nine SC-reserved seats constituencies.[64]

The study also found that the correlation between Brahmin majority areas and BSP's performance was not very strong.[65] Rather, the many Brahmin sammelans and rallies neutralized 'savarna caste anxieties'. By reaching out to Brahmins, Mayawati signalled to all the upper castes that she was willing to listen to their problems as well. Also, unlike the SP, the BSP would not be so favourably inclined towards Yadavs and other dominant OBCs. Considering the efforts put in to mobilize Brahmins, there was certainly a shift—of perhaps even '2 to 3 per cent of upper castes'—in her favour as she had hoped, significant enough in terms of tilting the balance.[66] This was possible due to the image of Mayawati, built in the 1990s, as a strong leader able to withstand the challenge from the BJP and to ensure the prevalence of law and order.

Rather, the BSP benefitted from greater support from the OBCs and Muslims.[67] The strategy of giving tickets to 110

OBCs contributed substantially to its victory, getting it seats and votes from the Kurmi, Lodh, Jat and other peasant castes. It also increased its vote share among Muslims to 17 per cent, compared to 10 per cent in 2002 and 2004, which resulted in twenty-eight out of sixty-one Muslim candidates of the BSP winning. The SP lost about 7 per cent support of the Muslims to the BSP.[68]

Moreover, the percentage of Brahmin votes rose for the BSP, which gained 16 per cent, 11 per cent higher than in 2002. In the past, despite giving tickets to upper-castes, it had received the electoral support of only a small segment, compared to the BJP and the Congress.[69] More importantly, in 2007, the BSP obtained a *massive 86 per cent support from the Jatavs*, and 58 per cent of the other SCs.[70] Thus, despite forming coalitions, giving tickets to upper castes in the 1990s, and in 2007 a direct outreach to the Brahmins, the BSP remained a Dalit party. Its big push towards widening its base with upper-caste support and gaining a majority was clearly and effectively communicated to and supported by its Dalit voters.

The results set the stage for an uneasy relationship between Brahmins and Dalits during Mayawati's regime (2007–12). On the one hand, there was a strong perception among Brahmins that it was their support that made the victory of the BSP possible, and they expected political power, position and some benefits. On the other hand, the Dalits believed that by accommodating the upper castes and consolidating Dalits behind Mayawati, they had scripted the historic win. They were also wary of Mayawati's attitude and the possibility of larger benefits to the upper castes, especially Brahmins. These perceptions were bound to create contradictions in the working of the sarvajan regime. However, for our larger story, this was also the last time the BSP was able to consolidate the Dalit vote from all sections of the community. Once the sarvajan regime fell under the weight of these contradictions in 2012, the process of unravelling of the BSP began. It is to these questions that we now turn.

2

Sarvajan in Practice

～

Today we are witnessing the Raj Tilak of a Dalit, and that too of a woman, virtually conducted by hundreds of thousands of Brahmins.

—A BSP supporter at the swearing-in
ceremony of Mayawati[1]

In December 2021, during the campaign for the 2022 UP assembly elections, the Yogi Adityanath-led government ran a series of expensive, front-page advertisements in leading newspapers that claimed per capita income in UP had doubled in the four years of the BJP government, and four lakh jobs had been created since 2017.[2] However, the government's own data tells a different story. Official estimates show that the gross state domestic product of UP rose at a compound growth

29

rate of only 1.95 per cent per annum, and per capita income increased by merely 0.43 per cent on average over 2017–21. In sharp contrast, the growth rate was 6.92 per cent during 2012–17 under the previous SP government, and GDP grew to 7.28 per cent as against a target of 6.10 per cent under the Mayawati government of 2007–12.[3] The performance of UP was worse under the BJP regime despite the 'double engine' of Modi and Adityanath, where both had the largest majority that any government in UP's history has had in the last three decades.

In contrast, in her five years, Mayawati pumped in over ₹1 lakh crore into various schemes, particularly for the Dalits and the marginalized. Economic growth was also spurred by heavy investment in real estate in the National Capital Region, in expressways, in the power sector and in small and medium enterprises.[4] A number of the expressways inaugurated by Modi prior to the 2022 assembly elections were actually begun by Mayawati and taken forward by Akhilesh Yadav. The story of Mayawati's sarvajan regime is undoubtedly one of achievements but also failures: achievements witnessed in the economic progress during this period, and failures leading to the ignominious defeat in 2012. While the latter is well known, the former has been largely ignored. It is on this contradiction of success and failure, and its long-term implications for the BSP, that our narrative is focused.

The capture of power by the BSP in 2007 was a historic occasion with a Dalit party forming a majority government for the first time in post-independence India, in the state of UP. The celebratory crowds that streamed in to Lucknow on 13 May, the day Mayawati took over as chief minister, were not only massive but consisted of both Dalits and Brahmins.[5] But most Dalits, *despite the collaboration with Brahmins, saw it as a victory against the upper and backward castes.* A group of Dalits who had come from Karchana in Allahabad district 'to take part in Behenji's swearing-in ceremony' saw it as an occasion to 'celebrate their own victory against the Thakur-dominated Samajwadi Party in their area'.[6] While they were aware of the dissimilarity between them and the rising Brahmin support base of the party, their perception of the differences and their interpretation of the new socio-political collaboration had dimensions beyond the conventional. The leader of the group, who has been with the BSP right from the mid-1980s when Kanshi Ram started the party, held that the day was monumental for members like him. 'It is not merely because the party has won a majority on its own, but because the elections and the swearing-in ceremony overturned a rigid Brahminical socio-cultural custom that persisted for centuries, right from the period of mythical history,' he said.[7]

The upper castes and the Dalits had different perceptions and expectations from the government. During the campaign, Mayawati was able to convince her Dalit followers that the BSP remained 'their' party despite it mobilizing the upper castes; but she would have to do the same when in power, which, as we shall see, was not easy. Senior BSP leaders were more cautious and understood the situation better. Sukhdev Singh Rajbhar, speaking soon after the results were declared, held that the core Dalit base understood that the aspirations of the Dalits should not manifest themselves as demands immediately, and that this victory was to be seen only as one step in the struggle of the marginalized sections to assert their rights.[8]

At the same time, apprehensions were expressed by the upper castes that Mayawati would forget them after winning the elections. But of the total of forty-nine ministers sworn in, the cabinet with nineteen ministers comprised eight leaders from other backward castes, six from the upper castes (three were

Brahmin), four Dalits and one Muslim. Two of Mayawati's close confidants—Naseemuddin Siddiqui and Satish Chandra Mishra—were the first to be sworn in after Mayawati. But it was Mishra, member of the Rajya Sabha, who took his seat behind her, the only BSP leader to be seated on the stage besides her.[9] Mishra quit his post a few months later, as it was decided by Mayawati that he would devote his energies to the important task obtaining the support of the upper castes in other states for the BSP.[10]

The caste composition of her ministry allayed the fears of upper-caste BSP MLAs, particularly the Brahmins. By giving more cabinet berths to Brahmins, she tried to send out the message that their interests were secure in her regime, which had been otherwise known for its aggressive Dalit agenda during her earlier three stints as chief minister. While a number of OBCs were included, it was felt that since they were from different castes, they would compete with one another for social, economic and political supremacy. A large number of ministers of state with independent charge were also sworn in. Here, Mayawati catered to her loyal vote bank of Dalits, appointing nine leaders from the community. Interestingly, a majority of the ministers from the upper castes, OBCs and Dalits at the swearing ceremony touched Mayawati's feet, a Hindu act of much significance in the cow belt, though many Brahmin ministers preferred not to, only bowing low with a 'namaste'.[11]

However, at this moment of triumph, few Dalit leaders realized that the sarvajan experiment faced a paradox that contributed to the BSP's defeat in 2012: on the one hand a bad slump in the economy, and on the other the rising aspiration among Dalits that their 'party's own government' would provide them rapid material advancement. The slump was a result of the politics of 'competitive populism' in UP during the

1990s. As no party was able to gain a majority, the SP and BSP as well as the BJP, when in power, vied with each other to make and fulfill populist promises in order to gain the support of various social groups, and showed little political will to mobilize additional resources, putting a tremendous burden on public expenditure.[12] Mayawati had made no effort to conceal her pro-Dalit agenda, arguing that 'only those schemes that are in the interest of the Dalits and other downtrodden sections would be carried forward'.[13]

Moreover, while in power in the 1990s, Mayawati had spent a considerable amount on building Ambedkar parks and creating and naming new districts after Bahujan saints and gurus.[14] Work on many memorials and parks, such as the Dr Bhimrao Ambedkar Samajike Parivartan Prateek Sthan (Social Transformation Symbol Spot) and Dr Bhimrao Ambedkar Smarak in Lucknow, were begun during the earlier Mayawati governments in the 1990s, and completed after 2007 at considerable cost.[15] These programmes had emptied the state treasury in the 1990s, leaving little for investment in key sectors such as education, infrastructure and health. UP, a revenue surplus state in the 1980s, entered a 'debt trap'—a vicious circle of low-growth rates, fiscal crisis and stagnation.[16] Consequently, by the 2000s, the condition of the poorer sections—which included a major chunk of the Dalits—worsened. The National Human Development Report 2001 revealed that per capita consumption expenditure fell between 1993–94 and 1999–2000, indicating deterioration in living standards.[17]

This meant that despite heading a majority government, the BSP would find it difficult to address the issue of uplifting Dalits—or the requirements of the upper castes—without first addressing the larger issue of the lack of development and economic collapse that the state was facing. Mayawati faced the daunting task of balancing the aspirations and needs of the Dalits and the upper castes, which could lead to rivalry and conflict. It is against this background of aspirations, hopes and apprehensions that the story of the sarvajan regime in UP under Mayawati needs to be told.

Sarvajan Policies

All this, however, was in the past; a different Mayawati rode to power in 2007. On assuming office on 13 May 2007, she made it clear that her government's focus would be the welfare of all sections of society, not only the Dalit–Bahujans.[18] The economic agenda announced by the new BSP government provided room for some *cautious optimism* as it was radically different from that of the retributive social justice agenda of the past. On 20 July 2007, she sought a special development package of ₹80,000 crore from the Centre for the Eleventh Five-Year Plan. The 'priority areas' of her government were spelt out as 'rural development, agriculture, social development and infrastructure, all-round development of all social segments and regions, and making the state conducive for attracting investment'.[19] Her request included a 'special area incentive package' of ₹9,400 crore, and ₹4,700 crore separately for developing infrastructure in the two most backward regions of the state—Purvanchal and Bundelkhand. In addition, she asked for ₹22,000 crore for the development of agriculture and allied sectors, ₹6,500 crore for rural development, and ₹13,300 crore for other important proposals for the integrated development of the state.[20]

Mayawati announced a target of 10 per cent growth rate and reduction in the number of people below the poverty line by half, during the plan period. In contrast to her earlier exclusionary policies, she requested the Centre to consider reservations and job quotas for the poor among the upper-castes.[21] To win over industrialists and yet help disadvantaged groups, Mayawati offered a voluntary scheme of 'incentives' and 'facilities' in the form of tax and other rebates to the former to set up units in UP if they reserved 30 per cent jobs for members of the SC, OBC, minorities and 'economically backward upper castes' groups.[22]

It was only after months of negotiation with the Centre that Mayawati was able to obtain ₹80,000 crore for UP on 18 February 2008; not as a separate package, but as part of the overall resources provided to the state under the Eleventh Plan.[23] According to the Prime Minister's Office, the total amount made available to the state under the plan was ₹2, 80,000 crore, amounting to three-and-a-half times the resources made available in the Tenth Plan. The decision came despite the fact that the Planning Commission's expert committee, which looked into Mayawati's demands, observed that ₹1,81,000 crore of resources for UP would need 'major increase in the absorptive capacity, improvement in governance structures and major reform of the delivery system'. The expert committee further observed, 'If ₹80,000 crore as requested by the state government is added to it, the total investment of ₹2,60,000 crore will certainly be unmanageable and clearly beyond the capacity of the state to spend.'[24] The funds were clearly part of a political deal, as the announcement from the Prime Minister's Office came a month after Mayawati threatened to withdraw her support to the Congress-led UPA government if it did not meet her demands.

Armed with these funds, Mayawati attempted to change the face of UP. Our analysis of her policies and programmes suggests that the BSP government—the first majority government since 1991—did attempt, and successfully introduced, substantial development in UP. A central feature of her economic agenda and budget expenditure to meet it was the attempt to achieve *a fine balance* between the expectations of the upper castes and the general population and the needs and aspirations of the Dalits, particularly the poorer sections. This is reflected in the pattern of budgetary expenditure of the BSP government over the period 2007 to 2011 (see Table 5, Appendix 1).[25] Expenditure in departments such as education, social welfare (for SC/ST), women and children welfare, health and urban development nearly doubled compared to the pre-2007 period. The government spent the largest amount of its budget on social security for these groups. Minority welfare expenditure increased nearly four times. Expenditure in agriculture and housing increased significantly but remained constant on energy. Sugarcane development (including the sugar industry), though increased for the first three years, decreased in the last year, to make way for other small-, medium- and large-scale industries that were neglected in the previous three years.[26]

Mayawati's developmental programmes fell into roughly three categories: social security for the poorer sections such as welfare, housing, education, health, a part of which was kept aside for Dalits; provision of infrastructure, which would help all social groups; and specific programmes for Dalits.[27] The average per capita expenditure on social security per year in the first three years was ₹805.20 on social welfare, backward classes welfare, welfare of physically handicapped persons, minority welfare, and women and children development.[28] The Uttar Pradesh Mukhyamantri Mahamaya Garib Arthik Madad Yojana was the most important scheme started in January 2010 on Mayawati's birthday. Under it, at least 50 per cent of poor SC/ST families, not included in the below-poverty-line survey 2002 or pension or food security, received ₹300 per month, the aim being to benefit 30 lakh people in its first year of implementation.[29]

A study by Shyam Singh argues that BSP's performance in the scheme Housing for All, which provided housing security in rural and urban areas and city slums, was 'very impressive'.[30] It provided three urban housing security schemes: Kanshi Ram Sahari Gareeb Awaas Yojana (KSGAY) for the urban poor in the general category, in which OBCs and SCs received 23 per cent and 27 per cent of total benefits, respectively. For city dwellers, 1.01 lakh houses were to be built, and in three years 96,418 houses were constructed. For the rural poor, two new schemes were started: Mahmaya Awaas Yojana (MAY) exclusively for SC/ST under which 3.06 lakh SC/ST families benefited at a cost of ₹949 crore; and Mahamaya Sarva Awaas Yojana for non-SC/ST poor under which 50,000 families benefitted at a cost of ₹180 crore.[31] The Sarvajan Hitay Garib Awas (Slum Area) Malikana Haq Yojana provided slum-dwellers with access to legal possession over a minimum of an area of thirty square metres and benefitted nearly 7,232 families.[32] For SC/ST categories, under the Manyawar Shri Kanshi Ramji Sheri SC/ST Basti Samagra Vikas Yojna, 250 slum areas were developed as model bastis, with 25 lakh houses at a cost of ₹3,000 crore.

The study also points to some 'remarkable steps' taken by the government for the uplift of girl children and women.[33] The Mahamaya Garib Balika Ashirvad Yojana begun in 2009, again on Mayawati's birthday, provided (only two) girls born in families below the poverty line on or after 15 January 2009 with a fixed deposit for a period of eighteen years, to be paid to the girl if she remained unmarried until then. The three-year achievement report of the government indicates that 'more than a lakh' girls benefitted from this programme. The government also provisioned ₹11,000 for a widow who wished to remarry. For child development, an Anganwadi programme provided cooked food for children.[34] Similarly, for young girls pursuing higher education, the government provided ₹15,000, a bicycle on reaching class ten, and an additional ₹10,000 on promotion to class twelve under the Savitri Bai Phule Shiksha Madad Yojana. A total of 'more than 6.8 lakh' girl students had benefitted from this scheme by May 2011.[35]

Under the Janani Suraksha Yojna, a centrally funded scheme, the state government provided ₹1,000 to urban women beneficiaries and ₹1,400 to rural beneficiaries. A study shows that the amount spent on the healthcare of women increased, particularly in the first two to three years of the government; nearly 65 per cent of pregnant women went to public health centres for delivery, while 27 per cent opted for private hospitals in the rural areas, though this is lower than in other states.[36] However, Shyam Singh's study argues that the government's response in the field of health was not satisfactory, with mostly old schemes and some new ones funded by the Centre being implemented by the state government. In the field of education, only one new social security scheme was financed by the government for girl students of classes eleven and twelve: one bicycle, a sum of ₹25,000 in two instalments and scholarships to pre- and post-metric students of all categories. Government reports showed that the quality of primary and secondary education had gone down during the first three years and the overall progress of the government during 2007–09 was 'lagging'.

On completing six months in office in November 2007, Mayawati claimed that her government had put into place a slew of inclusive developmental and pro-poor policies, a number of which she claimed were aimed at the all-round development of the state.[37] Her government also claimed that the establishment of an anti-terror squad[38] to deal with terrorist activities had helped in eliminating the land mafia, professional killers, the liquor and drug mafia, kidnappers and extortionists; 23 per cent of all thana heads were appointed from scheduled castes and tribes, 27 per cent from backward categories including minorities, and 50 per cent from other caste groups to ensure that people belonging to all sections of the population had confidence in the police.

A number of big infrastructure, power, healthcare and educational projects were initiated by the BSP government, a number of them based on public–private partnership.[39] In fact, many expressways inaugurated by PM Modi during his campaign for the 2022 assembly elections were actually started during Mayawati's regime and continued under the SP government of 2012–17. Some important projects that were started include the Yamuna Expressway which had been stalled in 2003; the Ganga Expressway to connect Noida with Ballia;[40] the Sanauta–Purkazi Expressway project along the upper Ganga Canal bank; an eight-lane expressway from Varanasi and Ballia to Noida connecting eastern UP to western UP;[41] and a ring road at a cost of ₹1,100 crore in the Taj city, Agra. The first phase of the Delhi–Noida–Greater Noida Metro Rail Link, first phase, from Delhi to Noida was completed.[42] Two international airports were planned at Kushinagar and Jewar but did not take off. An amended special economic zone (SEZ) policy[43] and an investment of ₹9,209 crore in flood control was put in place. In the power sector, the government planned to generate 30,000-megawatts of power by setting up new thermal power plants, many to be built by the National Thermal Power Corporation, eight of which were together expected to add an installed capacity of 7,200MW by 2011.[44] It also built the first solar power plant in Naini, about twenty-five kilometres from Allahabad.[45]

The BSP government built a number of hospitals and educational institutes, among them a 286-bed super-speciality centenary hospital and a fifty-bed critical care unit at the King George's Medical University, Lucknow.[46] In 2007, work on the ₹500-crore Manyawar Kanshiram Multi-Speciality Hospital in Greater Noida[47] and the Dr B.R. Ambedkar Multi-Speciality Hospital in Sector 30, Noida was initiated.[48] Constructed at a total cost of ₹600 crore, four institutions were established in Noida—Mahamaya Girls' Inter College in Sector 44, Panchsheel Boys Inter College in Sector 91, Savitri Bai Phule Girls' Inter College in Kasna (Greater Noida) and Gautam Buddha Boy's Inter College (Greater Noida). They have continued even after her term was over to provide good quality education.[49]

For the benefit of entrepreneurs, in 2011 the government launched a revamped Nivesh Mitra, an online investment-friendly, time-bound, single-window clearance scheme that had been conceptualized in 2006, using advanced internet-based facility.[50] In sharp contrast to earlier trademark pomp and splendour celebrations, on her fifty-second birthday on 15 January 2011, Mayawati dedicated to the people of Lucknow a new sewage treatment plant, the largest in Asia, which could treat 345 million litres of sewage, as against the existing plant which processed only 42 million litres, sending most of the waste back into the river Gomti.[51]

Interestingly, the Mayawati government inaugurated, on 18 October 2011, India's first Formula One (F1) event, the Grand Prix. Built at an estimated cost of about ₹20 billion,[52] in public–private partnership with the Jaypee group, the 5.14-kilometre-long Buddh International Circuit at Greater Noida was considered a massive success. Used for about three years, the race track generated much criticism about whether a government committed to removing poverty should have taken up such an elite project. An editorial in a leading daily commented that in a poor country, F1 racing, catering to a class of new rich Indians, was 'a criminal waste of money'. Yet, it also argued that F1 was both 'a sport and a business' and 'indeed a fantastic medium for promoting brands in overseas market'. Top business houses vied for advertising space during the Grand Prix and the tournament which had a total global television audience of 527 million, and attracted 95,000 spectators at the first race, opened a new chapter in Indian sports as a powerful platform for the steadily growing Indian automotive sector to position its brands globally.[53] The next SP government, however, refused to accept F1 as a sport and classified it as entertainment, which meant that high taxes would have to be paid, much to the disappointment of racing enthusiasts.[54]

At the same time, Mayawati paid special attention to the needs of Dalits through a number of schemes. She revived the Ambedkar Village programme[55] in September 2007, creating a department headed by a principal secretary-rank officer to oversee development at regular intervals.[56] The government emphasized upon creating cement concrete village roads, kerb channel drains and link roads connecting villages to the main road, electrification, providing hygienic toilets, drinking water, housing for the poor and schools in the selected villages.[57] A number of other schemes benefitted SCs: loans amounting to ₹77.75 crore released between 1985 and 1997 through the UP SC Finance and Development Corporation were waived off, benefitting more than five lakh families, continuous enhancement of budget allocations for SC welfare and for the SC Component Plan, as Table 5 shows, fair price shops allotted to more than 17,000 SC/ST persons and 202 hostels built for students belonging to the SC/ST and OBC categories.[58]

Return to Dalit Agenda

Despite these efforts to satisfy all social groups through her programmes, within a few months of Mayawati assuming office, there were rumblings of discontent, particularly among the powerful Jatavs, who felt their needs were neglected. Hence, she had to take some decisions to satisfy her core constituency. She requested an additional ₹23,000 crore as special assistance from the UPA government for SC/ST, OBC and minority welfare. The budget for SC welfare was increased each year from 2008–09 onwards, as Table 5 shows. She also supported the demand that reservations be extended to the private sector and put into the Ninth Schedule of the Constitution, and announced, in June 2010, rigorous implementation of a law enacted in 2002 to ensure actual possession by Dalits of land allotted to them.[59]

But the most controversial step by Mayawati was to restart the building of memorials and parks dedicated to Dalit icons. An important example of this was the decision to demolish the Gomti Nagar cricket stadium in Lucknow July 2008, built just ten years earlier, so that its land could be included in an adjacent Ambedkar memorial project.[60] The demolition caused much consternation and anger among the sports community as it destroyed one of the best sports grounds, the only one with an Olympics-size swimming pool, a cricket hostel and facilities for other sports including basketball, table-tennis, badminton and tennis.[61] With total disregard to public criticism, Mayawati continued building memorials with greater vigour to reassure the Dalits that the BSP remained 'their party'. As many as ten memorials were built at prime locations in Lucknow. Some were new; others were constructed on land available after demolishing projects built only a few years ago, some built during Mayawati's previous regimes.[62] Some of the most important were the Dr Bhimrao Ambedkar Samajik Parivartan Prateek Sthal and the Manyavar Shri Kanshi Ramji Green Garden in Lucknow, one of the biggest ecological parks in the world with 500 artificial animals made of bronze, ten bronze fountains with water bodies and a pathway of about thirteen kilometres surrounding it, which opened on 3 March 2011.[63] The Noida park, on the outskirts of New Delhi, that houses a social transformation gallery and a social transformation museum, was built at a cost of around ₹300 crore and inaugurated by Mayawati on 14 October 2011.[64]

The statue-building spree led to tremendous criticism. As one media report said, 'Money, land, manpower—nothing comes in the way, not even the fact that the high court was seized of the matter.'[65] Critics described it as a waste of resources in a state where social and economic indicators were among the lowest in the country. She was accused of narcissism—in at least four of these places, statues of Mayawati herself were installed and more were being built. As her political biographer put it, eager to promote symbols of the Dalit community, 'she soon, however, displayed a personality cult which materialized in "pharaonic" works: giant parks, giant monuments, giant statues of herself and Kanshi Ram, to the extent that all these constructions had to be veiled for the 2012 assembly elections on the order of the Election Commission'.[66]

But nothing deterred Mayawati. For her, it was BSP's way of expressing its gratitude to the great men who inspired the movement. Regarding her own statues, she had a stock reply: she was fulfilling the wish of her mentor Kanshi Ram, who had willed that her statue be installed wherever his statue was put up.[67] Pointing to the crores of rupees spent in constructing memorials of the Nehru–Gandhi family, Mayawati argued that the BSP government's creation of cultural symbols was out of sheer compulsion as no other government had bestowed appropriate honours on these 'great leaders' of the Dalit–Bahujan community.[68] 'Now we have given them that honour,' she would proclaim. She asserted that 'this memorial is for so many Dalits who now live in the capital and also for the people of western UP who can't visit Lucknow'. Contrary to reports that she had spent 1 per cent of UP's budget on her dream projects, she said that most of the funds were based on donations.[69]

As a defiant gesture to critics who held that Mayawati had used public funds to build statues, amass massive personal wealth, throw lavish birthday parties and accumulate diamond jewellery, her party presented her with a garland made of 1,000-rupee notes on 15 March 2010, estimated to have cost between $400,000 and $2m (₹3,26,68,700 and ₹16,33,66,100) and a second one at a party meeting a few days later, this time worth ₹18 Lakhs (US $ 22,050.04).[70] State minister Naseemuddin Siddiqui told the media: 'We today presented another garland of ₹1.8 million to the party supremo collected by party units in all eighteen divisions in the state. Wherever she goes, she will henceforth be greeted with garlands of notes and not with garlands of flowers.'[71]

Evaluating Sarvajan

How did the people of UP evaluate development during Mayawati's tenure as CM? The question is significant not only because of the defeat in the 2012 assembly elections but the sudden loss of Dalit support following it, which weakened the BSP and hastened its decline. During our interaction with Sudhindra Bhadoria, senior BSP leader and former party spokesperson,[72] he forcefully argued that Mayawati had introduced immense development in UP. According to him, no chief minister, 'has done as much for the state in recent decades'. Following her defeat in 2012, in the context of the September 2013 riots in Muzaffarnagar, political leaders such as Digvijaya Singh,[73] Sonia Gandhi[74] and Beni Prasad Verma[75] pointed out that there was better maintenance of law and order, no communal riots and better economic development for all sections during her regime than under Akhilesh Yadav. The imam of Jama Masjid, Maulana Ahmed Bukhari praised Mayawati, saying 'only she knows how to rule'.[76]

In spite of the criticism regarding expenditure on statues, reports in the media pointed out that the vital parameters of the economy had changed for the better in UP. The human development index report showed that its net state domestic product grew by 76 per cent over five years (2006–2011), almost at par with Gujarat.[77] The planning ministry reports revealed that UP was among five states with higher growth rates than their Eleventh Plan (2007–12) targets. As mentioned earlier, the GDP of UP grew to 7.28 per cent; it was also considered the 'best performing state in agriculture' by the UPA government. But the same report also emphasizes some harsh realities. Other parameters on UP's human development index remained below the national average of 0.467 due to poor health services and low incomes. Those at the grassroots level did not enjoy the benefits of welfare schemes due to corruption. But the report held that whatever be the case, there was no doubt that Dalits were seeing better days, at least in cities. It cited the example of Para, a locality in Lucknow, where Dalits now lived in houses donated by the government. For Shweta, a Dalit student, the free bicycle from the government revolutionized her life. 'Now girls can easily go to school and run errands,' she said.[78]

At a seminar in 2008, retired IAS officers who had served in UP said there was hope within the civil services that, having obtained a full majority in 2007, Mayawati would attempt all-round development and improve governance in UP.[79] V. Ravi Shankar pointed out that whenever Mayawati was chief minister, even for short periods, her grip on the administration was strong, with better maintenance of law and order.[80] He highlighted some achievements of her government: improvement in the fiscal position with a surplus in 2007; introduction of value-added tax and public–private partnership enabling the government to work with industry; simplification of regulatory controls leading to big projects such as the Taj and Ganga Expressways; and the promise to restore stability of tenure, accountability and rationalize transfer of officers with reactivation of the Civil Services Board. Anand Swarup[81] pointed to a more mixed record: the performance of NREGA was judged as average or below average by the Citizens Report on Governance and Development 2007, but the employment provided under it was 95 per cent; percentage of farmers indebted in UP was 40.3 per cent, lower than the national average of 48.6 per cent, with no reported farmer suicides. But little attention was given to the need to decentralize power to panchayats or to impart training in capacity building to gram sabhas.

Hari Singh Tyagi, a former Member of the Legislative Council from Meerut, described the 2007 election strategy as 'essentially opportunistic' and held that though it paid electoral dividends, it 'blunted the sharpness of the revolutionary movement of Dalits and upper castes'. Kanshi Ram, he argued, had worked hard to give this movement a steady momentum. Mayawati came to it when it was in its glorious phase, but with her idea of sarvajan, all programmes 'of Dalit uplift and consciousness have slowed down and at places even become defunct'.[82]

Senior journalist Venkitesh Ramakrishnan described the strategy as an 'effective campaign slogan for mass mobilization, a potent election strategy ... not an instrument of social reform'. He pointed out that immediately following the elections there were several instances when neither sections of Dalits nor Brahmins were keeping to the bhai-chara deal. Six months later, he found that in scores of villages in the districts of Baghpat, Muzaffarnagar and Meerut, the upper castes refused to allow Dalits to occupy the *patta* land[83] allotted to them by the government. He strongly felt that this inability to reconcile the conflicting political and economic interests of the two communities at two ends of the caste/class hierarchy required that it was time the BSP evolved a clearly laid-out ideological position on important social and political issues that would reassert its predominantly pro-Dalit position.[84]

Far more damning was the report of the Comptroller and Auditor General (CAG) tabled soon after the SP government took office in 2012,[85] which pointed to financial irregularities of over ₹10,000 crore, corruption and mismanagement of funds during the Mayawati regime. It showed large-scale financial irregularities and carelessness in monitoring the implementation of the National Rural Mission (NRHM), the release of 100 per cent funds to construction agencies without obtaining estimates and utilization certificates, and the procurement of goods and services not in consonance with the tendering process. The State Health Mission, a body headed by the chief minister to monitor the NRHM, did not meet even once during the 2005–10 period. CAG reports on 'commercial' and 'revenue receipts' revealed mismanagement in financial transactions made in various departments, including transport, excise and power supply. The CAG recommended a thorough probe by the Enforcement Directorate. In its report on state finances for 2010–11, it observed that the fiscal priority given by the previous Mayawati government to development, social and education sectors was not adequate in 2010–11, in spite of an overall increase by 15 per cent in the revenue receipts over the preceding year.[86]

How did Dalits themselves evaluate Mayawati's development policies, particularly the building of Ambedkar memorials and parks? This is an important question. The message Mayawati tried to send to Dalits through her memorials was *cultural symbolism*. The aim was to empower Dalits through the twin strategies of 'presence in space' and 'presence in time', both of which had been denied to them, literally and symbolically, for centuries.[87] Described as a 'modern-day female Ashoka', Mayawati claiming Dalit space and establishing a Dalit style of architecture—visually demanding that their icons were recognized—was integral to her brand of assertion, meant to unite Dalits in a singular 'imagined community'. As a Dalit member of Mayawati's cabinet remarked, 'The statues have given Dalits a place in the history of this country. Nobody can change that.'[88]

Yet, they were divided over whether Mayawati should have built so many memorials. On 5 December 2009, thousands of Dalits had thronged to the Dr Bhimrao Ambedkar Samajik Parivartan Sthal, opened on 17 September 2009, to mark the leader's fifty-third death anniversary.[89] But in 2012, a Dalit art student standing at a memorial pointed out that the money would have been better spent on schools. This literate and politically conscious student, however, does not represent the tens of millions of other Dalits who see these parks as a testament to Mayawati's 'zero to hero' story.[90] A cobbler who had travelled for a whole day to see one newly opened monument in Noida said, 'She makes me proud. I will vote for her, and my children will vote for her when I am gone.' Her personal wealth—she wore diamonds on special occasions—is justified similarly. All her wealth, said R.A. Mittal, a BSP organizer in Lucknow, came from donations from her supporters. As she had no children, the funds would be returned when she died so there would be no impropriety.[91] But former IPS officer and Dalit activist, S.R. Darapuri, viewed the memorials as a criminal waste of money. 'Babasaheb was not in favour of installing statues. Mayawati could have done wonders had she established Ambedkar libraries in every village,' he said.[92]

Over time, the controversy seems to have subsided and the memorials in Lucknow have become a sacred space for Dalits in UP and a major tourist attraction. Speaking to *The Hindu* newspaper prior to the 2019 Lok Sabha elections, visitors to the Ambedkar Memorial Park on the banks of the Gomti praised the beauty and architecture of the memorials, linking it to Dalit pride and the movement for social uplift. Vijay Pratap, a visitor, felt it was unfair of the Supreme Court to observe that Mayawati might have to 'deposit' public money spent on the memorials.[93] Pratap, who works for the National Rural Livelihood Mission in Bahraich district, claimed the issue was being raised before the 2019 Lok Sabha election to create 'negative thinking' among voters towards the BSP supremo. He said Mayawati was being targeted for her caste. Had Ambedkar been a savarna, the park would have been glorified. 'Why are these memorials (considered) a "wastage"? According to the caste structure, all castes have memorialized their icons. But when it comes to Dalit icons, they are pained and only see corruption. Nobody has a problem with the statue of Sardar Patel,' said Pratap. Ahmed Khan, a student at Lucknow University called it 'Lucknow *ki shaan*' (pride of Lucknow). 'It is a historic place, not a wastage of money. By that parameter then, the money spent on the Patel statue should also be handed back.' Staff at the park held that around 1,000–1,500 persons visited it daily, and more than 2,000 on weekends.[94]

However, by the time the 2009 Lok Sabha elections came around, there were reports of Dalits complaining that their villages lacked water, roads, schools and power while Mayawati was building parks and memorials. With the BSP unable to improve on its earlier tally of twenty seats in the Lok Sabha, a slew of changes were initiated to reassure its Dalit constituency: the marginalization of Brahmin leader S.C. Mishra and renewed importance to old-timers such as OBC leader Babu Singh Kushwaha and minority leader Siddiqui Naseemuddin Siddiqui; the replacement of 100 chairmen/vice-presidents of various local boards; a reshuffling of top bureaucrats to induct lower-caste officers; the gifting of 'currency garlands' by Dalit supporters to Mayawati at public rallies; hinting at a possible ministerial reshuffle, and the announcement of a Dalit mega rally in Lucknow in March 2010.[95] Prior to the 2012 elections, Mayawati declared that in her next term she would not build any more memorials but concentrate only on development; the phase of building parks and installing statues was over.

Crushing Electoral Defeat

Despite these controversies, Mayawati was able to manage the Dalit–Muslim–Brahmin alliance up to 2012. The BSP won three assembly and two Lok Sabha seats in the by-elections held in April 2008. The Congress, BJP and SP were badly defeated.[96] Brahmin candidates of the BSP won in Khalilabad and Bilgram constituencies, demonstrating that the upper castes still enjoyed support. BSP won the Muradnagar seat despite the Rashtriya Lok Dal (RLD) fielding a Muslim; its candidate, Akbar Ahmed

Dumpy, won the Azamgarh seat. The SP lost Azamgarh and Khalilabad, both Yadav bastions, despite fielding Yadavs in both constituencies. The results also pointed to the BJP being squeezed out of the state. It obtained 1.35 per cent of the vote in Muradnagar, 3.5 per cent in Colonelganj, 5.03 per cent in Bilgram and lost the deposit in Khalilabad.[97] The BSP also virtually swept the panchayat polls held in late October 2010, with BSP-supported candidates winning the maximum number of seats.[98]

But, as Table 1 (see Appendix) shows, the BSP suffered a crushing defeat in the 2012 assembly elections, obtaining only eighty seats and 30.43 per cent of the vote, compared to 206 seats and 23.92 per cent of the vote in 2007. The BSP obtained *more* votes from the Brahmins, Rajputs, Vaishyas and other-upper castes in 2012 than in 2007; in contrast, the Dalit votes dropped sharply.[99] Mayawati lost badly despite her efforts to implement numerous welfare programmes for Dalits and other poor sections and introduce all-round development for the general population. A post-poll survey[100] revealed a desire among a section of Dalits for expenditure on *development*, rather than *identity*; most were unhappy with the construction of memorials for Dalit icons which, it was felt, left little funds for better education, health, roads and other facilities. Corruption in the government and the wealth amassed by Mayawati was another reason.[101] But an important reason, which showed the change in Dalit thinking, was that Mayawati's victory had roused more aspirations and expectations among all sections of Dalits than could be fulfilled in the span of five years. The euphoria following BSP's victory was tremendous. However, UP is a backward state, and with the sharp deterioration of the economy, it would take a long time for the differences between the upper castes, who had long formed the elite, and the Dalits, who constituted the poorer sections, to be bridged.

The BSP's ignominious defeat in 2012 was significant for not only did it lose Dalit support, it marked the beginning of the swift decline of the party, a situation from which it has not recovered, as subsequent elections, including the recent 2022 assembly elections, show. It is to the reasons for the defeat and the process of continuing decline and existential crisis visible from 2012 onwards that we now turn.

3

Disillusionment, Decline, Existential Crisis

～～～

As someone told me during the elections, the BSP was not fighting this election for power. It was fighting this election (2012) to save its core.[1]

Even before the results of the 2012 assembly elections were announced, an observer pointed out, 'Mayawati knew that she was going to lose, and the cabinet passed a resolution dissolving the assembly. Never before has an incumbent shown such confidence about losing. Mayawati's body language during the campaign was proof of the same lack of confidence.'[2] However, another held that though she was subdued, she did not seem down, as seen from her words to the press: 'Across the state, Dalits have voted for the BSP. That is why the BSP is number two. Otherwise, my position would have been like Lalu's in Bihar.'[3] The defeat of the BSP was not surprising; what was surprising was that its tally of seats dropped by more than half. It lost 126 seats, and 4.5 per cent in votes; it won only fifteen out of eighty-five reserved seats.[4]

From 2012 onwards, Dalit politics in UP underwent a profound change; the defeat of the BSP began a process of rapid decline, visible in electoral results, organizational strength and leadership. In the 2014 Lok Sabha elections, the BSP won no seat, in the 2017 assembly elections just nineteen seats, and in the Lok Sabha elections of 2019 just ten seats, though in every election it retained around 20 per cent of the vote. This changed in the recently concluded 2022 assembly elections in which the BSP obtained one seat, but its vote share dropped to 12.9 per cent, which it last obtained in the mid-1990s.[5]

More important than the loss of seats, the BSP began to lose support from its core group—the Jatavs, who were deemed close to Mayawati. As Table 2 (see Appendix 1) shows, from the high watermark of 86 per cent in 2007, Jatav support fell to 62 per cent in 2012, a drop of 24 per cent; Balmikis went from 71 per cent to 42 per cent, a drop of 30 per cent; and other SCs from 58 per cent to 45 per cent. The bulk of this vote, at this point, shifted to the SP. This indicated *a seminal shift in the pattern of electoral support to the BSP*. Over the previous two decades, the success of the BSP had rested on a strategy of securing the votes of the vast majority of the state's Dalits, who made up 21 per cent of the electorate,[6] and supplementing this core with a smattering of votes from the backward sections of other communities, including Muslims and Brahmins. This pattern disappeared and has not reappeared.[7] These trends continued in the 2014 and 2019 Lok Sabha elections and the 2017 assembly elections, with the BJP successively grabbing more votes from Dalits, almost 50 per cent in the case of the smaller Dalit castes, though a lesser percentage from the Jatavs, who remained with the BSP in substantial numbers.

How does one explain these setbacks to the BSP post-2012, pushing it into an extreme crisis? In 2012, a commentator held that 'Mayawati's defeat is the BSP's victory ... Right now in UP, you will be told wherever you go that Mayawati's government benefited only Dalits, just as Mulayam's benefited only Yadavs. I met Brahmins and Bhumihars who would rather vote for the BJP or the Congress, but who said they were voting for SP this time to make sure the BSP loses.'[8] By 2020, the same commentator was more forthright: 'The Mayawati era is over. Bye-bye, Behenji.'[9] Also, following the rise of the Bhim Army, it was held that a new phase of assertion had begun and the BSP had competition from a younger generation of Dalits.[10] However, others have argued that 'political analysts and adversaries keep writing her (Mayawati) off, but the BSP remains a national entity. She has always tamed competition from within the Ambedkarite universe and kept her party a coherent and dominant force in politics ... There are today competing armies of "Bhim" and it remains to be seen who will take the movement forward.'[11]

Electoral defeats provide only part of the story of the tremendous change in Dalit politics. Our narrative of the political trajectory of the BSP post-2012 is woven around four developments, which are in line with important changes sweeping UP due to the waning of caste-based identities in the 2000s. First, a steady depletion of its social base and organizational strength due to considerable groups of smaller Dalits and some Jatavs moving towards the BJP post-2014. Second, despite her best efforts, Mayawati has not been able to rebuild the Dalit–Muslim alliance which was an important addition to Jatav support in the 1990s and which broke down due to the Muzaffarnagar riots of 2013. Third, equally important has been the departure of some of her closest and trusted lieutenants from the Muslim, OBC and Dalit communities in 2012, who had provided the BSP its varied support base, either through expulsion or poaching by the BJP. Fourth, the rise of the BJP under Narendra Modi, which pushed the BSP into the margins of the polity, an aspect that will be dealt with in greater detail in the second part of the book. As a result, since 2014, Mayawati has been struggling with little success to rebuild the BSP and her own image. Using these arguments, our narrative will trace the rapid electoral and organizational decline of the BSP since 2012.

Electoral Contests, Loss of Support Base: 2012 and Beyond

In 2012, the poor performance of the BSP was attributed by the media to the failure of Mayawati's sarvajan policy and it was felt that the BSP would be able to bounce back in the next elections. The parameters used to judge the defeat remained within the older political framework; the arrival of the BJP and particularly Modi at centre-stage in UP had yet to take place. The Centre for the Study of Developing Societies (CSDS) post-poll survey 2012[12] revealed evidence of dissatisfaction among Dalits with many aspects of governance by Mayawati, such as lack of quality education, employment, facilities in villages, failure to build roads, as well as corruption scandals. Although Dalits tended to judge the performance of the BSP more favourably than other communities, only one in four Dalits said conditions had improved; 43 per cent of Jatavs were 'very satisfied' and 30 per cent were 'satisfied'. Similarly, 31 per cent among other

Dalit groups were 'very satisfied' and 30 per cent 'satisfied'. While 75 per cent of the Dalits who thought development in UP had improved voted for the BSP, only around 40 per cent felt that development had stagnated or worsened.[13] Moreover, the construction of Dalit memorials and statues proved to be unpopular among a section, including Jatavs. While 73 per cent of Dalits who fully supported building statues voted for the BSP, only 57 per cent of Dalits who somewhat supported this did so, and this fell to less than 50 per cent among those who did not support the move.

Dalits who perceived that they did not get 'their share' of welfare 'patronage' through programmes for the poor and Dalits appear to have punished the BSP. A good example of this is the Uttar Pradesh Mukhya Mantri Mahamaya Garib Arthik Sahayata Yojana, inaugurated on Mayawati's birthday, under which poor SC, ST and families with female heads would get ₹300 per month. But data shows that due to poor communication, just under half the population knew about it, and only 53 per cent of Jatavs and 41 per cent of other Dalit communities were aware of it. Consequently, hardly 15 per cent of Jatavs, 13 per cent of other Dalits, and 5 per cent of Muslims benefitted, while 15 per cent of Yadavs and 6 per cent of upper castes did.[14] At the same time, Mayawati's personal wealth had increased considerably; she reported assets totalling ₹87.27 crore, according to an affidavit submitted to the Election Commission of India. This dented her image among Dalits, some of whom perhaps felt she had kept the spoils of office for herself rather than sharing them with her caste.[15]

The survey showed that while the older generation of Dalits, despite their unhappiness with Mayawati's policies, continued to vote for the BSP, the younger, better-educated, urban-based Dalits, with high level of expectations and likely to think the BSP was corrupt, were more likely to vote for other parties. Poorer Dalits and those involved in small businesses, farmers and low-grade professionals were the least likely to support the BSP; fewer women voted for the BSP.[16] In sum, the high expectations of Dalits were not fulfilled and Mayawati's policies seemed to be out of sync, particularly with the thinking of the younger generation.[17]

A long-drawn-out, acrimonious electoral campaign helped turn the tide against the BSP, with old foe Mulayam Singh saying he would 'do a Mubarak'[18] to Mayawati and recapture the state.[19] Mulayam was worried that Mayawati had done a lot to develop UP, which explains the shrill and nervous urgency with which he began his campaign. Three issues were used by the SP and the Congress to attack Mayawati: law and order, expenditure on statues and corruption, which helped move public opinion, including that of Dalits, against Mayawati. The first issue, as a leading newspaper pointed out, was not true since Mayawati had actually restored order. But the SP and the Congress, by focusing on rapes, violence against women and robberies, projected a picture of complete collapse of law and order.[20]

It was particularly the issue of corruption that gave Mayawati a poor image. By the end of her tenure, she had removed thirteen, that is, 40 per cent of her ministers in charge of important portfolios, such as health, education, agriculture and technology, for corruption after being indicted by the Lokayukta.[21] The UP-CAG report 2011,[22] which hauled up the government for spending more than the sanctioned amount on construction at the Bhim Rao Ambedkar Parivartan Sthal and Kanshi Ram Smarak Sthal in Lucknow, was widely reported in newspapers.[23] Finally, the review of the working of the NRHM revealed a huge scam, including a murder, leading to the resignation of family welfare minister, Babu Singh Kushwaha.[24]

The most damaging in the eyes of the Dalits was Mayawati getting the UP assembly to pass a supplementary budget that would provide funds for 'personal needs' at a time when the health sector, roads, education, water and sanitation conditions—which directly concern common people—were in poor shape.[25] Media reports pointed out that Mayawati owned thirty cars but wanted an additional twenty new Ambassadors and ten new jammer-fitted vehicles in her security cavalcade, and ₹26.4 crore had been sanctioned for this 'need'. Apart from the chief minister's official residence, two new houses had been built in Lucknow in the posh Mall Avenue area, at a cost of ₹50 crore, and more was being sanctioned for renovations.[26]

Accordingly, the run-up to the 2014 electoral campaign was one of intense struggle for Mayawati to sustain her relevance in UP politics. The BSP campaign, unlike earlier elections, was late, beginning from Lucknow in early 2014, and low key. Mayawati's speeches were targeted at the SP, whom she blamed for deterioration of law and order leading to 'jungle raj', and of being hand in glove with the BJP to create communal tension prior to the elections, resulting in the Muzaffarnagar riots.[27] Moreover, Dalit–Muslim clashes during the riots, in which Dalits for the first time supported the BJP and showed sympathy with riot-affected Hindus, damaged the base of the BSP. Mayawati, despite being popular among her cadre, did not put forward any strategy to respond to the intense Hindu–Muslim polarization facing Dalit workers. Consequently, while the party condemned the riots, BSP leaders and workers found it difficult to handle relations between Dalits and Muslims in many places since its base and particularly the local leadership straddled both communities. During communal incidents, BSP leaders like Kadir Rana, elected MP from Muzaffarnagar in 2009, often rushed to support the Muslim community that was involved, angering Hindu and Dalit supporters who also expected support. Rana, accused of rioting and making inflammatory speeches at a Muslim panchayat by the special investigation team looking into the incident, was not sure if he would be allowed to stand for election in 2014. Meanwhile, his wife Syeda Begum filed her nomination as an independent candidate for the same seat. Her nomination came as a surprise to the other parties as there was no known report of any friction or marital discord between the couple. Although Kadir Rana was not available for comment, sources said that he might have got his wife to file her papers as a 'dummy' candidate. 'Rana has already been charge-sheeted in connection with the September communal violence in the district. He may have fielded his wife to make sure that someone from his family remains in the fray in case his nomination papers are rejected, or if the BSP decides to drop him,' said local BSP leader. This created further tension between Rana and BSP workers.[28] These developments contributed to the break-up of the BSP's once-strong Dalit–Muslim alliance in western UP.

How did the BSP deal with these challenges? Mayawati reached out to the Muslim community during the 2014 campaign, pointing out that the BSP was a secular, Dalit-based party with whom they had much in common. She gave tickets to eighteen Muslims, as the return of riot victims to their villages suggested they were considering voting for a party that would defeat the BJP. She pointed out that while the BSP was in power (2007–12), there had been no riots as Muslim–Hindu bhai-chara committees were set up in many constituencies, and the Dalit–Brahmin–Muslim alliance was an attempt to take this concept further.

Second, during the initial stages of the campaign, the BSP continued to use its sarvajan strategy. At the same time, aware that the Dalits were unhappy with this strategy since her defeat in 2012, Mayawati had been quietly working to bring all sub-castes, particularly the non-Jatavs, back into the BSP's fold, trying to convey that the party was still committed to its original path of social transformation. But just before the 2014 election, an attempt was once again made to construct, in selected constituencies, a Dalit–Brahmin–Muslim alliance based on the sarvajan ideology.[29] She hoped to unite Dalits by giving tickets to both Jatavs and other sub-castes, and also to Muslim and Brahmin leaders ignored by the BJP. Fifteen OBCs, twenty-two Brahmins, eighteen Muslims, eight Thakurs and seventeen Dalits were given tickets. These shifts in campaign strategy confused its workers and did not help the BSP.[30]

Yet, despite the BJP's attempt to capture the Dalit vote-bank, the BSP emerged as the third-largest party in the country in terms of vote share (4.1 per cent), but did not win a single seat. This surprised even BJP leader Amit Shah, who had predicted that it would be the second-largest party in the state.[31] The most plausible reason was fragmentation of the non-BJP vote and numerous multi-cornered contests, which made converting seats to votes difficult within a first-past-the-post system. Hence, it was argued that it would be incorrect to write off the BSP in UP politics. The party had secured the second position in a total of thirty-four constituencies and increased its absolute number of votes in 2014 over the 2009 national elections, in forty-six parliamentary constituencies, emerging as the biggest challenge to the 'Modi wave'. More importantly, the BSP's challenge to the BJP was spread across all parts of the state, particularly in the northern districts of central and eastern UP; it was in

western UP and some parts of Bundelkhand that the party's
vote share fell.[32]

2017: Competition for Dalit Support

The BSP was significantly weakened by the movement of a
section of Dalits towards the BJP in 2014. However, this was
in the general elections and on this platform the BSP viewed
itself as having a strong position in UP. The period between
the 2014 general and 2017assembly elections was one of
heightened competition between a right-wing, upper-caste
Hindu party and a Dalit-based party attempting to hold onto
its support base.

Stung by the poor performance in 2014, Mayawati flagged
off an early and aggressive electoral campaign in 2016. Known
for working silently on the ground, the BSP began to use social
media, tweeting short, crisp messages and forming mutually
reinforcing links across Dalit social media groups. Along
with dividing UP into four zones under trusted lieutenants,
Mayawati planned big rallies in Agra, Allahabad, Azamgarh
and Saharanpur—all districts with large Dalit and Muslim
populations. At a well-attended rally in Agra on 21 August
2016, she attacked the BJP by calling it an anti-Dalit party and
one that treated Muslims badly.[33]

It is noteworthy that our fieldwork in riot-affected districts
in January 2017 indicated that the division between Jatavs and
non-Jatavs, a key feature of the 2014 CSDS survey, was, at least
at that point, not very clear.[34] While Dalits shared some of the
Hindutva constituent's anti-Muslim outlook in riot-affected
districts like Muzaffarnagar, Shamli, Mau and Gorakhpur, it was
questionable whether this would translate into a positive vote

for the BJP in an assembly election. Non-Jatavs like Balmikis in Muzaffarnagar and Shamli, and Pasis and Khatiks in Mau and Gorakhpur expressed a strong preference for the BSP, but admitted they had voted for other parties in previous elections. This indicated that the gap between their socio-cultural and political outlook could get narrower in some contexts or further widen in others.

Fieldwork also suggested sharp competition for Dalit votes between the BSP and the SP, which had gained Dalit votes in the 2012 assembly elections. The SP tried to divide the Dalit vote by recommending inclusion of seventeen non-Yadav OBC castes into the Dalit fold to unsettle the political calculations of the BJP and the BSP. But many Dalits did not want the SP back and seemed to prefer the BSP.[35] The pro-BSP sentiment of non-Jatav Dalits was articulated by a Kori Dalit at Ayodhya: '*SP ke raj me hum logon ki police me sunvayi nahi hai*' (The police are non-responsive to us during the SP rule). Similarly, a group of Pasi respondents, living in makeshift roadside accommodation near Jhansi in Bundelkhand, pointed to abandoned apartments built for the poor and the Dalits in the Kanshi Ram Awasiya Colony nearby during Mayawati's tenure. They said that within six months of the SP coming to power in 2012, water and electricity supply to the colony had been discontinued, forcing them to move to makeshift accommodation. Some of them were also critical of the BJP's rule after 2014, which, they felt, resulted in a loss of power to their community. A Pasi respondent at Faizabad said he voted for Modi in 2014 as Mayawati was not in the race for the PM's post; now he would vote for the BSP rather than Modi as the latter would not be the CM.[36]

Two significant developments during this period were Dalit protests against rising atrocities and the formation of the Bhim

Army under Chandrashekhar Azad in 2015 to deal with them. The fact that Modi took a long time to reach out to victims of these incidents led to a perception that his statements, which came very late and were largely symbolic and political in nature, would result in little action. The BJP's anti-Dalit image was further highlighted when senior party member Dayashankar Singh abused Mayawati in vile language, prompting her supporters to take to the streets in protest.[37]

In this situation, BJP leaders believed that some form of outreach to Dalits, particularly in western UP, was needed. It organized a huge Dhamma Chetna Yatra (Buddhist pilgrimage for raising consciousness) with about forty Buddhist monks, to cover all 403 constituencies in UP.[38] Starting on 24 April from Sarnath, it ended on 14 October in Lucknow, the day B.R. Ambedkar took *diksha*[39] and Ashoka is believed to have converted to Buddhism. The yatra bore the name of the All-India Bhikshu Sangh but was organized by BJP's state SC and national OBC morcha leaders. The attempt, as Harit, a Dalit BJP leader, pointed out, was to spread the message that while all other parties merely paid lip service, only the BJP worked for Dalits and respected Babasaheb Ambedkar. The BJP estimated that UP had at least 50,000 SC votes in almost each of its 403 constituencies, with the figure rising in some, making up 22 per cent of the total voters, of which over 60 per cent were Jatav supporters of Mayawati. The party was aware that it had no Dalit leader comparable to Mayawati. As BJP's Agra MP Ramshankar Katheria pointed out, 'You cannot win the election without creating a dent in Mayawati's votes.'[40]

The Dalits organized protests and there was an almost complete boycott of the Dhamma Chetna Yatra; rallies against it were held at Aligarh, Hathras and Mathura, where local BJP leaders were chased away. Describing the yatra as 'Gumrah Chetna Yatra'—the word 'gumrah' means to confuse or lead astray—they called their head monk Dhamma Viriyo an 'RSS agent'. Hathras BSP president, Dinesh Kumar Deshmukh, pointed out: 'The BJP knows that it cannot get Dalit votes. It needs a plan to enter Dalit colonies. Now they have purchased some fake Buddhist monks.' The yatra also drew strong criticism from the All-India Bhikhu Sangh which distanced itself from the programme, terming it an 'insult to Buddha and to Buddhism'. The Bhikhu Sangh president, Sadanand, was critical. '*Kharcha*, *parcha*, *charcha* (money, newspapers, publicity)—that's what politics is all about. For six months, you are in the news. What more do you want?' he asked. On 24 July, the monks of other factions drove away the local BJP leaders from a meeting in Aligarh after the Dalits present there protested against 'atrocities under BJP governments'.[41] Following this, a number of developments reflected the growing anxiety of the BJP, among them its claim that Rohith Vemula was not a Dalit[42] and its strategy of using nationalism through the Tiranga Yatras[43] to mark the seventieth year of independence to win over Dalits and backwards.

The BSP's efforts to woo Muslims, due to the perceived disenchantment and insecurity the community felt under the Akhilesh Yadav government, received a boost in August 2016 after four sitting opposition MLAs joined the BSP: Nawab Kazim Ali Khan from Swar (Rampur), Dilnawaz Khan from Sayana (Bulandshahr), Nawazish Alam Khan from Budhana (Muzaffarnagar), and Mohammad Muslim Khan from Tiloi (Amethi).[44] While the first moved from the SP (though he had won on a BSP ticket in 2007) and was a minister before leaving the party in 2012) the other three were from the Congress. Former BJP minister, Awadesh Kumar Verma also joined the BSP in the presence of Naseemuddin Siddiqui, party general secretary, and Gaya Charan Dinkar, leader of Opposition in the state assembly.

Accordingly, Mayawati gave 100 seats to Muslim candidates, including the four who had joined the BSP.[45] It was hoped that her reputation of being a tough administrator capable of maintaining law and order would appeal to Muslims who found that the SP government did not take action when atrocities were committed on them, particularly in western UP. Yet, it was known that the Muslims would choose between the BSP and SP closer to the elections, depending on which party they felt would perform better in relation to the BJP. But if the BSP was able to gain a large section of the Dalit and Muslim votes, it was felt that Mayawati could probably form a government, considering that both the BSP and SP were able to obtain majorities in 2007 and 2012 by obtaining about 29 per cent of the votes.[46]

Despite the efforts put in by Mayawati, both the BJP and SP performed better in the elections, getting 312 seats and 39.7 per cent, and forty-seven seats and 21.8 per cent of the vote, respectively. The BSP obtained nineteen seats, down from eighty in 2012, though it got 22.2 per cent of the vote;[47] it could win only two of the eighty-four reserved seats and fared badly in most districts with a large Dalit population, such as Agra, Sitapur and Kaushambi. Mayawati's attempt to forge a state-wide Dalit–Muslim combine also failed; only five Muslim candidates could win. The BJP managed to gain 66.1 per cent of the upper-caste vote, 58 per cent of the OBC and 55 per cent of the Kurmi–Koeri vote, 8 per cent of the Jatav vote and 37 per cent of the other Dalit votes.[48]

Rapid Decline Post-2017: Organizational Breakdown

The ignominious defeat of the BSP in 2017 led to its rapid decline due to the crumbling of its once-strong organizational structure, particularly at the district level. The decline had begun in 2012 but now became more pronounced. As veteran journalist Harish Damodaran[49] pointed out, Kanshi Ram built institutions like the BAMCEF, DS-4[50] and the BSP, but it was Mayawati who built the party organization to fight elections. Her success had been 'electoral' as she was a good strategist and planner. She created the post of district coordinator, a nodal position with considerable power and responsibility, always held by a Jatav or Chamar, on whom she depended heavily and with whom she consulted and strategized. Today, however, it was the district level and lower structures that had broken down, due to which the BSP was unravelling: 'Mayawati built it and she destroyed it.'[51]

A more detailed story of the organizational breakdown was recounted by Shrawan Kumar Nirala,[52] Mayawati's trusted lieutenant for almost twenty years before he left the party. As zonal and district coordinator, he was in charge of many districts in eastern UP in the 2000s, including Gorakhpur, Basti, Devipattan and Azamgarh among others.[53] Recounting his unhappy experience, Nirala told us that after the defeat of the party in 2012, the party organization had begun to break down, and money had come to play a major role in getting election tickets. Following her second defeat in 2017, Mayawati became reclusive and it was difficult to meet her. Nirala related stories of many capable, hardworking leaders who were refused tickets and were compelled to leave the party. He suffered the same fate. He was promised a ticket for the 2022 assembly election, but it was not given to him as he was unable to generate funds. Nor was he prepared to beg for a ticket. He left the party in late 2019. Although he was approached by the BJP, Congress and SP, he started his own organization—Ambedkar Jan Morcha— in eastern UP and put up candidates for the 2022 UP assembly elections. According to him, Mayawati's changed attitude and behaviour contributed to the quiet exodus of large number of cadres, which largely went unnoticed by the media.

Exodus: Hollowing Out of the Party

Parallel to these changes is the exodus of important party leaders even before the defeat of 2017 and afterwards, almost all of them to the BJP, which has sharply depleted the organizational strength of the BSP. The defeat in 2014 had dented its 'winnability' image, affecting Mayawati's ability to hold her flock together, and the BJP's capacity, with its image of being a stronger party, to poach them. The exodus had begun earlier but gathered momentum post 2014 and points to Mayawati's highly suspicious nature, impulsive temperament and inability to share power with rising leaders in the party. The first to leave in 1995 was Raj Bahadur, a Dalit leader associated with Kanshi Ram; he took nine MLAs along with him. In 2001, Mayawati sacked another Kanshi Ram aide, Barkhu Ram Verma, who had stood by her when she was attacked by SP goons in the guest house incident in 1995.[54] But it was prior to the 2017 election that the large-scale departure of old warhorses, who had risen through the ranks, hollowed out the party, affecting its organizational strength on the ground.

The exodus began with Daddu Prasad in 2015[55] and Jugal Kishore in January 2016, both accusing Mayawati of putting a price tag on tickets. This marked the beginning of a number of leaders being either thrown out or leaving. Dara Singh Chauhan, from the backward Loniya-Chauhan caste with influence in east UP, who had started his career with the BSP in 1996 and been its Rajya Sabha member, was expelled in 2015. He joined the BJP and won comfortably as an OBC leader from the Madhuban constituency in 2017 and held many important posts in the party and government.[56] Equally, if not more damaging, was the exit of two key BSP leaders from the OBC community who joined the BJP prior to the 2017 election: Swami Prasad Maurya and R.K. Choudhary. Both left on the invitation of the BJP but seemed to have been unhappy in the BSP. While leaving in June 2016, Maurya, the OBC face of the party, accused Mayawati of deceiving Dalits and taking bribes for election tickets.[57] Belonging to the biggest caste group among OBCs after Yadavs and Kurmis, known by the surnames Kachhi, Maurya, Kushwaha, Saini and Shakya, Maurya's caste group is present in most assembly seats from east to west UP. Similarly, R.K. Chaudhury while leaving in July said that he would form a new party; many BSP leaders were getting ready to leave the party and he planned a rally of these members.[58]

More shocking was the expulsion or perhaps departure of an important Brahmin leader, Brajesh Pathak, responsible for the sarvajan strategy and media convener for Mayawati's election rallies. An influential leader in central UP, he was ousted over accusations of 'anti-party activities'. He together with his wife and other supporters joined the BJP so soon after the expulsion that it looked as if he had been planning the move and was expelled to save face. Pathak's move was a major loss to the BSP's bid to secure Brahmin votes in the 2017 assembly elections.[59]

Most surprising, following the poor performance by the BSP in the 2017 elections, was the expulsion of Mayawati's trusted confidant Naseemuddin Siddiqui. He was part of the famed 'Banda trio' of Mayawati—Naseemuddin Siddiqui, Babu Singh Kushwaha and Gaya Charan Dinkar—who had contributed tremendously to building the party and her own image.[60] Babu Singh Kushwaha was removed from the party by Mayawati in 2012 due to the National Health Rural scam in which he was involved. The Central Bureau of Investigation (CBI) for long hesitated to target Kushwaha in the probe concerning the scam but finally filed a charge-sheet naming him. In 2015, the Enforcement Directorate (ED) attached his assets worth ₹196 crore. Yet, his expulsion proved costly. He had the support of the Kushwaha community in eastern UP. After being suspended from the BSP, reports said he was in touch with Rahul Gandhi to join the Congress, and two of his family members were in the SP. Kushwaha finally joined the BJP. He tried forming his own party, Jan Adhikar Manch, ahead of the 2017 assembly election but it failed to make an impact.[61]

Of all the BSP leaders who were either expelled or left, none had enjoyed Mayawati's trust for as long as Siddiqui (as described in Chapter 1), one of the architects of the sarvajan policy. As a bitter Siddiqui told us during an interaction in Lucknow,[62] the expulsion was sudden and came with no warning. Mayawati had continued to rely on him when the party was defeated in 2012, appointing him the leader of Opposition in the legislative council and coordinator for Bundelkhand and central UP. Again, when the party failed to win a seat in 2014, Mayawati gave him and his family members the responsibility of western UP and Lucknow division. Siddiqui claimed he worked hard for the 2017 elections, campaigning for most seats, reaching out to Muslims including clerics, some of whom declared their support to the BSP. He claimed that his success lay in his ability to mix with both Muslims and

Hindus, including Dalits, and he respected all religions. During the campaign, when BJP leader Dayashankar Singh made a derogatory remark comparing Mayawati with a prostitute, it was he who forced the BJP to expel Dayashankar, though it was later revoked in March 2017.[63]

At a meeting of party workers in April, Mayawati publicly questioned Siddiqui's approach, saying Muslims could not be wooed by visiting mosques or clerics. Siddiqui said that earlier she had never blamed Muslims for the party's electoral defeat, and her comments were resented by the community. Soon after, she stripped Siddiqui of all his responsibilities in the party organization in UP and transferred him to Madhya Pradesh (MP). BSP general secretary Satish Misra, who announced the expulsion, said Siddiqui did not go to MP as directed, and 'indulged in indiscipline' by remaining in Lucknow. Addressing party workers on Ambedkar's birth anniversary, Mayawati once again criticized Siddiqui for the privatization of sugar mills. It was clear that the gap between the two had widened beyond resolution. After Naseemuddin's expulsion, she seemed to prefer her brother Anand Kumar, making him the party's vice-president.

The expulsion led to unseemly public wrangling between Mayawati and Siddiqui. At a press conference on 10 May 2017, a bitter Siddiqui held that 'whatever charges have been levelled against me, applies to her [Mayawati] and I can prove those with evidence'. Holding Mayawati's 'wrong policies' responsible for the BSP's poor performance in 2009 and 2014 (Lok Sabha), and 2012 and 2017 (UP assembly), Siddiqui alleged that the BSP chief levelled 'false and misleading' allegations against Muslims and also made objectionable comments against them, especially in the 2017 polls. 'Unhone kaha ki maine blackmail kiya ... par aap se bada blackmailer maine pure desh mein nahi *dekha*' (She said I had blackmailed, but I haven't seen a bigger blackmailer than her [Mayawati]).[64] Further, he claimed that his expulsion from the BSP was because he had failed to fulfil a ₹50-crore demand by Mayawati, in support of which he also played audio clips as evidence.[65] The charge was rubbished by Mayawati in another press conference a little while later. 'He provokes other members of the party and then records their comments,' she said.[66] In turn, Siddiqui, recalling his ties with BSP founder Kanshi Ram, said, 'I was associated with his ideology for over three decades. For the sake of the party, I did not even visit my ailing daughter who died due to lack of treatment as Mayawati wanted my services during elections and did not permit me to go for her self-interest.'[67]

But party members have alleged that once Siddiqui rose in the party, he attempted to remove, through false allegations, senior leaders like Swami Prasad Maurya, Daddu Prasad and Babu Singh Kushwaha. Siddiqui's stature increased once Mayawati expelled them from the party. Sudhindhra Bhadoria, senior BSP leader, mentioned during our interaction that Siddiqui had received much support from the party and from Mayawati, but proved to be ungrateful, which underlay his downfall.[68] Soon after his expulsion, Siddiqui joined the Congress party.[69] It is also alleged that as Siddiqui rose in the BSP, so did his assets. In August 2012, the Lokayukta recommended a CBI and ED probe in the disproportionate asset case, grabbing of *nazul* (government) land and allotment of *patta* (contract) for mining in violation of rules.[70]

The expulsion of Siddiqui, considered number two in the BSP, gave the BJP an opportunity to make derogatory remarks against Mayawati. UP BJP leader Rakesh Tripathi alleged, 'Senior BSP leader Naseemuddin Siddiqui was merely playing the role of a cashier, while the real "trader of Dalit votes" was the BSP chief Mayawati. A number of BSP leaders who left the BSP have levelled this allegation against the BSP chief.' After the BJP won in March 2017, Chief Minister Yogi Adityanath ordered a CBI probe into the sale of twenty-one public sector sugar mills during the BSP regime.[71]

Of the Banda trio, only Gaya Charan Dinkar remains with Mayawati, the last confidant standing. Dinkar, a Dalit, worked extensively with Kanshi Ram and is one of the trusted aides of Mayawati. He won four elections—1991, 1993, 2002 and 2012—and was a minister in the Mayawati cabinet from 2002 to 2003. When Maurya left the BSP, Dinkar, an expert in parliamentary affairs, was appointed the leader of Opposition in the UP assembly in 2016. However, he was lesser known and lacked the stature and political contacts of Siddiqui.[72] It appears that Mayawati eliminates leaders whom she feels might threaten her position, unlike Kanshi Ram who fostered and trained a number of leaders.

An incident in 2017, following the defeat of the BSP due to its rapidly declining image, exposed the diminishing importance of Mayawati as a national figure. Mayawati resigned from the Rajya Sabha in a rather dramatic manner in July 2017, with the complaint that her 'voice was being muzzled'. It appears the chair had not allowed her to extend the three minutes' time allotted for her speech on the atrocities against Dalits in Saharanpur following the formation of a BJP government.[73] She said, 'I have no moral right to be in the upper house if I'm not allowed to speak on atrocities against Dalits.' Few members supported her and though nine months of her tenure in the upper house still remained, an angry Mayawati resigned. The BSP, with just nineteen seats in the 403-member UP assembly, did not have sufficient numbers to ensure her re-election, a little less than a year away.

2019: Defeat of the Mahagathbandhan

The victory of the BJP in the 2017 assembly election, which reduced the SP and BSP to just seventy-five seats in all, led to demands from within these parties for an alliance in the 2019 general elections. SP leader Shakir Ali who lost his seat to the BJP claimed there was 'polarization of non-Yadav OBCs and non-Jatav Dalits in favour of the BJP and against the Yadavs and Muslims ... SP and BSP should come together now. That is the only way ahead.'[74] There was a growing realization that without an alliance neither party could defeat the BJP, which was absorbing an increasing number of OBCs and Dalits; it was a strategy born out of desperation to keep their support base alive.

Accordingly, the BSP and SP leadership decided to bury their differences and joined hands to fight three important by-polls in 2018: Gorakhpur and Phulpur in eastern UP in March, and Kairana in western UP in May.[75] The coming together, quietly engineered by both parties, was a momentous decision after years of bitterness and rivalry between them, particularly the personal enmity between Mulayam Singh and Mayawati—the latter not having forgotten the guest house incident of 1995. It was possible due to the mediation of a young Akhilesh Yadav, whose persuasion was more acceptable to Mayawati. Calling her *bua* (aunt) and deferring to her age and seniority in politics, he was able to win her trust.[76]

In one of the most competitive, abusive, but watched election campaigns, the SP–BSP combine clearly rattled the BJP.[77] In eastern UP, Chief Minister Yogi Adityanath equated the SP–BSP alliance as 'a snake and mole coming together' and 'a coalition of thieves'. At a Phulpur rally, UP cabinet minister Nand Gopal Nandi compared Mulayam Singh Yadav to Raavan, Akhilesh

Yadav to Meghnad and Mayawati to Surpanakha—three demons and antagonists from the Ramayana. BSP support boosted the SP's morale and that of the politically emerging Nishad community in eastern UP as Akhilesh nominated Praveen Nishad, son of Dr Sanjay Kumar Nishad, president of the newly formed NISHAD Party, to the Gorakhpur constituency. The latter, who had long maintained that the Gorakhnath temple belonged to the Nishad community, was quick to campaign for the alliance. At Phulpur, Patel, Bind, Pasi and Muslim voters were the decisive factors, and some local SP leaders from these communities with the support of the BSP worked hard for a victory. The Brahmins, too, were unhappy with Yogi Adityanath who favoured the Thakurs, and this also proved to be an important factor against the BJP. Moreover, when the SP–BSP announced their decision to join hands, the BJP was caught unprepared with its campaign, still low key, as these constituencies were viewed as the strongholds of Adityanath.[78]

In Kairana, the BJP campaigned on the issue of 'Hindu exodus' due to an alleged threat by Muslim terrorists.[79] The death of sitting BJP MLA Hukum Singh, a strongman of the region who had attempted to spread this idea in the city, necessitated the election, and the BJP nominated his daughter. Here, the opposition campaign was led by Jayant Chaudhary, son of Ajit Singh, leader of the RLD, whose candidate Tabassum Hasan was supported by the SP, BSP and the Congress. Ground reports also pointed to Dalits playing a big role in the outcome, with the Bhim Army supporting the alliance candidate.

The victory of the SP–BSP alliance by a high margin on 14 March 2018, in the prestigious seats vacated by Chief Minister Adityanath and Deputy Chief Minister Maurya in Gorakhpur, Phulpur and Kairana was viewed as the revival of the social justice parties, and the deepening of the divide between the Dalits and the BJP.[80] It provided the SP–BSP the template for a major political realignment in the 2019 Lok Sabha elections. On 12 January 2019, SP–BSP–RLD announced their decision to form an alliance. The BSP and SP would contest 38 seats each, leaving two seats for smaller parties. It was also decided not to contest Amethi and Rae Bareli leaving the two seats for the Congress.[81]

Observers were optimistic, holding that in 2014, Modi had both maths and chemistry on his side, but the combination might not be as potent in 2019.[82] A number of factors encouraged this prospect: the combined vote-banks of the three partners comprising Dalits, Muslims, backwards and Jats could defeat the BJP. The combined vote-share of the SP and BSP in the 2014 elections (42.98 per cent) was slightly more than that of the BJP (42.3 per cent). It was also felt that both parties could ensure transfer of their votes to each other in their corresponding seats; more than demographic arithmetic, there would be positive chemistry between the workers of the three parties. The SP–BSP–RLD alliance was viewed as a turning point in west UP politics after the Muzaffarnagar riots in 2013, which would help in mending relations between the Hindus, Jats and Muslims, and give a tough fight to the BJP in a region where it had won all the seats.

Jointly announcing their decision, at a press conference, Mayawati reminded the electorate of the 'bahujan' Kanshi Ram–Mulayam alliance of 1993 which 'had outsmarted the BJP that was riding the Ram Temple wave at that time. The alliance will repeat the same feat by crushing the BJP in Lok Sabha election.' But she pointed out the context was different: 'This is not the coming together of two parties, but getting all the people together, including the poor, backward and minorities.' Akhilesh Yadav on his part made it clear that he wanted the next PM to be from UP, and he would support Mayawati.[83] They held joint meetings across the state. In the first-round, there were meetings of workers of all three parties, after which rallies were conducted often jointly by party leaders. The RLD was allotted seats in its traditional stronghold of Baghpat, Muzaffarnagar and Mathura; the BSP in west UP where the Dalit vote is decisive; while in the Muslim-dominated Rohilkhand region, the SP was given the lion's share.[84]

However, the magic of 1993 did not work in the 2019 elections. The BJP and its ally Apna Dal(S) won sixty-four of the eighty Lok Sabha seats; the BJP increased its vote-share from 42.3 per cent in 2014 to 49.4 per cent; in fact, it crossed 50 per cent if one considered that it contested only seventy-eight seats. The SP–BSP–RLD alliance won barely fifteen seats, but the shocking news for the SP and the BSP was that despite getting 38.92 per cent of the vote-share, they actually did a little worse than their cumulative vote-share of 2014, when they had contested separately.[85] Of the alliance partners, the Mayawati-led BSP won ten seats, the SP five seats, and the RLD could not win a single seat. The alliance did well in western UP, winning at least half of the fourteen seats of the Meerut, Moradabad and Saharanpur divisions; elsewhere it lost badly, particularly in eastern UP where it had won Gorakhpur and Phulpur in the by-polls in 2018.[86] Equally important, the alliance did not attract many Dalit votes. In the 2019 election, the BJP gained 48 per cent of the votes of Other Dalits[87] which was more than the 42 per cent gained by the SP–BS–RLD.[88]

Thus, 2012 marked a turning point in the history of Dalit politics in UP. In a period of twelve years between 2007 and 2019, in over five successive electoral defeats, the BSP lost the strong support base it had built with considerable effort among Dalits in the 1990s. The election results reflect the breakdown of the party organization and exit of key leaders, which have been traced by many leaders to Mayawati's changed outlook and corrupt behaviour, and which resulted in the unravelling of the party and a serious crisis of identity. A major challenge is whether Mayawati can once again build the party and unite all Dalit sub-castes. The BSP's strength has been the leadership provided by the Jatavs, but unifying under their domination is no longer acceptable for the rising poorer sections. Obtaining the support of other social groups, Muslims, backward and upper castes is also required as the BSP has a specific social base, due to which there are inherent limitations to the party obtaining a majority on its own.

The BSP is facing a strong, right-wing, upper-caste party in the BJP, which has managed to absorb a substantial section of Dalits and backward castes, marginalizing both the social justice parties, the SP and BSP, making it a dominant force in the state. The successive electoral defeats since 2014, including in the recent 2022 assembly elections, have significant implications for the future of Mayawati and the BSP, beyond electoral defeat. The strategies used by the BJP under the Narendra Modi leadership to bring Dalits into the saffron fold this shift by Dalits into the saffron fold, using both electoral and cultural means, are significant and are discussed in the next chapter.

PART II

Dalit Interface with Hindutva

4

BJP's Politics of Dalit Inclusion

Achhe din aane wale hain[1]

—BJP campaign slogan

On the bright winter morning of 8 November 2013, at the Vijay-Shanknad campaign rally in Bahraich—a backward region in eastern UP—Narendra Modi promised the enthusiastic crowd that if they voted him to power in 2014, he would transform their lives. Evoking the 'Gujarat model', he promised to bring about rapid economic development so that UP could catch up with the better-off states and improve the economic status of the poor and disadvantaged sections. Pointing to the apathy of earlier state governments headed by the SP and the BSP and the problems faced by poor and disadvantaged, he spoke about his own credentials as an

81

effective administrator in Gujarat. Drawing attention to reports by migrant workers of the availability of jobs in Gujarat, he said that 'there is no district, tehsil of UP, whose youth don't stay in Gujarat. When they can do wonders for Gujarat, UP can also utilize their skills.' Projecting development as his prime agenda, Modi assured them that he was their 'sevak' (servant) and the nation's 'chowkidar' (guard).[2] The crowd cheered when he repeated the BJP campaign slogan, '*Achhe din aane wale hain*' (better days are coming), first used by him in a speech on 8 January 2014.[3] In this way, Modi effectively gave voice to the frustrations of the voters, especially the unemployed youth in UP, and gave a fillip to their aspirations. He became a beacon of hope for disillusioned villagers, particularly those from the poorest sections of eastern UP who found themselves in the midst of constant violence and gangsterism and had little hope of their own state.

The BJP under Modi's leadership won a resounding victory in the 2014 national elections, obtaining seventy-one seats in UP with 42.3 per cent votes, while its ally, Apna Dal (AD), won two seats in eastern UP.[4] In the 2019 general elections, too, it performed well in UP, gaining sixty-two seats, less than in 2014, but grabbing almost 50 per cent of the votes. In the UP assembly elections in 2017, the BJP with the Apna Dal won 321 of the 403 seats, gaining two-thirds majority.[5] For the first time in thirty-seven years, a party had bagged more than 300 seats in the UP assembly.[6]

What surprised most observers was the shift of a substantial number of Dalit and backward caste votes to the BJP in 2014. The BJP gained only 18 per cent of Jatav votes but as much as 45 per cent from the other smaller Dalit groups, which rose to 17 per cent and 48 per cent in 2019, respectively.[7] In the 2017 assembly elections, too, the BJP managed to gain only 8 per cent of the Jatav vote but 37 per cent of the smaller Dalit groups. While the BSP managed to retain the support of its core constituency, the Jatavs, the support of other smaller Dalit sub-castes over three elections has steadily moved towards the BJP. Even among Jatavs, while as many as 68 per cent of them supported the BSP in 2014, there was a drop of 16 per cent in the 2019 elections; in the case of smaller Dalit groups, there was a significant decline of 35 per cent from 2009.

This move by the Dalits towards the BJP is of great significance as it has introduced a marked shift in the politics of UP. We analyse the electoral campaigns because the BJP is a party that is constantly in election mode. The period since 2014 has witnessed heightened contestation between an upper-caste, right-wing Hindu party and the two social justice parties—the SP and BSP—for the vote/support of the Dalits and backwards. While the former tried to co-opt them, the latter had earlier mobilized them, brought them into politics and long enjoyed their support. What is more important to note is that the aim of the BJP–RSS was twofold: *electoral*, that is, to defeat the social justice parties, marginalize them and gain control over this key state; crucially, it was also *cultural*, that is, to bring the Dalits and backwards into the saffron fold in order to build, over time, a Hindu Rashtra based on a consolidated Hindu identity.

While the rising aspirations among Dalits for upward mobility and its impact on Dalit politics leading to the defeat of the BSP was dealt with in earlier chapters, in this chapter we will concentrate on the methods and strategies used by the BJP under Modi to win the support of a considerable section of the Dalits. Why and how was the BJP able to attract a sizeable section of the non-Jatav smaller Dalits in UP, who until then were staunch supporters of the BSP?

Significant changes had been sweeping across UP since the late 1990s, affecting Dalits and other sections of the population. The heightened economic aspirations and desire for upward mobility among the Dalits due to the twin forces of globalization and cultural modernization, created extreme volatility in politics. UP experienced a quick political turnover in three successive elections: the BSP gained a majority in 2007, the SP in 2021 and the BJP in 2014. While all castes and classes shifted their preference, the shift in Dalit preference made a significant difference. Dalits, both the educated youth and particularly the smaller sub-castes,were disappointed with the lack of economic development under the BSP, which increased with the perceived failure of the sarvajan experiment. Also, the smaller Dalit sub-castes, feeling marginalized and neglected within the BSP vis-à-vis the Jatavs, were looking for greater recognition of their specific social and cultural needs and desires; this made them susceptible to the strategies of mobilization devised by the BJP during their successive campaignsin 2014, 2017 and 2019.

Two mobilizational strategies were employed by the BJP: One, a multi-layered, inclusionary, socio-economic and cultural discourse over elections, ranging from promises of rapid development, reinventing Hindutva as a subaltern ideolgy to appeal to the lower castes, charismatic speeches using a heady mix of promises of economic advancement to the use of religion to attract the electorate, including the Dalits, in more recent years. Two, the strategy of election management through the use of advertising companies and social media to build the brand image of a party and its leader. Both methods worked seamlessly, counterbalancing each other. While marketeers and publicists worked to create an image of a messiah of the poor and disadvantaged, Modi bolstered this image through his speeches and promises to the disadvantaged.

The 'Marketing' and 'Management' of Elections

Unlike in earlier decades, from 2014 onwards elections under the leadership of Modi have been 'managed' and 'marketed' by advertising companies. The BJP campaign in 2014 was the closest any Indian party till then had come to waging an American-style political campaign. Companies such as Soho Square, Ogilvy and Mather and Madison World were hired to build the image of the party and its leader, which helped sweep the BJP to power in the Lok Sabha elections in 2014 with the biggest election victory in thirty years; this trend continued in subsequent elections.[8] Neither the theories of *political economy* nor *rational choice*, used traditionally to explain voters' choices, are helpful in explaining the electoral outcome. The voters did not vote along the lines of their economic self-interest but were persuaded by Modi's charisma. Modi was projected as not only an able administrator but a man who had risen from humble origins, an OBC, a chaiwallah who went on to become the leader of his party, a messiah and a strong champion of development, good governance and welfare.[9] Once Narendra Modi was declared BJP's prime minister designate, the party invested heavily in creating a 'Modi brand' across UP and the rest of the country. The party distributed Modi T-shirts, masks and held 'chai pe charcha' campaigns which highlighted Modi helping his father sell tea at Vadnagar station in Gujarat, thereby underlining his humble background.[10] Thus, the *psychology of the voter* and, more importantly, the *war of perception*—personal and digital—was used by the BJP to 'manufacture' voter consent.[11] The PM's image and voice have been omnipresent since his 2014 victory.

Other political parties, such as the Congress, also employed similar services but without achieving the same success. The head of Ogilvy and Mather pointed out that they were 'provided a clear and focused strategy by the BJP, which we were asked to translate into people's language in a creative fashion. We recommended that we must lead with our biggest strength: Mr Modi.'[12] The BJP's success in attracting the poor and disadvantaged castes, despite being a conservative upper-caste party, can be attributed to the personality of Narendra Modi, which was further projected skilfully by such companies. As a TV anchor exasperatedly asked, 'What is it that separates Modi from star politicians before him? Is it a constant hunger for success, a personality-centric approach, a politics of hope and aggression, or a combination of all of these?' These qualities are evident in the final leg of the 2014 general elections when Narendra Modi dramatically announced at a rally in Himachal Pradesh: 'Yeh dil maange more' (The heart wants more). It was a quintessential Modi sound bite: the BJP's internal polls had captured a surge but the leadership of Modi and his lieutenant Amit Shah were determined to push beyond 'Mission 272' towards a triple hundred (literally, to obtain more than 300 seats in the parliament). The rest, as they say, is history.[13]

A related reason is the BJP's effective use of social media since 2014. The party set up a 'war room' in Delhi under Arun Jaitley, and one in Lucknow, popularly called the 'call centre' which, based on data mining of the electorate, sent out WhatsApp, email, Facebook and Twitter messages to people from various regions in UP, particularly to those from the lower castes.[14] The digital reach of the party was enormous: it set up 161 call centres across India and sent out 93.8 million text messages. While 2014 was the first digital election in which technology was used by the BJP to contact voters, by 2019, with Jio's ultra-cheap data almost doubling internet users, the IT cell undertook data collection to map potential voters. Local level workers were then used to spread messages on non-affiliated WhatsApp groups in their neighbourhood; the number of digital and personal workers far outnumbered those of the Congress and other parties. The party also used paid advertising, spending ₹21 crore on Facebook and Google, compared to ₹4.5 crore spent by the Congress.[15] The party's experiments were particularly successful in UP where the mission was to take Brand Modi to the youth, especially in the rural areas.

Equally important, the BJP had a a well-oiled, organized and effective election mechanism established by Amit Shah, who was brought specially from Gujarat to UP for the 2014 elections. Under him, the party designated BJP leaders to each region within UP, keeping in mind its distinct culture and the caste groups present, and recruited local leaders for mobilization on the ground, drawn from existing caste and class groups. Shah devised specific strategies to reach out to obtain Dalit votes, especially that of the non-Jatavs (Balmiki, Pasi, Dhobi, Kori etc., who constitute 9 per cent of the total population of UP) and decided to appropriate the legacies of Dr Ambedkar and other Dalit icons. Shah organized meetings in several Dalit villages and promised the Bharat Ratna for Kanshi Ram. The party arranged for over 400 GPS-installed digital 'Modi-vans', with campaign material and speeches to cover areas beyond internet reach. Modi's second 3D rally, telecast live at several locations across India on 14 April 2014, began with garlanding the statue of Ambedkar.[16]

Politics of Dalit Inclusion: Ideology and Methods

The successful mobilization of the lower castes by the BJP has been attributed to the generational change within the party. On 13 September 2013, the BJP appointed Narendra Modi as the new leader of the party and the prime ministerial candidate, effectively replacing the older leaders/founders—Atal Behari Vajpayee, L.K. Advani and Murali Manohar Joshi. He superseded the younger generation of leaders due to his three consecutive victories in Gujarat, for his reputation of having developed the state and his close association with the RSS. Soon after being designated leader of the party, the BJP introduced substantial changes in the party's ideology and organization, keeping the election of 2014 in mind.

Modi was keen to perform well in UP in 2014 as it was a key state that sent eighty members to Parliament. Early on, he realized that for the Dalits in UP, rather than identity, aspiration for economic advancement had become very important. He also recognized that winning power in UP required the support of the backwards and the Dalits, who together constitute almost half the state's population. He, therefore, redefined the party's core ideology of subaltern Hindutva to be more inclusive, which was tied together with an agenda of rapid economic development aimed to create a strong nation to improve the lives of all castes and communities, but specially the disadvantaged. Unlike in the 1980s and 1990s when the support base of the party was the upper castes and classes, in the 2000s the attempt was to co-opt the non-Yadav and non-Jatav sections of the backwards and Dalits as they were no longer attracted to the SP and the BSP.[17] The strategies used in the 2014 elections to obtain support of the Dalits provided the BJP a template, which was carried forward in subsequent elections not just to maintain but, in fact, to gain greater support from these groups.

Why was Modi able to use the ideology of Hindutva so effectively in gaining the support of the lower castes, particularly the Dalits? The reasons, according to Swapan Dasgupta, a close political observer,[18] lie to a considerable extent in the nature of Hindutva itself. According to him, any attempt to define the concept of Hindutva takes us into complex territory as there is 'no single interpretation' that can 'accommodate' all viewpoints. It is a 'bhavana' or emotion, a loose form of belief that resonates differently with different people, and hence appeals to both the middle-class and the Dalits. It is characterized by 'nebulousness' and 'ambiguity', which is both a help, as it leaves the door open to many diverse strands, as well as a hindrance, since there is a tendency to include a range of ideas, even those of the extreme fringe elements. He illustrated the fluidity of the idea with the example of V.D. Savarkar who, he thinks, committed a 'cardinal error' in trying to elaborate and define the philosophy of the then Hindu Mahasabha. His attempt to 'codify' Hindutva ran into problems because it is at best a 'sentiment', a loose construct, which forms, according to Dasgupta, the very bedrock or underpinning of India as a Hindu nation.

Dasgupta pointed out that it was the upsurge over Mandal and the parallel Ram Mandir agitation that brought issues of caste and community into the Hindutva debate. There was no conscious effort made to bring in caste; it was part of the unfolding politics of the time. The upper castes and, more importantly, the backward castes, participated in both movements, leading to a conscious breaking away from the high Brahminical thinking of the RSS. It produced many backward caste leaders such as Kalyan Singh, Uma Bharti and Vinay Katiyar; large numbers of sadhus in the Ram Mandir movement were not Brahmins either. Dasgupta interestingly described this new form as 'evangelical Hindutva'. He held that the attempt to attract the Dalits towards the BJP in UP is a more recent idea introduced by Modi, but rather than being planned, it was an offshoot of the Ayodhya movement.[19]

Dasgupta believes Modi brought the strategy of including the Dalits within the saffron fold from Gujarat. During the 2002 riots, a large number of tribals, Dalits and other poorer sections participated, which helped in creating a sizeable Hindu vote-bank, enabling a BJP victory. Replicating the Gujarat subaltern strategy in UP was possible because Hindutva is a 'malleable ideology' that can be refitted to the regional specificities and local cultural features on the ground. It needs to be interpreted differently in different geographies; local traditions, history, folklore and culture have to be brought in. Mobilizing Dalits, he points out, means targeting micro-communities, moving away from the Brahminical approach and making Hindutva attractive to them. For example, the Dalits have not undergone the rigorous process of indoctrination into the RSS philosophy or lifestyle, but they were given the slogan of 'Jai Shri Ram' which they could identify with, as it was also a part of the little tradition and folklore of the Hindi heartland. The BJP also identified a fault-line, of Jatav versus non-Jatav, that other political parties had not seen.[20] Hindutva, Dasgupta argued, has 'no geographical limits'; it is not limited to the Hindi heartland. The BJP can become the 'natural' conservative party of India if it attempts to mould its ideology and strategy to the culture of various regions. But he felt that this is still a 'project in the making' as this idea has not fully penetrated or been understood by the party workers.

To use its newly minted subaltern ideology to obtain Dalit support in UP, the BJP used a twofold agenda: developmental and cultural. Our fieldwork prior to the 2014 elections[21] pointed to two stages: the first being grassroots mobilization by the RSS–BJP from the late-1990s/early-2000s onwards, and the second, largely the handiwork of Modi, deploying the party's twin strategies, beginning with the campaign for the 2014 national elections, continuing into the 2017 and 2019 elections.

Modi's success lay in his ability to harness the early work by the RSS at the grassroots, including in the rural areas, and bring together the desire for development and social inclusion among the lower castes, and take it forward in UP.

Phase 1: Early Grassroots Mobilization

From the late 1990s, the BJP under the RSS had begun working silently and ingenuously at the grassroots in UP among the backwards, using a socio-cultural strategy suited to the region to revive the base of the party.[22] This plan of action was extended to include the Dalits in the early 2000s. As Dalits are fragmented along regional and sub-caste lines, an approach of attracting individual sub-castes was used as each had its own heroes and stories which could be employed for mobilization.[23] Local RSS leaders began finding histories and myths by which they could link Dalits to Hindutva. The attempt was to gradually build walls between them and 'others'—the Muslims—who had formed the composite culture of the villages. Three Dalit communities— Pasis, Musahars and Nishads—were particularly targeted by linking them with the Ramayana and Ram during his sojourn in the forest of the region.[24] Similarly, in the Bahraich region, the BJP attempted to create anxiety among Hindus, including Dalits, against the Muslims by counterpoising the myth of Ghazi Mian as a foreign intruder and Suhaldev as a Pasi Hindu, a Dalit king who protected the Hindus from the intruder's evil designs, which led to a small riot over this issue in 2003.[25]

Simultaneously, in eastern UP, Mahant Yogi Adityanath, a non-Brahmin leader, had begun to quietly mobilize the backwards and non-Chamar Dalits from the early 2000s onwards.[26] In the Mau–Gorakhpur region, he tried to create a more broad and inclusive Hindu identity by bringing the Dalits and backwards into the saffron fold. Using his Hindu

Yuva Vahini, a group consisting mainly of members from Dalit and backward communities, he was able to extend his influence to the entire terai (Himalayan foothills) region by 2017. This Hindu mobilization, combined with his Robin Hood image of providing welfare and economic opportunities to the underprivileged in an underdeveloped region with few opportunities, enabled the BJP to make inroads into a region where the SP and the BSP earlier had strong bases.[27]

These strategies proved useful, as the smaller and marginalized Dalit groups, who had recently entered the mainstream, were undergoing a process of modernization in which culture played an important role. In this process, the Hindutva ideology could influence some sections that aspired to be a part of the larger 'Hindu' identity. This is because culture is about relationality—relationships among individuals within and among groups—and is concerned with identity, aspirations, structures and practices that serve relational ends such as ethnicity.[28] Culture is not a set of primordial phenomena permanently embedded in blood relationships, language or culture but a set of contested attributes constantly in flux that can be constructed by political action, and identities 'invented' or 'imagined'.[29] The process of modernization often tends to proceed unevenly, benefiting some sections more than others, leading to conflict and competition for political power, economic benefits and social status among social groups, both within and among different ethnic categories.[30]

Hence, what we are witnessing in UP is 'politically induced cultural change', the process by which political elites select some aspects of a group's culture, attach new value and meaning to them, and use them as symbols to mobilize the group.[31] Consequently, identities have undergone constant change and revision in response to the changing social and political context.

Phase II: The Electoral Campaign

The long campaign for the 2014 national election in UP constituted the second phase of mobilization, in which Modi creatively forged the idea of development and cultural inclusion. The shift towards development had in fact begun in Gujarat where Modi as chief minister had moved to replace the 'old style, twentieth-century, Gujarat-based RSS chapter that had brought him into public life', with a new, more development-oriented style.[32] He promoted loyalists who had an activist-style commitment to development, rather than those who advocated older, more divisive Hindutva issues which had been used to take a 'jaundiced view towards Muslims and other minorities'. His selection of Amit Shah as his campaign manager in UP in 2014 was part of this shift.[33] He shifted his political repertoire from that of the 'Hindu Hriday Samrat'[34] as his admirers had hailed him, to 'Vikas Purush' or 'Development Man'. Accordingly, during the electoral campaigns, Modi gave importance to good governance and development. Realizing that mere caste calculations would not suffice, contrary to his party's attempt to build caste alliances, in several rallies he openly criticized the idea of caste in politics and also attacked the corruption and slow growth under the previous UPA government. Modi packaged development for the lower castes as something denied to them by earlier governments.[35]

Aware of the rising aspirations of Dalits, in 2014 Modi promised to bring in rapid economic development in UP by introducing the policies and programmes that had brought great success in Gujarat.[36] Industrialized and urbanized Gujarat is the third preferred destination for migration from UP, after Delhi and Maharashtra. It attracts tens of thousands of migrant workers from the backward areas of UP.[37] The issue of migration from UP due to lack of development provided him a handle. Among Indian states, UP has the largest number of poverty-stricken, inter-state migrants—12.32 million—who move to other states, and 52 million internal migrants, who move from the poorer to the better-off western districts in search of livelihoods. The 2011 Census shows that as many as 27.7 per cent of them are SCs who, the data reveals, migrate as employment is not available in the state, whereas OBCs and upper castes migrate to obtain better employment, or take to business or studies.[38] During his campaign speeches, Modi made excellent use of the issue of migration to spread the message of availability of jobs in Gujarat for Dalits from the backward areas of UP.

The BJP manifesto, released on 7 April, titled, 'Time for Change, Time for Modi', in the making of which Modi was closely associated, also reflected the developmental issues raised in his speeches.[39] The manifesto makes only a brief reference to Hindutva issues such as construction of a Ram temple in Ayodhya and a uniform civil code; it focused on development instead. Moreover, once in power, Modi held that his model of governance would be '*sabka sath, sabka vikas*' (development with everyone and for everyone). Emphasizing on unity and togetherness, he argued that all sections of the people should work together for the advancement of the country.

Simultaneously, during the campaign, the BJP invoked the cultural aspects of the ideology of subaltern Hindutva. An attempt was made to create a Maha Hindu identity, and based on it, a social coalition consisting of the upper castes and sections of the OBCs and Dalits, to give the lower castes a feeling of being included within the 'Hindu' fold. In the 1990s, for the Dalits and backwards, the Hindu upper castes were the 'other' to be challenged.

The electoral campaign for the 2014 elections in UP began early. In western UP, the Muzaffarnagar riots of 2013 provided an opportunity to mobilize the Dalits who were moving away from the BSP into the Hindu fold. During this period, the SP which was in power did not make a concerted effort to control the riots as it hoped to benefit from the resulting Muslim consolidation. While the riots witnessed violence between the Jats and Muslims in western UP villages, the social equations between Jats, Dalits and Muslims underwent a change. The equation between the Jats and Dalits, traditionally opposed to each other as land-owning and landless sections, improved, but there was increasing animosity between Dalits and Muslims; the latter were now characterized as the 'other', with whom Dalits had lived side by side in the villages. This brought the Dalits closer to the other Hindu communities in the region. Media reports show that the Dalits did not try to protect or help Muslims; rather, in many cases they actively participated in the riots, starting with attending the mahapanchayats,[40] to attacking Muslims in villages where the riots spread. This is seen in the many first information reports (FIRs) filed by Muslims, in which Dalits are also accused as culprits along with Jats, and many were jailed.[41]

Data from police stations across UP show that out of 605 communal incidents in the state in the ten weeks beginning with the Lok Sabha election results of 16 May, sixty-eight—or every ninth incident—involved Muslims and Dalits in rural areas. Forty-eight of these incidents—over 70 per cent—took place in and around twelve assembly constituencies where by-elections were due.[42] These clashes signalled a fracture in the BSP's once strong alliance between Dalits and Muslims. The weakening of this coalition made it difficult for the party's mixed leadership in these areas to take sides—and individual leaders often rushed to align with their respective religious groups, alienating members of the other group.

A number of clashes were reported in the media; for example, a minor argument over widening a village road resulted in a violent clash between Muslims and Dalits in Katauli Kala, in the Deogaon police station area of Azamgarh district. The superintendent of police, Vinod Kumar, said there was no history of tension between the two communities in that area. Again, according to a diary entry at Rani Ki Sarai police station in Sonvar village of the same district, on 4 July, an argument between a Muslim and a Dalit family over the boundaries of their fields resulted in a communal clash in which eight people were injured. In several cases, communal tensions polarized communities that had had no history of animosity and had lived in harmony for decades.

In many cases, tensions between Dalits and Muslims began after a relationship between, or elopement of, couples from the two communities. In many of these cases, local BJP units and leaders emerged as the 'protector' of Dalits. In the course of our fieldwork, the perception of the BJP leaders as saviour of the Dalits against Muslims resonated among the former.[43] This aspect has been reported by media and led to police cases. For instance, a media investigation in the police records showed the following:[44]

Village Gaineridan, Police Station Jahanabad, Pilibhit, 20 May: A Muslim family took away by force their girl, who had married a Jatav boy. Local BJP leaders demanded security for the Hindu family and the return of the girl, leading to tensions.

Village Lisadi, Police Station Lisadi Gate, Meerut, 30 May: The local BJP leadership got involved after a Jatav girl eloped with a Muslim boy.

Village Neta Nagar, Police Station Karari, Kaushambi, 6 June: A local BJP leader got involved after an incident of stone-throwing between Pasi and Muslim groups. Hindus complained to the police and an FIR was registered against the Muslims.

Village Kasba, Police Station Thana Bhavan, Shamli, 14 July: BJP leaders led protests after a Khatik girl eloped with a Muslim boy.

Mohalla Naurangabad East, Police Station Sikanderarao, Hathras, 15 July: BJP leaders led a protest roadblock after a Jatav girl committed suicide, allegedly after having been raped by a Muslim man.[45]

In fact, the aggressiveness of the Dalits became a significant aspect of the communal tension in the state in this period. In the Saharanpur riot on 25 July—in which Sikhs clashed with Muslims—half of all incidents of arson and violence took place in Dalit and Muslim areas.[46] According to a senior police officer who was involved in tackling the fallout of this riot, Dalit rioters were involved in around 70 per cent of the cases of destruction of property. In Kalasi lane on the outskirts of Saharanpur town, an area that is surrounded by Muslim and Dalit neighbourhoods, only three shops in a shopping complex were set on fire—all belonging to Muslim tailors. All the suspects that the police caught were Dalits.

2017 and 2019: Changed Political Discourse

The political discourse prior to the 2017 and 2019 elections underwent a marked change. The BJP adopted a new two-pronged strategy during the campaign: it decided to project the many welfare schemes that the party had implemented in UP and took recourse to a discourse of nationalism and religiosity during the campaign. This twofold strategy was employed to neutralize the difficult economic problems that the ruling BJP increasingly faced by 2017.

Having gained power at the Centre, the BJP was keen to capture power in UP in 2017. It was, however, a challenging task, given that three developments had taken place by 2017: the sudden announcement of demonetization on 8 November 2016; the implementation of GST, which replaced the numerous federal and state taxes in June 2017 and slowed down economic growth, leading to rising unemployment; and increased atrocities against Dalits, which led to confrontation, particularly in western UP, and the formation of the Bhim Army by Chandrashekhar Azad. The first two policies caused economic chaos and suffering that affected everyone, particularly the poor and disadvantaged and small businesses, and was expected to create a backlash against the government. But Modi in an ingenious twist made demonetization into a class issue, explaining it as one that would extract black money from the rich, which would help the poor and the country as a whole. Following this, large sections of the population, the most affected, including the poor and disadvantaged, defying popular analysis, rationalized their suffering as contributing to the move for ridding the country of black money. Similarly, pointing out that the previous government had not implemented GST which would take the economy forward, Modi counselled patience as the government dealt with glitches in the implementation of the GST.

Despite all the problems which hurt the population, particularly the poorer sections, the UP electorate rewarded the BJP with an astounding electoral victory in the assembly elections in March 2017. Modi's almost iconic figure and message—that he alone could fix these problems, if given one more chance—seems to have resonated among the electorate, particularly the younger generation and aspirational Dalits.

By the 2019 elections, the economy was in worse shape. As a scholar pointed out, 'years of mismanagement' by the BJP government resulted in a progressive decline in growth and rising unemployment.[47] India's GDP growth has been declining since 2017–18; in the financial year ending March, GDP only grew at 4.2per cent.[48] The impact on workers was massive since there was an increase in unemployment from 2017–18 when it averaged 4.6 per cent. In 2018–19, unemployment rose to 6.3 per cent, in 2019–20 to 7.6 per cent, and in June 2020 it reached 11 per cent, being 29.22 per cent in the urban areas as against 26.69 per cent for rural areas.[49] 'Over-promise and under-deliver', according to an economist, was a succinct summary of the economic outcome of the last five years.[50] Moreover, the victories of the Congress party in December 2018 in Chhattisgarh, MP and Rajasthan, and the formation of the SP–BSP alliance in UP prior to the 2019 election were challenges that troubled the BJP.

At that point, one of the most successful policies of the BJP, which helped the party overcome the image of a declining economy, were a series of welfare schemes, and based on them, the able marketing of a massive welfare state. Rather than attempting to deliver intangible traditional forms of redistribution, such as health and education, the BJP used a distinctive approach of 'new welfarism'[51] which has given rise to the category of the 'labharti' or those persons who have benefitted by this approach and in turn have supported the BJP. This policy of new welfarism was based on the 'political calculation' that there is 'rich electoral opportunity' in providing tangible goods and services that are easier to deliver and monitor, which can be delivered in the political present, as opposed to intangibles, such as education that would deliver benefits in the distant future. They provided subsidized essential goods and services, normally provided by the private sector, such as bank accounts, cooking gas, toilets, electricity, housing and, more recently, water and also plain cash.[52] Moreover, data showed that the percentage of labharti households that have gained access to these goods and services each year had accelerated since 2015, especially in rural India; a good example being helping women acquire bank accounts, cleaner cooking fuels and electricity. In some aspects, though, there was less success, such as clean sanitation. To ensure that the deliverables were attributed to the Centre, and thereby the BJP, the central bureaucratic machinery has been used as much as possible. The policy has also been followed by a strong and persistent messaging highlighting the benefactor, particularly Modi.[53]

The method by which this scheme was implemented is also important. Beginning in 2014, the government had introduced beneficiary schemes like Ujjwala and PM Awas Yojana, distributed through a huge personal and digital outreach, which connected it to, as claimed by Amit Shah, almost 22 crore beneficiaries.[54] Importantly, this economic intervention was undertaken by the government through a more flexible 'deprived category' index developed with the help of the Socio-Economic and Caste Census instead of the old 'below poverty line' (BPL) concept. The use of Aadhaar to pinpoint individuals within this category and transfer benefits electronically, allowed the government to create a class of beneficiaries that may come from different caste groups but have a similar economic profile. While this did not remove caste affiliations, it gave value to the economic identity of smaller caste groups that, until now, were hoping to corner benefits by showing caste solidarity with dominant groups like the Yadavs and Jatavs in UP. Thus, the Modi government created new, workable, credible options to old caste alliances by establishing a new paradigm for accessing state resources.[55]

The work of data collection began soon after the 2014 victory and closer to the 2019 elections; beneficiaries were contacted through call centres. The constituencies which saw the most beneficiary outreach, were nineteen in UP and four in Maharashtra, amounting to 8 lakh beneficiaries. In February 2019, under the Mera Parivar BJP Parivar programme, workers and sympathizers visited the beneficiaries with the soft message: 'Modi has given schemes to these many families in only five years. Give him another five and you can make that number even more.' This raised the aspirations of many families in the selected areas who supported the BJP irrespective of how many persons had actually benefitted from the schemes.[56] This strategy contributed to retaining the support of the electorate in UP and, in fact, increased support from Dalits.

Parallel to this was the use of the discourse of nationalism, or 'desh bhakti', reinforced by constant references to Pulwama and the Balakot 'surgical strike' against Pakistan, to move the mood away from the economic decline among the party's supporters. The strategy was highly successful. As Swapan Dasgupta pointed out, because Indian nationalism and Hindutva are closely connected in the minds of citizens, Hindutva is being viewed as a symbol of national pride.[57]

This was evident in our field work during the 2019 campaign[58] which showed that upper castes, non-Yadav OBCs such as Kashyap/Dhimar, Saini, Badhai, Lodh, Kurmi and a section of non-Jatav Dalits such as Khatiks, Valmikis, Pasis and Dhanuks rallied behind the BJP quite enthusiastically, citing the Modi factor and nationalism as the most influential criteria for this. As the nation's most populous state, UP makes up 16.5 per cent of the country's population and its share in the rank and file of the army is 14.5 per cent.[59] In our field study, the state government's performance was not rated well—83 per cent of the respondents reported stray cattle menace to be a serious issue and over half blamed the government for it. But respondents held that Modi deserved 'ek chance aur' (one more chance) to complete the good work he had begun.[60] The narrative of nationalism employed in the campaign divided the electorate into Modi detractors and Modi supporters; the latter proved to be more in number.[61] Thus, for an overwhelming majority of upper castes, non-Yadav OBCs and non-Jatav Dalits, Modi appeared as a bold and decisive leader. None of the respondents in these groups were willing to link their precariat economic situation with their voting preferences; mention of welfare schemes like the PM Awas Yojna, Ujjawala Yojna were more a tactical, post-facto exercise to rationalize their pro-BJP stance.[62]

While the building of the Ram Mandir was repeatedly raised by the BJP in electoral campaigns, a strong religious feeling or belief had been employed prior to the 2019 elections. It marked the coming together of the notions of Vikas Purush and Hriday Hindu Samrat. While the upper castes have long been supporters of the BJP, the religious discourse was directed more at the lower castes.

In February 2019, Narendra Modi washed the feet of five sanitation workers, or safai karamcharis, in Prayagraj as part of his visit to the ongoing Kumbh Mela, hailing them as 'karma yogis' and thanking them for their 'tireless' contribution in keeping the Kumbh clean, thereby helping in the Swachh Bharat drive. Later, tweeting that he would 'cherish' this moment all his life, Modi justified his act by saying he was honouring the workers as 'no one can know the labour they (safai karamcharis) have put in the Kumbh. Cleanliness has been the trademark of this Kumbh.'[63]

Modi's cultural symbolism seemed to have clearly paid off. The sanitation workers were shocked and overjoyed at the PM's humility. The five sanitary workers whose feet were washed—Pyare Lal, Naresh Kumar and Chaubi from Banda, Hori Lal from Sambhal, UP, and Jyoti from Korba, Chhattisgarh—were in awe after this experience. 'It's nothing less than a dream. We will share this proud moment with everyone. Modi deserves another chance as the country's head,' said one of them. 'We were told that we will be honoured and were made to sit on chairs. We were speechless when we saw the PM approaching us. He was very soft-spoken and told us that he will wash our feet. He then washed and wiped our feet and felicitated us with an 'angavastram' (upper cloth or stole, a garment used by men especially in south India). He asked us about our problems and the experience of working at the Kumbh,' said Pyare Lal. Modi also invoked Mahatma Gandhi, saying the father of the nation had first thought about 'Swachh Kumbh' a hundred years ago when he had attended the Haridwar Kumbh.[64]

The second instance of the use of religion was in May 2019 when Modi spent eighteen hours meditating in the Rudra Meditation Caves, 11,700 feet up in the Himalayas, a kilometre from the Kedarnath shrine in Uttarakhand. The Rudra (Shiva) Cave is not a 'natural' one; it was built in 2018, at the suggestion of Modi himself, and is maintained by the Garhwal Mandal Vikas Nigam, Kedarnath.

Despite the floundering economy, the BJP managed to win sixty-two seats in UP, nine less than in 2014, but its vote share rose from 42.63 per cent in 2014 to 49.4 per cent. The BSP–SP alliance won barely fifteen seats, despite getting 37.22 cent of the vote. The expected transfer of core votes between the alliance partners did take place: the BSP improved its position, obtaining ten seats as against zero in 2014, the SP obtained five as in 2014.[65] But the BJP proved successful once more in appealing to the new voting bloc of the upwardly mobile, aspirational class of non-Jatav Dalits, who constituted a substantial section of the electorate who were profitably mobilized by the BJP, first in 2014 and then in larger numbers in 2019.[66] The BSP obtained 75 per cent or three fourths of the Jatav votes, which was higher than 68 per cent in 2014, but only 42 per cent of the smaller Dalits; 48 per cent of them preferred the BJP.[67] Clearly, the strategies aimed at obtaining Dalit votes had paid off.

Thus, the BJP under Modi has used a variety of mobilizational strategies to win elections and obtain the support of a substantial section of Dalits since 2014. However, Modi's achievement is only one part of our story. Two puzzling queries remain: While Dalits protest strongly against upper-caste atrocities, why do they vote/support the BJP in the next election? Also, is this support temporary and instrumental due to the decline of the BSP, or does it reflect conversion of Dalits to the Hindutva ideology of the BJP? These are the questions we take up over the next two chapters to complete our understanding of why Dalits have embraced the BJP in recent years.

5

Dalit Preference and Protest

Our child was raped and killed only because she was a Dalit. Our children have no safety here.
    —Ram Lal (name changed), uncle of a thirteen-
    year-old girl who was raped and murdered in
    Lakhimpur Kheri, UP, in August 2020.[1]

In recent times, a hotly debated issue on the shifting nature of Dalit politics is the puzzle of two parallel discourses: on the one hand, the consistent politics of agitation and protest across India against atrocities by dominant castes and the slow response of the BJP, while on the other, increasing political preference at every election for the saffron party. The former is revealed in incidents ranging from Una, Bhima Koregaon and Saharanpur to the Hathras incidents, while Dalit electoral support for the

BJP in these states in general, and UP in particular, testifies to the latter. Given the layered and complex nature of this puzzle, we provide a broad analytical framework for on the complex interplay of 'political dynamism' and 'electoral determinism'.

Political Dynamism and Electoral Determinism[2]

In September 2020, there was tremendous shock and anger over the gangrape of a Dalit woman by Thakur men in Hathras district of UP. However, the incident was one of many—the National Crime Records Bureau data showed an increase of 7.3 per cent in crimes against SCs with 45,935 cases, an increase from 42,793 cases registered in 2018. The data for per head cases for atrocities committed against SCs in 2019 showed that rape constituted 7.6 per cent of the total cases against them.[3] UP, official crime data showed, had recorded the highest increase in crimes against women, at 66.7 per cent, in the four years up to 2019.[4] The National Dalit Movement for Justice and National Campaign of Dalit Human Rights—coalitions defending the rights of Dalits—have said the recent rapes of Dalit girls in Lakhimpur Kheri, Hathras and Balrampur expose the existing situation of the lower castes in the country.[5] While atrocities including rape of Dalit women are not new in India, or in UP, the numbers have risen in recent years. Yet, a substantial section of the smaller Dalit groups in UP continue to vote for the BJP in both assembly and national elections.

Before unravelling the political psychology of Dalits, we need to understand the structural factors that shape the socio-political context of the community. Dalits being at the bottom of the pyramid, socially and economically, experience both aspirations and anxieties. They seek social recognition, respectability and eradication of all forms of stigma, an assertion in the normative realm. In economic terms, they need the welfare schemes offered by the government, making their dependence on the ruling dispensation much greater, compared to non-Dalits. In UP, the Ujjwala scheme, free rations and cash were welcomed by the smaller sub-castes among Dalits, most of whom are poor and suffered heavily during the Covid-19 pandemic. This explains the apparent paradox, otherwise difficult to understand, of alternating protest and preference by Dalits. This dichotomous choice vis-à-vis the BJP could be labelled as normative versus pragmatic, or the abstract versus the concrete. What helps navigate this maze is the reliance on the relative gain approach that the community makes while assessing the desirability and utility of their choices, wherein the new welfarism of the BJP wins the race. It is against this background, and drawing on both media reports and our field experiences, that we explain this phenomenon and what it means for Dalit politics.

The provision of welfare and economic benefits[6] are mentioned in the literature as reasons for Dalit preference for the BJP. Equally significant, as we learnt during our fieldwork, local conditions and village-level relationships play a key role. What seems like a puzzle at the state or national level is best understood through local level studies of various incidents which reveal the social and political inter-relationships between the various players involved. The smaller Dalit sub-castes long preferred to support the party that could provide them protection against the locally dominant castes, primarily the Yadavs, and the party representing them, the SP, was viewed as a goonda or mafia party. While in the 1990s it was the BSP that provided them protection of life and property, today they view the BJP as the only party that can protect their interests. In fact, during our fieldwork, they pointed out that they do not associate the BJP with atrocities committed by the upper castes, and that such incidents are not BJP-specific—they have faced similar if not more atrocities under SP rule.[7]

Sudhindra Kulkarni in our discussion endorsed our framework of 'two levels' of contradictory attributes of Dalit protest and preference: the political and the electoral, with a *gulf* between the two.[8] The political is very dynamic, full of contradictions and protest, but the electoral realm is different— it is insulated from the political. He agreed that Dalits in rural areas have little choice as the Yadavs constitute their direct oppressors. He pointed out that the BJP uses Hinduization to mobilize the Hindus, but it does not do 'anti-Yadav politics'. It does not need to, as ground reality shows that Yadavs dominate, so BJP becomes the party of 'natural preference' for the smaller Dalit sub-castes.[9] Having gained confidence and empowerment in the 1990s, the Dalits today have learnt to exercise their independent choice—and employ strategic voting in elections.

Further, Kulkarni held that both preference and protest will continue to mark Dalit politics because of the condition and behaviour of Dalit parties. The BSP in UP and the Republican Party of India (RPI) in Maharashtra, for example, kept quiet during atrocities at Saharanpur and Bhima Koregaon; there was symbolic condemnation but no agitation. This is because they need the support of the non-Dalits to gain even the few seats they can win in Parliament, or in the state assembly. Hence, anger is expressed through agitational, but not electoral, politics. So, while these two actions seem contradictory, there is an apparent coherence between the two; assertion and integration is taking place in a complex manner, side by side. There will be agitation as there is injustice against the downtrodden, according to Kulkarni, but it will not translate into an autonomous and successful Dalit politics.[10]

Another feature of Dalit protests in UP today is that it is led not by the BSP which, as most Dalit respondents pointed out, does not participate in protests, nor does Behenji step out of her residence to help the victims. The protests are led by the new Dalit organizations and activists—in western UP the Bhim Army, in Purvanchal the Ambedkar Jan Morcha, and other smaller and not so well-known organizations. Most of those protesting, as our field study shows, are Jatavs in western UP and Chamars who constitute dominant groups elsewhere. However, the division between Jatav and non-Jatav collapses in the case of rape of Dalit women or lynching of poor Dalits. It leads to entire villages joining the protest against delay in government action, or poor police intervention. At the same time, while the Dalits, particularly the Jatavs in western UP, support Azad when he fights against atrocities and are critical of Mayawati, as long as she is there as their leader, they will vote for her. There is an emotional attachment to the BSP, especially with Mayawati.

Equally important are the methods used by the BJP to obtain Dalit support, despite rising atrocities. The BJP, as our narrative has shown, has perfected new ways of doing politics. Effective communication—employing digital and personal methods, by cadres approaching and promising welfare and other benefits to convince Dalit voters—plays a significant role. Our fieldwork revealed what happens during the electoral campaign and actual voting is no longer important; most voters, including Dalits, had already made up their minds. Elections are no longer political occasions, but events that are 'managed' skilfully. There is a disjunction between governance and politics; only that which is visible, such as law and order and ration and subsidy, matters; the less-talked-about does not matter. Moreover, the candidate matters much less; it is the image of the leader—Modi or Adityanath—that matters. The

BJP enjoys the structural advantage of being in power and is able to influence voters.

In UP, this contradictory phenomenon of strong agitation against atrocities and inclination towards voting for the BJP reflects the fragmentation, both social and political, within the Dalit community, following the unravelling of the BSP post-2012 and the rise of the BJP. Deep-rooted differences between sub-castes have surfaced, and feelings of uncertainty, anxiety, internal competition and economic jealousies have replaced identification with and consolidation behind a strong Dalit party. Moreover, it portrays the problematic and constantly fluctuating interaction between the Dalits and the BJP with its massive Dalit outreach on both the material and ideological planks.

Based on these arguments, we document some atrocities in UP and discuss the Dalit outlook on the interplay between preference and protest. The related question of whether the shift towards the BJP is a tactical move during a period of vacuum when there is no strong Dalit party or whether it reflects an ideological-cum-cultural move towards the Hindu fold is discussed in the next chapter.

Rising Dalit Atrocities in UP

A major contribution to the BJP gaining a full majority in the Lok Sabha in 2014 was the Dalit (and OBC) support it received in UP. The new government, in a bid to consolidate and further increase its newly gained support base, made huge investments in the Dalit icon, Dr Ambedkar. Among them, a number of foundation stones were laid—for an international centre in Delhi, a memorial at the Indu Mills Compound, the Dr Ambedkar Memorial in London, a committee to celebrate his 125th birthday, and importantly, the election of Ram Nath Kovind, a Dalit from UP, as President of India, all during 2015.[11]

However, beginning in 2015, the rise in the number of atrocities against Dalits across India, and the lack of immediate remedial steps by the government, created a phase of confrontation, caste-based violence and anger. It led to the formation of Dalit organizations/movements such as the Una Aytachar Ladat Samiti in Gujarat, the Vanchit Bahujan Aghadi in Maharashtra and the Bhim Army in UP,[12] led by new Dalit leaders Jignesh Mevani, Prakash Ambedkar and Chandrashekhar Azad, respectively. The need for new organizations had been felt for some time with the vacuum created by the decline of Dalit parties such as the BSP and the RPI.

The rising atrocities led the new Dalit leaders to focus the community's anger primarily against the BJP on ideological grounds. They argued that the spike in violence against Dalits was linked with the political ascendency of the BJP. Privileging the ideological plank and going soft on the non-BJP parties, these new Dalit leaders employed a pan-India pattern and weaved together myriad and scattered incidents—like the case against Rohith Vemula, a Dalit student at Hyderabad University who committed suicide in January 2016; the July 2016 incident in Una, Gujarat, when some Dalits were assaulted by vigilantes for allegedly skinning a dead cow; and later the Bhima-Koregaon incident in January 2018—under a singular frame of anti-BJP-ism.[13]

In UP, then ruled by the SP, a large number of major crimes against Dalits were reported from across UP during this period. In Mainpuri district on 15 January 2017, Hari Om Katheria, his wife and brother were thrashed by an upper-caste Thakur in Daulatpur village for not greeting him with a 'Ram Ram'.[14]

In the same district, on 28 July a year earlier, a Dalit couple was hacked by an upper-caste grocer after they failed to repay a debt of ₹15. This was a few days after the Una incident.

But it was Dalit girls against whom the largest number of atrocities took place. An example was the gang-rape and murder, on March 2015, of three Dalit girls, an eighteen-year-old college student and two schoolgirls aged thirteen and ten, in Katiyari village, Deoria district. The girls had gone to the fields on Friday afternoon to collect grass for livestock but did not return home. The girls' bodies were found in neighbouring Pakaipur village, under the jurisdiction of Barhaj police station. The mother of one of the girls claimed, 'The rapists tried to chop their bodies as there were cut marks on their bellies and heads. This is the work of at least six people. There are some upper-caste affluent people who dislike upwardly mobile Dalit boys and girls and harass them. There are many instances when they have beaten up downtrodden boys and raped girls. But people are afraid of complaining against them to the police, which often sides with the rich.' The father of the youngest victim also alleged the police knew who were behind the murders. 'They want us to name them. Later on, the same police will terrorize us and protect them. We don't know what to do in this situation,' he rued.[15]

Yet, despite rising Dalit atrocities and protests in UP and elsewhere in the country, the BJP obtained an absolute majority in the 2017 UP assembly election, gaining just 17 per cent of the Jatav votes but as much as 48 per cent of the non-Jatav votes.[16]

2017 to 2019

The period between 2017 and 2019 witnessed both increasing atrocities but also increased support for the BJP, judging by the massive victories in the assembly and general elections. Although Dalit votes contributed to the victory of the BJP in UP in 2017, the state accounted for 43 per cent of the total number of cases of harassment against minorities and SCs registered in the period 2018–19.[17] Soon after the new government was sworn in, a major atrocity took place in UP that led to massive protests: violent clashes in two villages of Saharanpur district in April–May 2017, one between Dalits and Muslims and the other between Dalits and Thakurs. These violent atrocities and the protests that followed, it was held, 'heralded a new era in Dalit politics'.[18] The Dalits were also angry because the new BJP government gave plum posts to the OBCs and hardly any to Dalits. This coupled with the atrocities created antagonism among a section of Dalit youth, mainly Jatavs, towards the BJP.

Saharanpur has a large community of Dalits, mostly Jatav leather workers, some of whom are Buddhists. The violent clashes in March 2017 were the result of rising confrontation between pro-BSP Ambedkarites and pro-BJP Hindutvawadi Jatavs, following the revival of the BJP.[19] As Nepal Singh, our important Dalit contact in the city, told us, the divide between the Ambedkarites and the Hindutvawadis dates to 2013, when he and his followers shifted to the BJP. After this, the Ambedkarites and the Hindutvawadi Jatavs began celebrating Ambedkar's birthday separately, with BJP MLAs attending the event organized by the latter. In 2017, after Nepal Singh won a seat as a ward member from Jatav Nagar in the municipal election held in December 2017, five BJP MLAs including the local member attended the function organized by his groups.[20]

Till 1991, the Saharanpur Lok Sabha and Saharanpur Nagar[21] assembly constituencies had been largely peaceful, with the Congress or the Janata party winning these seats. But contestations for these seats began from 1996 after the

Ram Mandir agitation. Despite the large number of Dalits in the district, the Lok Sabha seat was held by the BJP with two exceptions: the SP in 2004 and the BSP in 2019. In the case of the Saharanpur Nagar assembly seat, with which we are concerned here, in 2012 the BJP local strongman Raghav Lakhanpal Singh won with 38.80 per cent of the votes, followed by Congress candidate Saleem Ahmed with 33.05 per cent but in 2017 the SP managed to win with Sanjay Garg, their local influential candidate who gained 46.68 per cent; the BSP's Mukesh Dixit came third gaining only 6.37 per cent But in 2019, as a part of the 'mahagathbandhan' (grand alliance), the BSP's Haji Fazlur Rehman won with 41.74 per cent votes, pushing Raghav Lakhanpal Singh to second place. Also, there was growing antagonism among the Dalits towards Muslims in the constituency with whom they had shared space within the BSP and in their villages. A schism had developed over time due to an earlier Dalit–Muslim clash in 2006, when the Dalits of a village were prevented by the Muslims from taking out a procession commemorating Saint Ravidas, which triggered protest across Saharanpur city.

Discussions with villagers during our field trip soon after the violence in 2017 revealed that the local BJP leaders and organizations were active at the grassroots in mobilizing Dalits, paralleled by assertion by upper castes against the rising lower castes. The two violent clashes involving Dalits were both due to attempts to hold processions to honour caste and community icons: a Dalit–Muslim conflict took place on 20 April 2017 at village Sadak Dudhali, due to an Ambedkar Shobha Yatra taken out by a Dalit group; and a Rajput–Dalit clash on 5 May 2017 at village Shabbirpur arising out of a Maharana Pratap Shobha Yatra by Rajputs. Sadak Dudhali, a village barely five kilometres from Saharanpur city, and now a part of the city municipality, comprises roughly 80 per cent Muslims mainly from the Gada caste, who claim to have converted from Hindu Rajputs, and 20 per cent largely Jatavs. While earlier the Dalits and Muslims had shared social space in the village, with instances of BJP confrontations rising every day, mundane issues became communalized.

On 12 April, Ashok Bharti, head of Ravidasiya Dharm visited Sadak Dudhali and, along with a few Dalit youths, planned to organize an Ambedkar Shobha Yatra there on 20 April to celebrate the birth anniversary of B.R. Ambedkar in the village. The local administration denied them permission as it apprehended trouble due to pre-existing tensions between Dalits and Muslims. Some younger Dalits, angry with both the Muslims and the administration, mobilized the youth and held the procession in the village, which was led by the sitting BJP MP Raghav Lakhanpal. He threatened to take the yatra through Saharanpur city, also saying, 'I will not allow Saharanpur to become Kashmir.'

Newspaper reports reveal that when the procession was about to enter the Muslim area of the village, it was attacked with stones and stopped. In retaliation, a mob of BJP supporters in Saharanpur city went on a rampage, attacked the house of the senior superintendent of police, allegedly broke CCTV cameras and furniture, and set public property on fire. The police ordered an FIR against Lakhanpal and over 500 others for the violence, vandalism and attack on the police officer's house and the district magistrate's office; order was restored only after the city of Saharanpur was turned into a fortress.

The 5 May incident took place in the neighbouring villages of Shabbirpur and Simlana in Saharanpur district. Rajputs are the dominant community in Shabbirpur but their socio-political pride and authority has been challenged more recently by politically mobile castes like Jats and Gujjars and the advent of subaltern Hindutva. Also, economic anxieties due to a deepening agrarian crisis have deprived them of their occupational identity as prosperous farmers. In this situation, the Dalits provided a soft target, particularly during a non-BSP regime.[22] In a striking similarity, the occasion involved the yatra of an icon taking place without the required permission. However, the participants were Rajputs and those who protested against the yatra were Chamar Dalits. Violence broke out when the Maharana Pratap procession was passing through the Dalit neighbourhood of the village of Shabbirpur; residents objected to the allegedly loud music, triggering an exchange of heated words. The altercation led to a violent clash with both groups throwing stones and bricks at each other. A stone hit a twenty-five-year-old Thakur man, killing him. His death further enraged the community and more Thakurs from neighbouring villages gathered at Shabbirpur, setting at least twenty-five Dalit houses on fire. The Dalits allegedly attacked police and fire brigade personnel who had rushed to the village. While Dalits in the village are divided, as elsewhere, into pro-BJP and pro-BSP groups, they united in their anger at their property being destroyed, attacked the Thakurs and engaged in skirmishes with the police. According to media reports, on 20 May, 180 Dalit families converted to Buddhism in protest against what they called unfair targeting of their community in Shabbirpur village, particularly the burning of their houses. They also alleged that the police did not allow them to hold a Dalit mahapanchayat. On 23 May, a Dalit was killed while returning from a rally held by Mayawati in Saharanpur, and on 24 May a Thakur youth was shot and sustained injuries.[23] Caught between loyalty to party and community, the BJP-affiliated senior Dalit leaders in the district, while showing solidarity with the Dalits of Shabbirpur, tried to keep out of the incident.

These two incidents, particularly the one at Shabbirpur, united the pro-BSP Jatavs of the district. However, the BSP leadership did not react immediately or support the protesting Dalits, which seemed to further alienate a section from the party. It was the Bhim Army, led by Chandrashekhar Azad, who organized a meeting at Jantar Mantar in Delhi on 21May—attended by at least 50,000 Dalits—to protest against atrocities against Dalits, particularly at Saharanpur.[24] It led to an upsurge in the popularity of the Bhim Army, witnessed in the use of the resounding slogan of 'Jai Bhim'. A worried UP government arrested Azad on 17 June 2017, and later detained him again under the National Security Act.

Outside the state, the year 2018 witnessed several incidents and increasing protests by Dalits. The year began with attacks on Dalits at Bhima-Koregaon, a village thirty kilometres from Pune in Maharashtra, where hundreds of thousands of people gather on New Year's Day to commemorate the victory of the English—whose troops comprised mostly of Mahar soldiers—against the Peshwa-led Maratha empire in 1818. The year marked the 200th anniversary of the Battle of Bhima-Koregaon. Violent clashes were reported between Dalits and those with saffron flags who pelted stones. At least one person died and three were injured in the clashes between villagers from Bhima-Koregaon, Pabal and Shikrapur, and those celebrating the event; clashes also took place in Pune and Mumbai. Dalit leaders Jignesh Mevani and Prakash Ambedkar were present at the Bhima-Koregaon protests and the Elgar Parishad rally.[25]

More important were the violent protests by Dalit groups in the Hindi heartland in March 2018 against the Supreme Court's

20 March order calling for changes in the SC/ST (Prevention of Atrocities) Act, 1989. It was felt that the changes would dilute the Act, which would have strong repercussions on Dalits who had recently experienced a series of atrocities, with little protection from the government.[26] While India has witnessed agitations by Dalits in the past, the scale of the protest, which spread across several states in the Hindi heartland, leaving eleven persons dead and many injured, and saw public property being damaged, the use of social media and anger visible on the street, was unprecedented in recent times.

The Act was, in fact, the end product of movements and the formation of the BSP in 1984 by Kanshi Ram, and the Dalit upsurge from below in many other states in the Hindi heartland. By the mid-1980s, the nature of crimes had changed, and the reasons were now as much economic and political as social; 'ritual untouchability' was replaced by caste atrocities, such as not allowing Dalits to vote, defiling statues of Ambedkar, burning houses and raping Dalit women. Much of this arose out of social jealousy as sections of Dalits were able to improve their economic condition owing to education and reservation to get government employment. Most of the crimes were perpetrated by the middle castes—the traditionally dominant landowning groups—who found that a younger generation of landless Dalits in the countryside was no longer willing to submit to humiliating practices as in the past. It was the formation of two coalition governments by Mayawati in 1995 and 1998 in UP and the rigorous implementation of the Act by her government that gave greater confidence to Dalits to use the Act and created a fear of punishment among perpetrators. Against this backdrop, the argument that the Act is often misused did not appeal as it was seen as the duty of the state to ensure that this did not happen.[27]

On 9 August 2018, the Centre passed a bill to overturn the Supreme Court order and restore the provisions of the Act.[28] However, on 12–13 September 2018, this reversal was strongly opposed by upper-caste Hindus and even a section of BJP party workers in Agra, Chitrakoot and Varanasi, and some other districts, demanding that the amendment be immediately reversed and threatening to hold a country-wide agitation.[29] While the BJP leadership dismissed these clashes as sporadic and which they could resolve, the protests occurred just when the campaign for the MP, Rajasthan and Chhattisgarh assembly elections had begun, leaving the party worried. The Congress party was able to defeat the BJP in all three states in November 2018,[30] fuelling the feeling that the BJP was losing Dalit support in the Hindi heartland, including in UP.

In this tense atmosphere, the defeat of the BJP by the grand alliance formed by the SP and BSP in early 2018 to fight three by-polls to the Lok Sabha in Gorakhpur and Phulpur in eastern UP on 14 March, and in Kairana on 27 May, led observers to point to the revival of the BSP and a deepening divide between the Dalits and the BJP in the state. The victory of the SP–BSP alliance by high margins in the seats vacated by Chief Minister Adityanath and Deputy Chief Minister Maurya, in Gorakhpur and Phulpur, just a year after the formation of the new government, were major victories for the opposition parties.[31] In Kairana, the deepening crisis in the sugar industry which affected the Jat farmers underlay the defeat of the BJP.[32] However, ground reports point to Dalits playing a big role in the outcome and the Bhim Army supporting the Muslim candidate Tabassum Begun, jointly supported by the RLD–BSP–SP.

Worried by the victory of the SP–BSP mahagathbandhan, the UP government announced that Azad would be released early, before the expiry of the NSA against him, on 12 September

2018. His early release was seen as a political move by the UP government to woo the Dalit voters ahead of the possibility of an alliance between the SP, BSP, Congress and other opposition parties for the 2019 Lok Sabha polls. However, the UP law minister said that Azad had been released on the basis of a confidential report that law and order had improved in the state.[33] After his release, Azad claimed that the BJP feared his detention might dent its Dalit vote-bank ahead of the 2019 Lok Sabha election.[34] Speaking to the media, he said, 'I am out, and the BJP is going to face the ire of the Dalit samaj. This time, the BJP will be out of power ... If the mahagathbandhan happens, the BJP will be reduced to single digits,' and he would 'definitely' support it. He reminded them that 'in the Lok Sabha by-polls, the BJP lost Gorakhpur and Phulpur and tasted defeat.'[35]

Enthused by the victory in the 2018 by-polls, the SP and BSP formed a mahagathbandhan together with the RLD for the 2019 Lok Sabha elections. A template existed; the two parties had managed this experiment in the Gorakhpur, Phulpur and Kairana by-elections. Also, it was felt that the parties could ensure shift of their votes to each other, and they could jointly defeat the BJP. But the alliance won barely fifteen seats, despite getting 38.92 per cent of the vote-share in 2019, while that of the BJP increased from 42.63per cent to 49.55 per cent.[36]

An important reason for the poor performance of the alliance was the failure of its caste calculations. The consolidation of the core constituencies of the alliance partners did happen: the SP's core voters, the Yadavs, fully supported the alliance, with three-fifths voting for the alliance; the BSP fared better, obtaining 75 per cent or three-fourths of the Jatav votes, higher than the 68 per cent in 2014. But in the case of the other SCs, it gained the support of 42 per cent, while 48 per cent preferred the BJP, as in 2014. It was the much larger 'non-core', that is, the new voting bloc of the non-Yadav and non-Jatav Dalits, who constituted a substantial section of the electorate that had been profitably mobilized by the BJP, first in 2014, and in even larger numbers in 2019.[37]

In fact, in 2019, the formation of the alliance created a sharp division between Yadavs and Jatavs versus the lower OBCs and smaller SCs. The ambitious slogan *'Ekbhi vote naghat-ne-paye, ekbhi vote nabat-ne-paye'* (Not a single vote should go waste, not a single vote should be split) raised on 7 April, at the first rally of the BSP–SP–RLD, was a call for the mutual transfer of votes between their core support bases, but it also came to be seen as a 'veiled suggestion' to other communities that they were not needed in this alliance.[38] This created a counter-mobilization of lower backwards and smaller Dalits, who, unwilling to return to erstwhile Yadav–Jatav dominance, moved towards the BJP in even greater numbers than in 2014. In fact, the anti-Yadav sentiment was the fulcrum in UP that helped the BJP enormously. Consequently, over four-fifths of upper castes, fourth-fifths of Kurmis and Koeris, and three-fourths of lower OBCs voted for the BJP. Along with non-Jatav Dalits, the three constitute around half of UP's population. Thus, despite the violent protests against rising Dalit atrocities, the BJP was able to once again obtain the support of the smaller Dalits. It was local relationships and power equations, along with relatively better incentive for the BJP, rather than the rhetoric of the social justice parties, that drove Dalit preference.

The Post-2019 Scenario

The process of protest and preference continued post 2019, and in the run-up to the 2022 assembly elections atrocities against Dalits and protests by them increased. UP registered the highest number of cases of crimes against women—59,853 in all—in the country from 1 January to 31 December 2019, according to the National Crime Records Bureau's 'Crime in India 2019' report. The NCRB report, published on 29 September 2020, showed that in terms of rapes committed, UP ranked second (3,065), behind Rajasthan (5,997). It also ranked third in terms of rape-murder cases. Out of 278 such cases in the country, 34 were committed in UP.[39]

A thirteen-year-old girl was gang-raped and killed in Pakariya village in Lakhimpur Kheri district in August 2020, following which the police arrested two men from the village in this connection.[40] The victim's body was found in a sugarcane field, reportedly owned by one of the accused, after a brief search by her family. A relative of the girl said three people were involved in the crime. The victim had gone missing on Friday afternoon after leaving her house at 1 pm. After a brief search, her body was found near a sugarcane field. The girl's post-mortem report confirmed sexual assault and strangulation. Mayawati condemned the rape case on Twitter and attacked the BJP government in UP. Bhim Army chief Chandrasekhar Azad condemned the incident, alleging that Dalit oppression was at its peak under the BJP government, and demanded Chief Minister Yogi Adityanath's resignation.

On 29 September 2020, a twenty-two-year-old Dalit college girl was gang-raped and assaulted in Balrampur, UP, and she died on the way to the hospital. According to her family, she was abducted on her way back home and raped by at least two men. The post-mortem report suggests she was badly tortured even after being raped.[41] The two main accused were arrested by the UP police, and the UP government offered financial assistance to the victim's family.[42]

But most important is the incident that took place in Hathras, which is known to have a history of anti-Dalit violence by the Jats and the upper castes.[43] On 14 September 2020, a nineteen-year-old Dalit woman belonging to the Valmiki caste was gang-raped in Boolgarhi village, Hathras, by four upper-caste Thakur men, and died two weeks later. Though all four accused were arrested promptly, the role of the district police came in for severe criticism on two counts, namely, deliberately underplaying the seriousness of the incident by denying rape charges and demonstrating insensitivity by cremating her body in the middle of the night against the wishes of the family. In fact, the state police ruled out rape by arguing that the victim in her first statement after regaining consciousness did not mention rape. Though the rape was confirmed subsequently in victim's dying declaration as well as in CBI's charge-sheet, senior police functionaries taking recourse to technicalities in a hurried manner and denying this aspect led to further agitation by Dalit activists and opposition parties. In fact, the public shock was so severe that the Lucknow bench of the Allahabad High Court took suo motu cognizance of the incident and indicted the role of the district police, district magistrate and others.[44]

The incident stuck in the public memory, particularly among Dalits, as it had created a furore nationally. In our fieldwork in September 2021 and February 2022, the Balmikis in western UP, while expressing anger and distress,argued that such incidents are not BJP-specific. Rather, they stated, under SP rule they have faced more atrocities. Recognizing the enormity of this incident, prior to the 2022 assembly election, the BJP used its cadresto micro-manage constituencies such as Hathras and Lakhimpur Kheri where strong Dalit protests following atrocities had taken place. Though the BJP had won in both constituencies in 2017, many observers believed that the BJP would face defeat in 2022. But in Hathras, BJP's Anjula Singh Mahaur won close to 1.55 lakh votes, three times more than the runner-up Sanjeev Kumar, a BSP candidate, who received approximately 54,000 votes. Similarly, in Lakhimpur Kheri, despite the nationwide outrage[45] and despite eight people including four farmers being killed on 3 October 2021 during a protest against the Centre's farm laws,[46] the BJP won all eight seats in the district.[47]

BJP's national secretary, Y. Satya Kumar, told the media, that they had earlier reached out to Dalit youth from the same locality and community in Lakhimpur Kheri and now the party had many workers from within the community, for future elections as well.

> The Pasi community was already with the BJP because of the influence of former BSP leader Jugal Kishor, who is now with the BJP. The Jatav votes were yet a concern for the party. However, the party through social outreach won all eight seats, which was a difficult task ... a similar practice was adopted in other parts of the state to reach out to Jatavs. In western UP, too, it paid dividends and despite farmer's agitation, the party gained the votes, which were micro-managed at each booth.[48]

In the aftermath of the rape and assault incident of the Dalit girl at Hathras and subsequently her death, opposition parties, particularly the Congress and the SP, began a state-wide protest. However, it was Chandrashekhar Azad who was at the forefront of the agitation to secure justice for the victim. He and his supporters were the first to protest at Delhi's Safdarjung Hospital, where the victim died on 29 September 2020, following which the UP police took the body to her village. Azad alleged that he was arrested by the state police while he was accompanying the family of the victim from Delhi to Hathras and was put under house arrest in Saharanpur.[49] At Jantar Mantar in New Delhi, Azad and the Bhim Army spearheaded the protest and were joined by other opposition leaders like the Delhi chief minister, Arvind Kejriwal, and members of the Aam Aadmi Party, Communist Party of India (Marxist) general secretary Sitaram Yechury and Communist Party of India leader D. Raja, among others.[50] Later, Azad was allowed to visit the victim's family, but the agitation continued until the CBI was asked to investigate the matter.

While Azad and other opposition parties were visible on the ground, the BSP and Mayawati faced angry criticism in general, and from Dalits in particular, for their complete absence from the scene. She tried to defend the absence of BSP's workers on the ground by arguing that BSP did not participate in protests[51] but angry Dalits in Agra burnt Mayawati's effigy over her silence on the Hathras incident.[52]

A comparative study of the Bhim Army and Azad and the BSP and Mayawati in various incidents of Dalit atrocities does indicate a shift in the Dalit discourse, with Dalits supporting the former and being angry with the latter. However, despite Azad's popularity, Dalits do not view him as a leader who can win elections. This viewpoint has continued even after the formation of his own party—the Azad Samaj Party—in March 2020. During fieldwork in in western UP in August 2020, Jatav respondents declared: '*Hum Azad ki izzat karte hain, par humara vote Behenji ke liye hai*' (We respect Azad but our vote is for Mayawati). Thus, Azad's BA and ASP are seen as social forces that protect them against atrocities but not as a viable political force that can make electoral gains. Also, despite the decline of the BSP, for the Jatavs of western UP Mayawati remains the tallest Dalit leader.

Thus, our narrative shows that Dalits close ranks and participate in the politics of protest and agitation whenever there are incidents of atrocities, rallying behind new-generation community leaders But they continue to vote for the BJP despite rising atrocities, due to the collapse of the BSP and to prevent the SP, representing the Yadavs in the countryside, from returning to a position of dominance. An equally important reason is the range of welfare and economic benefits that the BJP has provided them from 2014 onwards. Electoral results following major atrocities, such as at Lakhimpur Kheri and Hathras, suggest that a significant section of Dalits do not link the BJP to these.

The two social justice parties, the SP and BSP, have found that apart from their core supporters, the non-Yadavs and non-Jatav groups, the smaller Dalits and OBCs no longer support them; they prefer the support and protection afforded by the stronger party, which is the BJP. As our narrative has shown, they attempted twice—prior to the 2019 elections—by joining hands to win back the support of their erstwhile supporters. While they were successful in the 2019 by-elections, it was only in specific locales, and in the national election they moved back to the BJP. While opposition parties such as the Congress have been successful in Rajasthan and Madhya Pradesh, in UP the BJP has managed to obtain and sustain the support of Dalits as a part of the social coalition built in 2014. Dalits today, with rising political consciousness and aspirations, make their own choices, and in the final analysis, weighing the pros and cons based on a relative-gain approach, find the BJP better on the plank of protection, welfare and inclusionary social politics. It seems we are going to see the continuance of protest and preference as a parallel trend in Dalit politics for some time to come.

6

Dalit Shift: Tactical-Instrumental or Ideological

It is not a mechanical or transactional shift, but this section of society has begun to discover its Hindu roots. [1]

As our narrative has shown, the BJP under Modi has been able to obtain the vote of an increasing percentage of the smaller Dalit sub-castes in UP over the 2014, 2017, 2019 and 2022 elections. This raises the question whether this is a temporary and tactical decision on the part of a section of Dalits following the decline of the BSP, or whether it reflects an ideological-cum-cultural conversion to saffronization. The decision of tactic or ideology is of significance in order to understand the future direction of the Dalit movement.

127

A number of questions arise in the present context: If the BSP manages to recover, will the smaller Dalit sub-castes return to it? If the BJP loses, will Dalits leave and move to other parties, or has the saffronization project run deep enough for them to remain with it? Does this mean the Hinduization of Indian society is now irreversible, and what does this mean for the Dalit movement?

While it is an important and controversial subject, studies that analyse the shift by Dalits towards the BJP post-2014 do not explore if the support is limited to the electoral arena or if it has entered their social consciousness.[2] We argue, based on interviews and fieldwork, that this question *should not be viewed as a binary, in an 'either/or' framework*. Tactical or strategic decisions by nature are instrumental and pragmatic; the smaller Dalit sub-castes being poor and dependent on the support of the state tend to choose the party that dominates the political landscape. They supported the Congress during its heyday and with its disintegration moved to the ascending identity-based parties in the 1990s. Since 2014, with the electoral decline of the BSP and the spectacular rise of the BJP, they have moved to the saffron fold. The binary viewpoint assumes significance when we see the present-day political preference of the Dalits for the BJP as the product of the more *immediate* developments of the 2000s, but do not explore the underlying historical processes that have led them to make that choice. In an ideological shift, culture is the prime marker behind the positive interface of the Dalit and the BJP, and this is due to the historical process of Hinduization which has further intensified in the last decade. Along with emphasis on the material aspects, cultural issues pertaining to linking the Dalit sub-castes' histories with the deities of the Hindu pantheon of Hinduism have acquired a new momentum. With an ideological shift, the saffron embrace of the these Dalits could have a longer shelf life, irrespective of the electoral fortunes of the BJP.

These dual processes, electoral and cultural, should be viewed as working in tandem, sometimes alternatively and sometimes parallel to each other. A closer look on the ground level and past trends suggests a more complex mechanism of the shift; whether it is tactical or ideological is contingent on external factors like durability of the support and the role of prominent political elites from within communities. The initial shift is often driven by calculated considerations such as better and more credible incentives promised by the saffron fold, and their positive reception by the Dalit electorate. Thereafter, if the electoral support sustains for an extended period, as has been the case with the Valmikis—whose case we analyse in some detail—the initial considered move translates into an ideological shift. The Dalit sub-castes internalize their support to the saffron party and start identifying themselves as committed voters. However, if the duration of the shift were not to sustain in the future beyond one or two elections on account of disillusionment, or the role played by prominent political elites who help shape their political experiences, the Dalit interface with the saffron party could be said to be tactical. Thus, reversals back and forth are possible but do not seem likely in the near future, given the current hegemonic position of the BJP.

These intermittent patterns of tactic and ideology are visible historically in the trajectory of the Dalit movement on the subcontinent. In this chapter, we explore the working of both these processes, their inter-relationship in the past and present, and discuss the various views put forward by scholars and commentators, and what this means for the future of the Dalit movement.

Tacticality and Ideology: The Immediate and the Historical

Tacticality and ideology can be viewed as two sides of the same coin. Our narrative in the earlier chapters has shown that the two important decisions made by the Dalits in the 2000s have been to shift away from the BSP, which they supported since its inception in 1984, and to move towards the BJP under the leadership of Narendra Modi. While these decisions are no doubt the result of a number of immediate changes in UP politics, as our analysis will show, important historical developments, too, that impacted the Dalit movement underlie their decision to move to the BJP.[3] While the immediate tactical reasons for the shift have been dealt with in detail in the preceding chapters, we reiterate them briefly below, together with the critical viewpoints of observers, before we move on to present the historical–ideological forces underlying them that support this decision.

In the 2000s, the Dalits, particularly the smaller non-Jatav sub-castes, were unhappy and disappointed with Mayawati on a number of counts. While the BSP provided them self-respect, dignity and political empowerment, the waning of identity politics made Dalits part of the larger aspirational class in the country, creating rising aspirations for material advancement. Placed at the bottom of the pyramid, the Dalits today exhibit a higher level of individualization; aware that they are different from the upper castes, not a part of 'them', their main objective is 'what we can get from them'.[4] Their vote for the BJP today reflects a higher level of confidence and a sense of independent choice. Mukhopadhyay mentioned how the motorbike has become the symbol of upward mobility among the Dalits. This is borne out by what we too observed in our field studies, particularly in Saharanpur in western UP.[5] An erstwhile supporter and a prominent leader of the BSP in Saharanpur, Nepal Singh, argued that the BJP has earned Dalit support by providing both material and cultural inclusion to Dalits.

The gradual shift by Mayawati towards the ideology of sarvajan from mid-1990s onwards, giving up the ideology of social justice, created divisions. It was celebrated and hailed by some when the party gained power.[6] But it was also criticized as a move away from Ambedkarite ideology and loss of identity as a Dalit party.[7] There was a perception that the dissolution of the social justice parties was due to their failure to govern and deliver goods to their constituencies. Some continue to feel that Mayawati has 'squandered' the legacy of Kanshi Ram through the sarvajan shift and high levels of corruption while in office.[8] Others point out that 'there remains no Ambedkarite discourse'.[9]

The role of the BSP's leadership has been disappointing for Dalits, who have moved towards a stronger party. Mayawati has been held responsible for the breakdown of the party's organizational structure and the exodus of many trusted, capable leaders who had worked with her and Kanshi Ram. It is argued that she is not as dedicated an organization-builder as Kanshi Ram; she gave little importance to 'sangathan'.[10] Many Dalits feel the BSP is a party totally subservient to one person and can hardly be described as a democratic or transformative party.

Corruption destroyed Mayawati's image and made her vulnerable to the BJP; it also created a 'disconnect between the community and party leadership'—she is viewed as no different from other political leaders.[11] She had hoped that her display of wealth and the symbolic politics of building parks and memorials to celebrate Dalit icons would enthuse Dalits with the idea that 'we can do it too' but it proved to be 'counter-productive'. If she had continued on the path of clean politics, good governance and stable politics as in southern India, where the Dravida Munnetra Kazhagam[12] promoted literacy and focused on human development of the disadvantaged sections, there could have been a future. Mayawati's vast assets, acquired over her or during her active years in politics, have also punctured the myth that Dalit politicians are deprived.[13]

Nor, it has been pointed out, has Chandrashekhar Azad been able to build a new Dalit movement; he is seen as a 'hit and run' leader with little organizational strength or new ideology, without which the party formed by him cannot be sustained.[14] In this situation, given their historical animosity towards the Yadavs and the OBCs, and the SP as the party representing them, the only choice left for Dalits is the BJP.

Aware of their rising aspirations, the BJP has used social inclusion and welfare to satisfy their immediate needs and attract the support of the lower castes. The smaller Dalit sub-castes have welcomed the attempts by the BJP to include them within the larger Hindu identity as they have felt marginalized and neglected socially within the Dalit community, and politically within the BSP. Equally important, the BJP's conscious efforts to use the policy of 'new welfarism' which has created a category of 'labharti' (beneficiaries) [15]—or groups who should be provided benefits in order to gain their political support—has paid off. There are labhartis in every caste category, but the largest number is from the Dalits and OBCs.[16] This is a material approach underplayed in the media along with the cultural approach of nationalism and Hindutva. Describing Modi as the 'master of outreach', Mukhopadhyay argues that little has been done by the opposition parties to counter this method. The BJP finds out the needs of the lower castes in an area and provides for it without delay; their response time is very fast.[17]

It is these incentives that Kanshi Ram's sister Swaran Kaur, in an interaction with the media in their native village of Pirthipur in Punjab, pointed out that stop the Dalits from voting for the BSP. She believes that 'the biggest problem with the Dalits is that they are easily distracted by offers of free ration or petty cash subsidies'.[18] She said her brother used to say 'the only way to uplift Dalits is to ensure they receive good education, and to create suitable employment opportunities. If they are educated and have jobs, they will themselves buy ration from the market and take care of their families ... But the problem is that political parties have always used Dalits in vote bank politics and hardly worked to lift them out of poverty. The party founded by my brother was no different and, in fact, is now monopolized by those having deep pockets'.

At the same time, observers have pointed out that the decline of the BSP reflects a larger contemporary 'crisis in Ambedkarite politics' that Dalit political leaders and elites have not addressed. Arguing for a long-term ideological shift of the Dalits to the saffron fold, Sudheendra Kulkarni was very critical of present-day Ambedkarite politics, the weaknesses of which he located in the politics of Ambedkar and his legacies that have been uncritically accepted. There has been iconization of Ambedkar 'as (of) no other political leader'.[19] Ambedkar has now come to be accepted by all, but a lot of what he wrote, espoused and did during his life has 'now been washed away, and is not relevant', but unfortunately some myths are being created 'which are not critiqued based on hard facts'. For instance, Kulkarni holds that it is not true that he was the 'sole architect' of the Constitution. He points out that if we read Ambedkar's *States and Minorities*, which he presented to the Constituent Assembly, and compare it to our Constitution, there is 'absolutely no comparison even on fundamental rights, which means that very little of what he presented, was actually accepted by the Constituent Assembly'. He also points out that Ambedkar as a leader who espoused justice for the SCs stood 'very tall', but he was not successful as a party builder. The many political parties he formed beginning with the Indian Labour Party in 1936, the All-Scheduled Caste Federation of India, with a branch in the United Provinces in the 1940s or the Republican Party of India, formed after his death but based on his advice, made no mark on Indian politics of the time. The only time the aspirations of Dalits for self-empowerment succeeded to some extent was in UP in the 1990s, under the leadership of Kanshi Ram. In no other state has an Ambedkarite party been able to come to power.[20]

Similarly, he pointed out that Ambedkar's critique of Hinduism is now being discarded by the SCs themselves. The socio-cultural practices of the SCs are subtly undergoing change. Taking the example of Maharashtra, he says there is Hinduization of religious practices even among those who had converted to Buddhism. There is also resentment against the dominant Mahars to which Ambedkar belonged, as they occupy the entire Dalit space in economic and cultural terms. Other SCs in the state are very conscious and even proud of their Hindu identity. In UP, this is true of the Balmikis who trace their origin back to Rishi Valmiki. These feelings are part of the 'politics of memory and lived experience', not something they have created recently. Differentiation among the sub-castes has always existed, and the project to create a unified Dalit identity has not proved successful, whether in Maharashtra by the Dalit Panthers or in UP by the BSP. The leaders of the RPI in Maharashtra are 'hardly Ambedkarites'. One of their biggest leaders, Ram Das Athawale, was a member of Narendra Modi's cabinet in 2014 and in 2019.[21]

Yet, there is the iconization of Ambedkar today. His statue is one of the largest in the Parliament complex; political parties have reaped rich electoral dividends riding on his name. Invoking him has become convenient and politically useful for the BJP, and even the Congress party, which historically opposed Ambedkar's politics throughout the national movement and afterwards. But there is 'unfortunately not much critical appraisal of Ambedkar', his ideology and politics, and the irrelevance today, which might have helped in dealing with present-day problems, drawing on his ideas and charting a new direction.

In this situation, Dalit politics under the BSP, Kulkarni feels, has run its course, and its obituary can be written—this reflects the 'severe limitations of identity politics'. While Ambedkar will continue to remain an icon as there is a desire for social justice and equality which he certainly represented, there is little room for Ambedkarite politics of the BSP variety. Dalit assertion and discourse on the ground will continue as there is aspiration among Dalits for a better life, but for Dalit politics as a 'separate and successful politics', there is no future.[22]

Divisions and Hinduization

While the above proximate factors over the ideological/tactical nature of the shift underlie the decline of the BSP, a perusal of the existing literature on the subject shows that two historical features have impacted and determined the Dalit movement in UP: first, social divisions between sub-castes within the Dalit community given the nature of the caste system; second, a long-term process of Hinduization of Dalits, both during the colonial and post-colonial times.

As a consequence, there have only been brief periods in UP during which the Ambedkarite discourse and movement were able to challenge upper caste dominance and politically unite all sections of the community: first, the 'Ambedkar alternative' in the 1930s[23] which, though late compared to Maharashtra, created big leather merchants in Agra, Aligarh and elsewhere; second, the formation of the All-India Scheduled Castes Federation of India with a strong branch in the former United Provinces in the 1940s, the RPI in the 1950s and 1960s; third, and most important, the formation of the bahujan movement and party by Kanshi Ram in the 1990s. None of these movements, however, were able to sustain themselves over time, and declined. In each case, the existence of a strong dominant party that did not allow the Dalit movement the space to flourish was important: the Congress party in the colonial and immediate post-colonial period, and in the 2000s the BJP.

A major reason for the unravelling of the BSP today is because the term 'Dalit' hides the fact that the SCs or former untouchables are divided into a number of small sub-castes with multiple cultural moorings. Dalit is an identity 'created' in post-independence India; it did not exist during Ambedkar's time.[24] Politics was sought to be built on the basis of this unified Dalit identity, although they constituted a very diverse group. The importance of these divisions lies in the fact that in every region of India, one or two sub-castes are numerically and socially dominant and economically advanced. While in UP it is the Chamars, in Maharashtra it is the Mahars, in Andhra the Malas and in Gujarat the Vankars, etc. In UP, according to the census, there are sixty-six sub-castes or jatis identified as standing below the line of pollution,[25] with considerable differentiation among them. There is, in fact, a caste system below the line of pollution, and some sub-castes do not inter-marry or inter-dine with each other.[26] Historically, there has been a division between the Chamar–Jatavs of western UP and non-Jatav, smaller sub-castes both socially and politically; the Jatavs have been 'feared and respected' by the others[27] and have been in the vanguard of all movements in the colonial and post-colonial period.

In UP, the Jatavs have had a strong sense of pride in their lower-caste identity traditionally. As a result, though they experimented with Sanskritization and attempted upward mobility in the caste system, compared to the smaller Dalit sub-castes, the process of Hinduization has not had as much impact on them. As Owen Lynch's study on Agra shows,[28] they prospered due to the introduction of the leather industry by the British authorities after 1857, and big leather merchants arose who had the economic potential to challenge the upper castes. They were attracted initially to the shuddhi movement of the Arya Samaj, which attempted the task of re-incorporating the untouchables into the Hindu fold.[29] By 1910, between 60,000 and 70,000 shuddhi ceremonies had been performed in Punjab and the United Provinces. But the depressed classes, most particularly the better-off Chamar workers, discovered that it made no difference to their position in the caste hierarchy, as caste Hindus continued to treat them as untouchables.[30] Rather, as Lynch shows, they took to Sanskritization and the discovery of a new identity, creating a legend to prove this.[31] They put pressure on the British government to recognize them as Jatav-Kshatriya in the census and hoped the caste Hindus would accept this step, but this did not happen.

It is for this reason that the Jatavs are found in western UP, and elsewhere they are known as Chamars. Another reason for their dominance over smaller sub-castes in other regions of UP, especially the eastern region, is that during the colonial period due to the network of canals built and the early commercialization of agriculture, almost all economic development in the sphere of agriculture took place in western UP. As Mohinder Singh's study based in the 1940s shows, the Jatavs of western UP were more prosperous, better fed, housed and clad, and closer to their Punjabi neighbours than the Chamars of the other regions.[32] The condition of the smaller sub-castes in the densely populated poorer districts of central and eastern UP and Bundelkhand was one of extreme poverty, and heavy pressure on land led many to perform *begari* for the landlord.

It is the social divisions within the Dalit community that have made the non-Jatav, smaller sub-castes more amenable to the long process of Hinduization in the Hindi heartland. Hence, a significant reason for their decision to support the BJP today is not a 'mechanical or transactional shift, rather this section of society is beginning to discover its Hindu roots'.[33] Today, the process of Hinduization is visible practically all over India and has helped the BJP garner the votes of the Dalits.

Much literature shows that there was a process of Hinduization in north India among the former untouchable castes of Chuhras, Mehtars, Doms and Bhangis in the late nineteenth century—sub-castes whose traditional occupation was cleaning and scavenging. Contemporary developments have led to a renewed interest, among many scholars, in the process of the 'neo-Hindu politics' of the colonial period which tried to categorize the depressed classes as Hindus. The impact of Hinduization is best seen in the case of the Chuhras in Punjab and the Balmikis in the former United Provinces. Many scholars concur that these two groups were non-Hindu in their cultural traditions, and earlier were also followers of Muslim saints Bala Shah Nuri in Punjab and Lal begin the United Provinces.[34] The Balmiki movement was 'originally planned to redefine the community from above' by the upper castes who suggested they would attain higher Hindu traditions through worship of Rishi Valmiki.[35] Two reasons underlay this attempt: to prevent their conversion from the Hindu religion, and the 'politics of numbers' in which the Muslims claimed these sub-castes were a separate social category and not part of the Hindu community, which would increase their own numbers vis-à-vis Hindus in their attempt to obtain separate representation, while the Hindus claimed them as integral to the Hindu community.[36]

The Balmiki identity and its nominative politics of cultural persuasion were planned in the twentieth century in north India by Hindu missionary organizations, the Arya Samaj, the Hindu Mahasabha and the Harijan Sevak Sangh, which, it is alleged, were allies of the Indian National Congress.[37] Hindu culture was disseminated by organizing kathas, havans, rath yatras, bhajans, and processions in Harijan colonies. They took to the nomenclature of Balmiki and many Muslim traditions were replaced by Hindu ones.[38] An interesting story relates how an Indian historian visited Jalandhar and interviewed Om Prakash Gill, an ageing leader of the Balmiki community. He revealed that the old name of the Balmiki temple in Ali Mohalla was Darbar Sahib and 'it was a shrine to Bala Shah Nuri and Lalbeg'.[39] Many traditions influenced by Islam were replaced by Hindu ones. In many areas, self-ascription became a matter of political and economic pressure. Under this process of Hindu acculturation 'Chuhra sweepers' of north India established the Valmiki Sangh in 1910 to defend their interests. By the 1930s they liked to call themselves Balmikis after the name of their patron guru Valmiki and recorded themselves as such in the

Census of 1930.[40] Finally, this 'politics of cultural persuasion' was strictly legalized in post-independence India. The INC in 1950 approved reservation benefits as valid only if the Balmikis declared themselves Hindu.[41]

In contrast, in the United Provinces, following the creation of new military/civil administrations and cantonment towns like Lucknow, Allahabad and Benares built by the British after the 1857 uprising, led to a demand for scavengers, sweepers and conservancy workers. This prompted untouchable caste groups such as Mehtars, Doms and Bhangis to migrate to these towns from the late-nineteenth century onward.[42] Their jobs as paid labour improved their condition from being unpaid serfs or *harwahas* in the rural areas, providing them a feeling of liberation, creating hopes of education and advancement. Due to their unhappiness and frustration, they were strongly attracted to the Adi-Hindu movement based on religion premised on the concept of Bhakti or devotion, as it contained a message of social equality that enabled them to question the discriminations they faced.

The Bhakti movement propounded the theory—prevalent at that time among depressed classes in parts of the country— that untouchables comprised the 'Adi' or original inhabitants of India and were converted by the Aryan invaders, who used caste as a political and social instrument of subjugation, to make them into lowly individuals.[43] This provided a historical explanation for their poverty and deprivation, and a vision of their past power, and hopes of regaining such lost rights. They decided to shed their demeaning caste names and began to call themselves follower of Valmiki who, though from the lower caste, provided a link to the upper-caste Hindu tradition and took to the teachings of saints such as Ravi Das, Ramanand and Kabir.[44]

However, the benefits of the Adi-Hindu movement were limited, caste barriers remained in the towns and the depressed classes remained confined to menial jobs. This was because the movement did not constitute an attack on the caste system, even though their definition of caste as an instrument for imposing social inequalities and job discrimination in the towns, did imply a critique of ritual hierarchy. Bhakti was a form of personal worship and a denial of caste distinctions; it could not form the basis of action. The Adi-Hindu theory gave solace to the migrants as they recollected a glorious past or 'golden age' when as original inhabitants they enjoyed equality, which enabled them to 'bypass' the prevailing unequal order. It did not question the underlying ideas of purity and pollution or the inheritance of social duties. The movement ultimately was a protest against the attribution of 'low' roles and functions to the untouchables in urban society by means of a claim not to be Aryan Hindus; it did not develop into a 'full-blown' attack on the caste system.[45] The lasting contribution of the movement was *atma-anubhav* or 'thinking for oneself' without reference to the upper castes, which its leaders hoped would undermine the control of the upper castes. This tradition led to the building of many temples but did not lead to a movement.[46]

In post-Independence India, the task of bringing Dalits into the Hindu fold has been continued by the RSS.[47] Beginning in the 1970s, the RSS has worked on the ground consistently for decades to reduce the distance between the upper castes, the backwards and the Dalits. The first two 'sarsangchalaks' (leaders) of the RSS, Keshav Baliram Hedgewar, who formed the RSS in 1926, and Madhav Sadashiv Golwalkar, were not interested in politics despite the formation of the Jan Sangh during Golwalkar's period. Their primary objective was to awaken and harness Hindu consciousness and convert it into a cohesive ideology.[48] It was Balasaheb Deoras, a sarsangchalak 'with a difference' who, when appointed in 1973, visualized the need to change the direction and content of the work of the RSS. He brought many changes in its inherent character, thereby introducing a 'paradigm shift' on the caste question and the need to understand politics.[49] Supportive of affiliates such as the Bhartiya Mazdoor Sangh (BMS) and the Akhil Bhartiya Vidyarthi Parishad (ABVP), he believed that such organizations had the capacity to take up grassroots work and gradually enter into politics. In fact, even before he became sarsangchalak, in the 1960s itself, he had been advocating this stand and asking Golwalkar to support the Jan Sangh. He felt that if the RSS did not move ahead into politics, it would become a sect and loose its ability to participate in building society.

Deoras understood the need to broaden the base of the RSS by inclusion of the lower castes and held that *asprishyata* (untouchability) was a social sin; the RSS under his leadership did a lot of work to bring the SCs closer to the party. As a young RSS worker, he allowed swayamsevaks of other castes into his house and to eat from his kitchen. It was this conviction of viewing all Hindus from a common prism that led him to take a 'more egalitarian social path'.[50] This was done by introducing *samajik samrasta* (social harmony) and establishing Vanvasi Kalyan Ashrams and Shishu Mandirs. Similarly, other leaders such as Deen Dayal Upadhyay stood for integrative politics rather than ideological politics. In fact, the Jan Sangh supported Jagjivan Ram for PM in 1977 over Morarji Desai or Charan Singh, thereby sending a message that it stood for change.[51]

Deoras's vision of how to deal with the subject of Hindu consolidation, when major caste divisions existed in society, was enunciated at the annual Vasant Vyakhanmala (Spring lecture series)[52] held in Pune on 8 May 1974, titled 'Social Equality and Social Consolidation' where describing it as a 'watershed lecture', Mukhopadhyay argues, he stressed on the need to 'go beyond the savarna groups'.[53] Addressing the question of who is a Hindu he argued that except for Muslims, Christians, and Jews, every citizen was a Hindu. It was 'social inequality' that was the reason for the downfall of Indian society, and 'fissiparous tendencies like caste and sub-caste rivalries and untouchability, have been the manifestation of this inequality'. He was emphatic about the need to end caste divisions and recommended introducing reforms within Hindu society.

In 1979, Deoras urged the swayamsdsevaks to start service activities among the most neglected sections of society. This led to the establishment of the Sewa Bharati in 1979, which over time expanded its activities to running hostels, residential schools, and orphanages, in an effort to bring all groups under the umbrella of the Hindu religion. In fact, in 1952, Deoras had established a school in Gorakhpur called the Saraswati Shishu Mandir (temple of learning named after goddess Saraswati, the goddess of learning). The school provided the poor, who could not afford an expensive education, an alternative, were steeped in Hindu ethos and thereby had an impact on the lower caste groups that attended them. Gradually all these organizations were brought under one scheme—the Vidya Bharati—which currently has a network and seva kendras and employs lakhs of teachers and is the largest educational institution in the non-governmental sector. It has served a dual purpose, of educating the SC and ST children and Hinduizing them.

These ideas were subsequently taken forward by other RSS leaders. In the late 1980s, Govindacharya took up the issue of the 'need for social engineering'.[54] He began the practice of noting down the caste background of candidates—'jati kya hai'—and computerized analysis of how this might help the party win seats. It was this shift in thinking that brought in leaders such as Kalyan Singh, who belonged to the backward Lodh community, as chief minister in 1991, rather than the Brahmin leader Kalraj Mishra. Also, leaders such as Sunder Singh Bhandari were responsible for recognizing that politics in UP had changed in the 1990s, remarking that 'Pant *aur* Tiwari *ka jamana khatam'.*[55]* However, Nilanjan Mukhopadhyay argued that this aspect has not fully permeated the BJP even today, despite the success in bringing the smaller Dalit sub-castes into the saffron fold. The problem, he argues, is that the 'savarna mentality still lurks in the background'.[56]

Contemporary Politics: Tacticality and Ideology

While Hinduization of Dalits has been a feature of post-independence India, it has been a slow and quiet process. However, with the rise of the BJP under Modi in the 2000s, it has acquired a far greater momentum. It is both a societal and political project with reflection in the electoral process, which has 'taken a more open and aggressive stand' than in the past. We are witnessing, simultaneously, a tactical and ideological attraction of the smaller Dalit sub-castes towards the BJP. In fact, many opposition parties such as the Congress are feeling constrained to practice 'soft Hindutva', the difference between the two being one of degree and not of kind.

Unlike in the past, under Modi the process of Hinduization is characterized by two features: cultural inclusion of Dalits through religiosity, and 'othering' of Muslims.[57] The former is visible, as mentioned earlier,[58] in the inauguration of the Ram Temple and the Kashi Vishwanath corridor, washing of the feet of Balmikis at the Kumbh and celebrating Ravidas Jayanti. The BJP succeeded in this venture as it consciously moved towards the non-Jatav poorer sub-castes, amongst whom a gradual process of Hinduization was already underway. They were also unhappy by their marginalization in the BSP vis-à-vis the dominant Jatavs, who were able to corner the benefits of reservation and welfare. Dalits and OBCs are also impressed by the BJP's equation of Hinduism and nationalism, which has inculcated a patriotic feeling that 'to be Hindu is to be Indian'. Promoting social harmony through discussions and community lunches together, which has been used by the RSS in the past, has also continued.[59] Further, the BJP has tried to benefit out of Modi belonging to an OBC caste, a fact that began to be used in 2013 itself.[60] This has appealed to the OBCs and Dalits, together with the image of someone who came from a poor background and had risen from the ranks to become the PM.

Once in power since 2014, the BJP–RSS have actively worked to increase their support among the Dalits. Many Dalits are impressed by the fact that the BJP government has spent huge sums of money to acquire the places that Dr Ambedkar lived in London and in Mau, where he was born, or to build new Ambedkarite institutions. No other government including the Congress party has done as much.[61] Attempts have been made to take forward cultural mobilization of the smaller Dalit groups by providing them greater space within the Hindu community, acknowledging their specific sub-caste identity, right to practice local rituals and building small temples for their local deities, thereby according them dignity and respect. A good example is the Mata Shabari temple in the PM's adopted village of Jayapur in his parliamentary constituency of Varanasi in the Musaharbasti of the village. Although the basti lacks basic amenities such as roads, drains and pucca houses, and the Musahars are very poor, they are very happy to be provided a temple of their own.[62] In sum, the Modi phenomenon is as much societal and cultural as political.

Regarding the current anti-Muslim feeling, which is shared by Dalits, Kulkarni argued that it is not something 'manufactured' or 'created' by the BJP, or a deep-seated feeling since Partition, waiting to be pried open. Rather, it is part of the 'lived experience' of the SCs and OBCs. Historically, a majority of the Muslims in India converted from these lower castes, and so when a section of the Dalits is becoming upwardly mobile and feeling proud of its Hindu roots, they are susceptible to the propaganda of the BJP that this is true nationalism. The BJP, in contrast to the past, has taken a more 'open and muscular' form of 'othering' of Muslims, which it has tried to extend to the lower rungs of the caste hierarchy by use of 'love jihad', legislation against sale of beef and inter-religious marriages, the latest being the anti-hijab controversy in Karnataka. All this fuels the feeling that Muslims are the hurdle to creating a stronger India. The BJP has reaped the benefit of the 'Hindu concern' for the nation, there is an 'equation of being Hindu and national feeling'. All over the country, people are concerned about nation and nationalism; partition divided creating an uncompromising attitude to Muslims, which he argues is not limited to the upper castes but appeals to the Dalits as well. Thus, Hinduization has taken deep roots in Indian society and even if the BJP were to lose state power, it will not disappear.

However, Kulkarni strongly argued that even if the BJP was defeated in 2022 in UP and in the general elections of 2024, Dalits will make their own independent choices like all other groups. They may remain with the BJP, join some other party, or may even form a new party. He emphasized that none of this will lead to de-Hinduization among Dalits or in society in general, there will be no 'social reversal' irrespective of the

BJP's fortunes. The fascination with being Hindu has taken deep roots and will continue.

To sum up, it is obvious that the debate over the issue of Dalit support to the BJP needs to be seen at two levels. Electorally, some sub-castes may prefer the saffron party due to ideological affinity while others, tactically, for the material incentive. However, there is no denying the fact that a parallel socio-cultural process, of a positive interplay of the saffron and the subaltern, is going on.

PART III

New Stirrings: Emerging Dalit
Organizations

7

Azad, Bhim Army and Other Ambedkarite Fragments

———— ❦ ————

The unravelling of the BSP in recent years following its successive electoral defeats and the existential crisis it has been facing since 2014, has been accompanied by the rise of new Dalit organizations across UP. This is a phenomenon not limited to UP, but is seen in Gujarat with the formation of the Una Dalit Atyachar Ladat Samiti by Jignesh Mevani and the Vanchit Bahujan Aaghadi by Prakash Ambedkar in Maharashtra, following atrocities against Dalits in these states. Exploring the emergence and activities of the organizations in UP presents a picture of the Dalit movement in the state. Among them, the Bhim Army (BA) formed by Chandrashekhar Azad in western UP is the best known, but strong Dalit assertion at the grassroots has spawned others. Two of the most prominent that we have selected for analysis are the Ambedkar Jan Morcha

151

(AJM) in Purvanchal and the Bahujan Mukti Party (BMP) in Bundelkhand.

Small Dalit organizations at the grassroots level have existed in different regions in UP during the post-Independence period, thrown up due to rising democratization and political consciousness among Dalits. They were a product of Dalit assertion which, with a longer history in UP than the BSP, was effectively harnessed to create a movement and a party. In the 1990s, many existed outside the ambit of the BSP which, it was felt, was an opportunistic party keen to capture power, visible in the coalitions formed with the upper caste BJP.[1] Yet, despite being independent, they had a close relationship with the BSP and voted for it, being in most cases an 'outgrowth of the mobilizational drive by the BSP to create a distinct identity and social base'.[2] Many represented the smaller Dalit sub-castes and organizations formed by them, who felt that the BSP was dominated by the Jatavs, leaving little space for them.[3] These organizations actively protested against upper-caste domination and particularly the desecration of Ambedkar statues—such as the Shergarhi incident in Meerut in May 1994 when an Ambedkar statue was removed leading to large-scale protests by Dalit organizations.[4]

However, the organizations we examine are different, as they have emerged in various parts of the state following the decline of a strong Dalit party, the BSP, which enjoyed a phase of dominance in the 1990s. Their leaders represent a younger generation that has gained self-respect and confidence to oppose upper-caste domination and oppression and aspire for a role in the politics of the state. Also, in contrast to a section that since 2014 supports the BJP, they constitute Ambedkarites. This raises a number of questions that we explore. How does one explain the emergence of Dalit organizations in different regions? In the post-BSP phase, do they signify a transitory phase of Dalit politics before culminating into a pan-UP party, or do they herald the beginning of a new phase of sub-regional subaltern politics, thereby rendering the phase of pan-state Dalit discourse a matter of history, at least for the present?

Decline and sub-regional fragments

UP is a large state and the new organizations are a product of both the decline of the BSP and the emergence of sub-regional Dalit politics. At the same time, there are simultaneously similarities and differences between these organizations, rendering Dalit politics and discourse on the ground complex.

The BA formed by Azad represents an independent effort by a young leader as early as 2015 in response to rising Dalit atrocities by upper castes emboldened by the revival of the BJP. It was an effort motivated by the defeat of Mayawati in 2014, but equally by the lack of response of the BSP to atrocities against Dalit, and as a challenge to the rise of a hegemonic and oppressive right-wing BJP. It is an outfit located in western UP which has always been the region where Dalits are better-off and educated, Jatavs are in large numbers, and assertion has been strong. The AJM and the BMP, on the other hand, were formed by former members of the BSP who left the party unhappy with Mayawati's stewardship which, they felt, was responsible for its defeats in 2017 and 2019, leading to its decline. They represent sub-regional fragments or threads of the BSP and though they are critical of it, they would like to replace it. Both these organizations were formed in the more backward regions of the state where Dalits are poorer, but where the BSP had a strong base, and which has since collapsed.

Two features characterize these organizations. First, all three describe themselves as organizations based on the ideology of

Ambedkar and more immediately Kanshi Ram. In that sense, they all constitute a legacy of the strong Dalit movement mounted by Kanshi Ram and Mayawati since the late 1980s. Yet, at the same time, these organizations, despite describing themselves as Ambedkarite, are constantly competing with each other. Our discussions with the leaders of these organizations suggests that this competition is similar to the early rhetoric of the BSP used by Kanshi Ram when he was building the party. In that framework, the Dalit discourse was viewed as a perennial battle between 'selfish Brahmanical stooges' and 'authentic Ambedkarites', the former consisting of Dalit leaders within the Congress such as Jagjivan Ram and the latter the leaders of the BSP.[5]

Second, the unravelling of the BSP signifies the decline of 'institutional' Ambedkarite politics which has a more patient, long-term vision of social transformation. In its place, we are witnessing the emergence of a spontaneous and populist Ambedkarite Dalit discourse rooted in the politics of 'everyday agitation'. The BA led by Azad particularly represents this thread of impatient discourse that immediately resonated with a majority of the younger Dalits. To Azad, the ascendency of the BJP's Hindutva and its winning over a significant section of the Dalits, necessitates a politics of constant agitation, it is the modus operandi to rekindle the Ambedkarite spirit. Everyday agitation also acts as an ideological project against the politics of opportunism of the BSP. Here, Ambedkar's and Kanshi Ram's life aspects are selectively invoked to justify the BA's discourse. Naturally, the BSP and all other post-BSP Ambedkarite Dalit organizations are declared wanting in authenticity for failing to meet the criteria of everyday mode of agitation.

In contrast, the two other emerging Ambedkarite organizations, the AJM and the BMP, are attempting to build on the institutional emphasis by Ambedkar and Kanshi Ram. They see themselves as true claimants of the legacy of Kanshi Ram for adhering to the long-term institutional vision rather than being constantly distracted by the everydayness of Dalit problems. They claim to have a structural understanding of society and politics and, by extension, of the Dalit question, something the BA is labelled as colossally lacking. The AJM and the BMP are, hence, critical of Azad and the BA and their mode of politics, as lacking the structural and political nature of the Dalit discourse. At the same time, our narrative shows that all these organizations, despite their ideological positions and discourse, are experimenting with a variety of strategies such as agitational politics, service to the community, participating in elections, etc.

This constantly shifting battle of tactics and strategy by the new Dalit organizations has sent confusing signals to the majority of the Dalit youth, who are the prime mobilizational target of all three competing claimants. Based on the nature of their anxieties and aspirations they respond to different organizations, including the BSP, according to their suitability. Hence, one of the prominent features of the emerging Ambedkarite claimants seems to be a perennial battle for who represents an *authentic* Dalit discourse. This feature also helps explain the social and political fragmentation even within the arena of Ambedkarite Dalit politics, as well as the phenomenon of protest and preference in UP, described earlier.

All the new organizations we have selected for discussion have been formed by Jatavs who, as was famously pointed out by a British administrator,[6] 'are feared and respected by the others' and have historically been at the forefront of new challenges and beginnings, ready to revolt against upper-caste oppression. However, there are other small emerging organizations formed by other sub-castes described as the 'scattered and the invisible' in other areas of UP, locating which would require sustained fieldwork.[7]

At the same time, the complexity of the post-BSP Ambedkarite space on the ground is evident from the presence of Dalit organizations with affiliation to the BJP. A good example is the Uda Devi Pasi Manch formed in 2015 by Pasi youth in the rural area of Lucknow district.[8] Although it describes itself as an Ambedkarite organization, it was formed by Pasi leaders who had shifted to the BJP along with Kaushal Kishore, a Dalit leader twice elected to Parliament on a BJP ticket and made minister of state in the Union government in the cabinet reshuffle before the 2022 assembly elections. But prior to the election, many of its members joined the SP, complaining that Dalit leaders were not given space within the BJP. The BJP has encouraged such organizations; it celebrated the anniversary of Uda Devi, a woman who fought in the 1857 mutiny against the British army. Thus, our selected Dalit organizations face competition with Hindutvawadi organizations supported by the BJP, rendering their task even more challenging.

Against this backdrop we now examine the emergence and working of our three selected Dalit organizations and the inter-relationship between them.

Three Fragments of the New Ambedkarite Dalit Discourse

Saharanpur: The Agitational Politics of Azad and the Bhim Army

The Bhim Army formed by Chandrashekhar Azad, a young Dalit leader, has adopted the agitational path in its efforts to deal with rising atrocities by upper castes and opposition to the hegemonic position achieved by the BJP in UP politics. Azad was not a member of the BSP, he is a product of the new phase of Dalit politics of the 2000s, a part of the upwardly mobile and aspiring younger generation who, disappointed with the BSP, decided to enter politics. Educated, assertive, articulate and keen to wipe out atrocities against Dalits, he appeals to the younger generation in western UP.[9] In our interview, Azad recounted his early life in Dehradun in an educated household, his father being a schoolteacher. He did not experience open discrimination himself but was aware of its existence. Few know that he joined the Akhil Bharatiya Vidyarthi Parishad (ABVP), the BJP's student wing, as a law student, but left it soon afterwards as he found that whenever a Muslim–Dalit clash took place the ABVP was there, but when the violence was by upper castes against Dalits, it disappeared. This led him to read about the life and ideas of Ambedkar and, in 2013, with a law degree, Azad decided to return to his native village Chhutmalpur in Saharanpur district, western UP, with the 'urge to do something'.[10]

Azad, a well-built young man sporting an upwardly twirling moustache, immediately caught the fancy of the Dalit youth of Chhutmalpur who had been feeling aggrieved with the state administration for not taking action against the upper castes and the desertion of agitational politics by the BSP. The educated and politically assertive Dalits of Chhutmalpur, largely a Dalit village, decided to support Azad's organization. This was a period when, following the victory of the BJP in the 2014 general elections, the upper castes, particularly the Thakurs of the region, were boldly harassing Dalits. The Bhim Army, named after Ambedkar and formed by Azad and Vinay Ratan Singh in 2015, had the declared aim of 'direct action' based on

confrontation to preserve or restore the dignity of Dalits. This
was reflected in a poster in Azad's apartment with Ambedkar's
words, 'Go write on the walls that you are the rulers of this
nation.'[11] Azad's adoption of the name 'Ravan', depicted as
evil incarnate, despite being a King and learned man, the chief
adversary of Rama in the Ramayana, also reflects a cultural
counter to the BJP's upper caste god, Rama revered as a symbol
of the victory of right over the evil.

Initially, Azad attempted to cycle to villages, like Kanshi Ram
and Mayawati in the 1980s, to deal with atrocities and harness
Dalit anger and assertion. In western UP, agrarian distress
and the lack of non-agricultural employment had created
considerable frustration among Dalit youth. Azad mentioned
a large number of cycle yatras he has held regularly to instil
confidence in Dalit youth[12] as the upper castes and OBCs,
taking advantage of BJP's victory in 2014 at the Centre and in
UP in 2017, took every opportunity to attack Dalits, creating
an atmosphere of confrontation in Saharanpur district. The BA,
established as an organization to fight caste atrocities, would
'show up' *and* 'straighten things out' which often meant *beating
up those who used force against Dalits*. Azad declared, 'The aim
of the Bhim Army is to make west Uttar Pradesh atrocity-free in
one year. I don't want to read about another incident like this
… This has to stop.'[13]

An early example of action by the BA was at the Rajput-run,
Anglo Hindustan Public Inter-College (AHP) at Chhutmalpur
near Saharanpur city in August 2015, where Dalit students
were forced to sweep classrooms and drink water only after
the Thakur boys had used the water tap.[14] Two incidents
made Azad well-known. The first was the confrontation in
Gharkoli village over the signboard, 'The Great Chamar Dr
Bhim Rao Ambedkar Gram Gharkoli Welcomes You,' put up

by Dalit boys of the village. Despite threats by the Thakurs, the Dalits, supported by the BA, refused to remove it.[15] Following complaints, the police wanted to arrest Azad but a rally of Dalits from nearby villages and members of the Backward and Minority Communities Employees Federation (BAMCEF) forced them to release him. The second was at Gatheda village where a statue of Dalit saint Ravidas in a temple had been smeared with black paint. The arrival of the BA forced the police, initially reluctantly, to start an enquiry. The BA also acted when a Dalit groom was forced off his horse by Thakurs and when a temple dedicated to Sant Ravidas in Tughlaqabad, Delhi, was under threat of demolition in February 2020. Guru Ravidas is one of the most revered saints among Dalits in northern India and the Ravidasis (Jatavs) constitute the single largest Dalit community in UP. The silence of Mayawati (also a Ravidasi) on the issue endowed Azad stature as an alternative Ravidasi leader.[16]

Azad and his BA received tremendous support from Dalits in the area, encouraging Dalit shopkeepers, and those employed, to contribute to the 'cause' (the organization and its work for Dalits). While many Dalits realized that conflict with the police would not help build a small movement with little organizational strength, it made Azad very popular as they were happy to see a Dalit organization standing up to the police. Also, local newspapers such as the *Dainik Janvani* reported how the 'Bhim Army explodes in anger over idol desecration'.[17] It is important to understand that such confrontations do help. As Teltumbde points out, 'The spectacular brutality of these atrocities is deliberate and calculated to distinguish caste atrocities from other kinds of violence'.[18] The use of social media is also seen in photographs taken at incidents where the BA appears and these are then circulated widely on WhatsApp groups. Within three years, the organization had over 20,000 followers in the Saharanpur region.[19]

However, the event that made Azad a Dalit hero and well-known across UP and the country were two violent clashes in villages in Saharanpur district in April–May 2017, soon after the new BJP government under Yogi Adityanath was formed. As described in Chapter 5, both were due to processions held to honour icons of the Dalit and the Thakur communities: Dr Ambedkar and Maharana Pratap respectively.[20] The strong intervention of the BA increased its standing within the Dalit community and was symbolic of a new force capable of dealing with Dalit atrocities in a state where the upper castes felt they held power with the formation of a BJP government. The UP government, afraid of Azad's growing support, attempted to confine him. He was first arrested on 17 June 2017 and just as he received bail in November 2017, the UP government detained him again under the National Security Act. When he was released in September 2018, Azad had become a hero for many Dalits.

The Saharanpur incident increased the popularity of Azad, but it led to the political alienation of a sizeable section of the Dalit youth in the district who supported the BSP and Mayawati. In fact, the BSP leaders and cadres at Saharanpur were in a fix upon the emergence of Azad as a popular youth icon.[21] While they appreciated the action and leadership of Azad, they were also wary of and unhappy at his criticism of the BSP leadership, for not doing enough on the Saharanpur incident. In Jatav Nagar in Saharanpur city, until then a bastion of the BSP, with leaders who had been trained in Ambedkarite ideology by Kanshi Ram himself, the BSP cadres started describing Azad as a popularity-driven leader who lacked an institutional mode of Ambedkarite politics. To them, the Dalit discourse under the

BSP meant strategies for capturing state power, but through use of democratic means. Any attempt to break away from this shared responsibility, they argued, was tantamount to an irresponsible approach to politics that would only weaken the Dalit discourse, which was already under strain on account of the ascendency of Hindutva politics.[22]

Despite the involvement in agitational politics, in December 2019 Azad announced that he would form a new party to provide a political alternative to the Bahujan community and formed the Azad Samaj Party (ASP) on 15 March 2020.[23] During the interview, Azad explained that the ASP, based on the values and ideas of Ambedkar, aimed to accomplish the political goals of Kanshi Ram, invoking his ideological proposition: *Bahujan hitaya, Bahujan sukhaya*. Unlike Kanshi Ram, who dispensed of his grassroots organization BAMCEF in favour of the BSP, Azad said he planned to retain the BA and run it as a parallel outfit. The organization has units in Delhi and many states including Kerala, Tamil Nadu and Odisha, and Azad has visited most of them and met local Dalit leaders. Party activists point out that many spontaneous Dalit organizations have emerged across the country and the BA hopes to bring them onto a single platform. They claim to have received a positive response from some states and there is enthusiasm that if a determined effort is made, a strong party can emerge.[24] However, Azad's foray into electoral politics in the 2019 Lok Sabha and 2022 assembly elections once again drew sharp criticism not only from the BSP cadres and supporters in Saharanpur, but also from other organization leaders such as Shravan Kumar Nirala, who described Azad's mode of politics as irresponsible and devoid of a long-term vision.[25]

Notwithstanding the formation of the ASP, Azad stressed that he was currently focusing on education and building a strong organization for the BA. The BA, he pointed out, runs about 350 free schools for Bahujan children in Saharanpur, Meerut and Muzaffarnagar. Showing us pictures and videos of the schools, Azad argued that Dalit children require education to move ahead in society. Azad argued that the BA would establish itself as a strong organization in UP by taking action against Dalit atrocities and helping Dalit children get educated.

However, closer to the 2022 assembly elections, Azad decided that his party would participate in the polls, a decision perhaps fuelled by the formation of the SP–RLD alliance in western UP, a region in which his organization has a presence. Eventually talks with Akhilesh broke down as Azad was offered only two seats, which he held were too few, and refused. Azad claimed, 'After all the discussions, I felt in the end that Akhilesh Yadav does not want Dalits in this alliance, he just wants the Dalit vote bank.'[26] Many felt that he should have taken the seats offered as his organization was small with little support on the ground, and it was an opportunity to win and enter the assembly, thereby marking the presence of the younger generation of Dalits. Azad's decision to stand for election against Chief Minister Yogi Adityanath in Gorakhpur brought him a great deal of media attention, even though it was obvious he would not win. He finished fourth with 7,543 votes—behind the BSP and SP—and lost security deposit. But he held a number of rallies in Gorakhpur town and surrounding areas and this enthused the Dalits.[27]

An important feature of the BA, not evident in the narrower canvas of traditional Dalit parties, is the decision in 2019 to link atrocities to larger issues of national significance. Azad was proud of the BA's focus on such activities, linking them to his agitational approach to politics against the BJP. The BA took an inclusive stand on the citizenship issue and provided support to widespread protests by citizens of all communities against the Citizenship Amendment Act (CAA) and the National Register of Citizens (NRC). By upholding the secular fabric of the nation, Azad has endorsed the idea of a plural society in contrast to the attempt by the BJP to polarize Dalits and Muslims. This is seen in his 'dramatic appearance' at the Jama Masjid in Delhi and public reading of the Preamble of the Constitution, and support to the protests at Shaheen Bagh.[28] His support to rallies against the CAA and NRC widened his support base and provided him a new constituency comprising students, including Muslim and Dalit, from Jamia Milia Islamia, and from Jawaharlal Nehru University, to whom he extended support in their agitation on the fee hike in November 2019.[29] Recognizing that it is limited to western UP, the BA has also tried to register a pan-India presence. It supported violent Dalit agitations across the country such as at Una, Bhima-Koregaon and elsewhere, alongside other Dalit organizations led by Jignesh Mevani and Prakash Ambedkar.

Azad has kept his organization independent of both Dalit and non-Dalit parties. While he initially tried to move close to the BSP, criticism by Mayawati who viewed him as a rival, led him to move away. He also pointed out that the BSP had voted for reservation for the economically weaker sections,[30] removal of Article 370 and the CAA in Parliament, thereby 'murdering' the Constitution and weakening the Bahujan movement. Yet, during the interview, Azad refrained from criticizing Mayawati personally, according her the respect due to a senior Dalit leader. Azad also pointed out that the ASP had decided not to support the Congress party in the 2019 national elections as the party during its period of dominance in UP had opposed Ambedkar and done nothing for Dalits.

Azad is still the most popular Dalit icon at present and BA/ASP has become a popular platform. The BA has built a space

for itself on the ground in UP fighting against atrocities and
taking up unjust national issues. But in terms of agitational and
electoral politics, as its participation in elections has shown, the
outfit is confined to parts of western UP. Entry into electoral
politics, even within UP, given the forces ranged against it, will
be very difficult. At best, it represents a strong *social force* at
the grassroots against upper caste domination and oppression,
and the failure of the state to protect the life and property of
Dalits.

Purvanchal: Shravan Kumar Nirala and the Ambedkar Jan Morcha

The Ambedkar Jan Morcha formed by Shravan Kumar Nirala
represents a post-BSP organization founded by an individual
who had held responsible positions in the BSP. Nirala was
born into an educated family in Gorakhpur district; his father,
Ram Pyare Ram, had studied until intermediate and was also
a well-known wrestler in the locality. Nirala told us[31] that a
Dalit sugarcane development officer, Moti Ram, approached
his father to accompany him on his official tours and provide
physical protection as many upper-caste villages often harassed
the officers. To make the arrangement legal, he appointed Ram
Pyare Ram to the assistant cashier's post in the sugarcane
development department. As his father was often transferred,
Nirala went to school in many different places, and was thus
exposed to Dalit politics in many regions of UP.

Though Nirala was acquainted with Dalit issues, his political
journey as an Ambedkarite activist and BSP supporter began as
a student in Gorakhpur university in 1995, where the main issue
he took up was that of reservation. Beginning with assisting
new Dalit students during their admission process to raising

and fighting for issues concerning them, he started interacting with Dalit students at other universities, like Banaras Hindu University and Jawaharlal Nehru University. Soon, he was involved in organizing seminars and workshops at Gorakhpur University to create awareness among Dalit students and bring them in touch with Dalit leaders and intellectuals.

While at the university, Nirala's connection with the BSP was largely informal and emotional. But when he began attending functions of the party voluntarily, his active presence began to be noticed by local BSP leaders. As he had built a team of dedicated Dalit students committed to fighting for the community's rights, local BSP leaders began to approach him when they faced opposition from non-Dalits while organizing programmes. Very soon, Nirala became a full-time party activist and began to be assigned a formal role with responsibilities. After the fifteenth Lok Sabha, he was regularly entrusted with the responsible position of zonal coordinator for many regions: in Basti Mandal, comprising Basti, Sant Kabir Nagar and Siddharth Nagar districts, for three years starting 2009; in Devipatan Mandal, comprising Balarampur, Sarasvati, Bahraich and Gonda in 2012. Impressed by his efficient and energetic style of working, Mayawati began assigning him zones that required special attention: he was made coordinator of Faizabad Mandal comprising districts like Barabanki, Ambedkar Nagar, Sultanpur and Faizabad (now Ayodhya), and later of Azamgarh mandal, which included the districts of Ballia, Azamgarh and Mau. A year before the 2017 assembly election, he was made zonal coordinator of Gorakhpur mandal comprising districts like Dewaria, Kushinagar, Gorakhpur and Maharajganj.

During this period Nirala emerged as a trusted lieutenant of Mayawati and, as related by him, held weekly meetings with her to discuss party strategy. He said, '*Behenji ke liye dil laga ke kam kiya*,' (I worked with all my heart for Mayawati). At the time, she was highly approachable and he was often called to Delhi to consult her. But towards the end of her term (2007–12) and after the defeat in 2012, changes began to take place. The party structure began to break down as corruption crept in and money became important. No one could meet Behenji without paying for it, and money began to determine ticket distribution. Ministers shared their spoils with her, working on her weakness. Nirala pointed out that in the 1990s, all the BSP regimes headed by Mayawati had been overseen by Kanshi Ram and there were no allegations of corruption nor demands for money.

Despite the defeat, a month after the results of the 2017 assembly elections were declared, Mayawati sent for Nirala. Recognizing that the party had become weak in Purvanchal, he was put in charge of Bansgaon assembly constituency with instructions to prepare for 2022 as a candidate. Despite this, however, Mayawati gradually became reclusive and party workers found her unapproachable unless they had something to offer. Also, she was afraid that the BJP would put her in jail for unaccounted assets, though Nirala told us that this would get her 'tremendous support' from Dalits. Actively dedicating himself to his task, Nirala worked for the strengthening of the party and in the 2019 Lok Sabha election, though the BSP lost the seat, it secured 85,000 votes in the constituency, the highest for the party in the entire state among reserved assembly constituencies.

But on 9 July 2019, at a review meeting of the Lok Sabha results at Gorakhpur Club, when Bansgaon was discussed, Nirala was informed by the zonal in-charge, Ghanshyam Kharwar, that the party had decided to put him in charge of Maharajganj district. By this time, Nirala knew that changes were being made as he had earlier been called to Lucknow by Mayawati, where she told him that the candidate selection process had been started afresh. He was told that as he was a dedicated worker of the party, he was being given a ticket and he was to deposit the relatively lesser sum of ₹3 crore, though there were others willing to pay more. Nirala knew that the culture of selling tickets had been institutionalized, and had intensified following the party's defeat in 2012. This culture, he believed, was finally responsible for the denial of the rightful claim of committed party workers such as himself, who had given many years of their lives to the party and were now side-lined for candidates who had purchasing power. Consequently, at the Gorakhpur Club, Nirala publicly announced the cancellation of his promised ticket; this lead to altercations between his enthusiastic supporters and party officials. He also announced his resignation from the primary membership of the BSP the same day after having given it twenty-five years, for having been marginalized due to the prevailing money culture in the party.

Within two months of his resignation, Nirala and his associates formed the Ambedkar Jan Morcha. Nirala claimed he was approached by many political parties, including the BJP, but he decided to form an independent organization as he felt the need for a new intervention in the social and political realm, from the Ambedkarite vantage point. The AJM is based on the ideas of Ambedkar and Kanshi Ram, and Nirala strongly believes that there is need for long-term social movements at the grassroots to spread awareness, rather than the politics of power-grabbing, money culture and the personal interests of party leaders. Since 2020, the AJM has been actively mobilizing Dalit students and youth, and fighting for the revival of Bahujan unity by taking up issues like atrocities against Dalit, reservation and backlog recruitment for the SC, ST and the OBC groups. Besides, the AJM also conducts special sessions on Ambedkarite politics, endeavouring to disseminate the ideas of Ambedkar and Kanshi Ram. Nirala claimed that the AJM has succeeded in acting as an effective pressure group for Dalit interests and issues primarily concerning students.

Bundelkhand: Daddu Prasad and the Bahujan Mukti Party

Similar to Nirala, Daddu Prasad, a former member of the BSP formed the Bahujan Mukti Party in 2016. In fact, Prasad's association with the party was longer than Nirala as he had been an associate of Kanshi Ram and had held important positions in the BSP. Many leaders expelled by Mayawati had announced that they would form their own parties; it was Prasad who actually formed one.

Originally hailing from Banda, Daddu Prasad considers Chitrakoot his 'karma-bhoomi', the place where, it is believed, Rama spent his years of exile, along with Sita and Lakshman. Charting his career in politics through this karma-bhoomi, Prasad argues, has been a long and winding journey.[32] Born into a poor Dalit household, Prasad spent his childhood and youth understanding the true meaning of 'difference' and 'prejudice'. His father, Buddhua Prasad, worked as a bonded labourer while Prasad nursed dreams of studying to become an engineer. Fighting against social discrimination in a society that 'on the one hand, celebrates Gandhi and lauds Ambedkar as a great icon on the other', he finally gained a diploma. Greatly inspired by the ideas of Ambedkar, but more immediately Kanshi Ram, who had begun as a social reformer and formed the BSP, he decided to devote his life to uplift of Dalits. Unable to fulfil his own educational ambitions, his major concern was the distance of Dalits and Adivasis from education/knowledge and white-collar jobs, and their continued oppression.

Claiming that he was 'mesmerized' by the work of Kanshi Ram, Prasad formally joined the BSP in 1993. Working with both Kanshi Ram and Mayawati, he rose rapidly within the party. He was a BSP MLA thrice, and an important and highly trusted minister in Mayawati's cabinet from 2007 to 2012. During this period, he handled many important tasks and helped run the sarvajan alliance. However, after the defeat of 2012, his relationship with Mayawati changed. Many BSP leaders were unhappy with Mayawati's change in attitude and, along with others, he made accusations pertaining to her 'compromises' including 'selling seat tickets' at crores of rupees. For this he was expelled from the party in 2015.[33] Unhappy with the manner in which he had been treated by Mayawati, Prasad described to us in great detail the 'devious' ways in which Kanshi Ram was placed under house arrest by her when he fell severely ill and had to be hospitalized. He formed the Bahujan Mukti Party in 2016[34] which he claimed ran on the 'grand values of Ambedkar and Kanshi Ram'. However, he re-joined the BSP in 2017 following the party's defeat in the 2017 assembly elections in UP.[35]

But seven years later, in May 2019, following the massive victory of the BJP in the general election, Prasad left the party once again and decided to form a 'social organization'—the Samajik Parivartan Mission. This was because viewing the rapid decline of the BSP, he felt that there was an urgent need for a strong social movement as a precondition for the emergence of a truly transformative Dalit politics. He argued that individuals who are comfortable within our unequal society will not work to change the status quo; only a person from an oppressed community can introduce change. His organization has also distanced itself from all forms of messaging such as mass media, television, which he feels are largely upper caste oriented, to actively work at the grassroots among the people. As he said, 'Winning or losing doesn't particularly mean much to me now. What is important is the work.'

Sub-regional Fragments: Crisis or Regeneration?

Our narrative points to a steady dispersion of Dalit power in UP with the unravelling of the BSP since 2012. The state seems to be returning to its older form of Dalit movements limited to sub-regions. The BSP was the first pan-state Dalit party to be built in UP in the 1990s, with branches across the state, both during the colonial and post-colonial period. Today, with the decline of the BSP, once again each sub-region has thrown up its own Dalit organization/party with a limited reach. What are the possibilities of the various sub-regional political forces joining hands and forming a strong party like the BSP? Like the leaders who came together to form the BSP—Kanshi Ram and Mayawati—the current crop of Dalit leaders are young, educated and hostile to the BJP, just as the BSP was to the Congress and its Dalit leaders such as Jagjivan Ram. But the issue is not simply about coming together to replace the declining BSP. Rather, with contradicting visions, mutual rivalries and differing mobilizational strategies, each of the leaders of the various organizations wishes to replace the BSP. There is competition between the Dalit fragments, each claiming to represent the *authentic* Ambedkarite discourse and describing the other, as not genuine. While all the new threads of the Ambedkarite Dalit discourse swear by the ideals of Ambedkar and Kanshi Ram, they dismiss each other as misguided and, by extension, not representing the true Dalit self.

This is seen in the critique by Azad and Nirala regarding the ideology and methods used in Dalit mobilization in western and eastern UP. Azad holds that it is the Jatavs of western UP who have led the Dalit movement and historically acted as an emancipatory force for the downtrodden. Hence, implicit in his body language is an assumption that while there needs to be a united pan-UP Dalit discourse, the leadership has to be from the western region. More forthright on the sub-regional divide, Nirala emphasizes the fault lines of the new mode of Dalit politics. He has a pejorative view about the Dalits of western UP: 'Dalits of western UP are transactional by nature while those of eastern regions are simple and emotional.' He is critical of Azad for seeking an opportunistic alliance with the SP and then getting angry for not getting the desired deal, a telling comment on the nature of the emerging sub-regionalities of the Dalit discourse. Prasad, as an experienced Dalit leader with long years in the BSP, claims that he will soon succeed in creating a strong movement.

Thus, the emerging Dalit discourse in UP is characterized by extreme fragmentation, by the phenomenon of 'many Azads' on ideologically similar grounds but regionally and culturally divided, scrambling to fill the post-BSP vacuum. These fragments represent both the crisis that is affecting the Dalit movement as well as the hope of regeneration, which has yet to take shape. But the prognosis for the future of the Dalit movement is pessimistic. While each organization applauds the other in terms of having the right intention and seeks wider Dalit unity against the common ideological other, the BJP, each would like itself to be the anchor of that desired unity. Since there is no anchor or strong and trusted leader who can bring all of them together, the journey for a singular Dalit discourse is likely to remain elusive. What we may witness is the politics of, and by, Dalit fragments. These fragments derive their meanings only in relation to the whole. Every fragment aspires to become the whole, and therefore we see contested claims to being the key Dalit organization in UP. This elusive quest has already led to a clash of Dalit personalities. It has all the ingredients to metamorphose the structural question into a biographical one wherein the doctrine of 'my way as the authentic way' informs all three claimants.

8

Fragmentation of the
Dalit Movement in UP

⌇

The Dalit movement in UP has not been an incremental movement, gradually increasing in size and intensity. It has passed through phases of resurgence and decline with periods of hiatus in between, which has given it a complex nature. During its phase of decline, the Dalit movement has adapted and accommodated itself to other dominant political formations with little attempt to form a separate identity. The presence of a dominant, mainstream, upper-caste party during this period, which affords little space for narrower sectarian formations, is a key reason for the decline. In the colonial period and the early years of independence, it was the dominant position occupied by the Congress party with its leadership from the upper castes that did not allow room for a Dalit party to grow. In the present phase of decline of the BSP, it is the BJP once again an upper caste party with a broad spectrum of Hindu social support that constitutes a strong political force. While the desire to challenge domination and oppression by the upper castes and classes remains during this period, a dual process seems to be at work within the Dalit movement: opposition to and yet simultaneously a desire to become a part of and be accepted by the upper castes and classes as equals. It is hence a layered, multidirectional process, at times ambivalent, and on other occasions highly confrontational.

Separation, on the other hand, entails assertion and a revolt against societal oppression and domination by upper castes and parties representing them, and formation of a separate Dalit identity, and political party. This phase coincides with the decline of mainstream upper caste parties, providing room for identity-based parties with a communitarian ideology. A brief recap of these phases would enable a better understanding of the predicament that the BSP finds itself in today. For this, we must look back in order to understand the present-day situation, which in turn will help us look forward to the future of the BSP and the Dalit movement in UP.

Any attempt to analyse Dalit movements must take into consideration that it is a product of, and taking place within, the larger society in which it is placed. Dalit movements require a favourable social structure and climate to flower. Unlike southern and western India, a seminal feature of the Hindi heartland in the colonial period, continuing into the early years of independence, was the *delayed development of Dalit consciousness* among the large mass of persons considered ex-untouchables in the state.[1] This region did not experience any large-scale or sustained Dalit movement until very late in the colonial period; its mobilizational impact upon the vast mass of the depressed classes was limited. Rather, a series of small, widely separated and weak movements took place, that did not coalesce into one large movement as in the Bombay presidency until very late in the colonial period.[2] There was little economic development apart from commercialization of agriculture, the leather and a few other industries in western UP, which could have played a catalytic role in breaking down the oppressive village structure.[3] Most important, the impact of Ambedkar and his movement was felt only in the mid-1930s, and that too by a small, educated section of the better-off Jatavs of western UP, and it came too late to have a transformative impact.

In the absence of any large-scale, organized movement of the depressed classes, the pattern of mobilization in the United Provinces by the Indian National Congress (INC) during the freedom movement was significantly different, in so far as its impact upon the lower castes was concerned. The national movement came under the leadership of the INC and particularly Gandhi, while in western and southern India, due to the Mahar and non-Brahmin movements, it was profoundly influenced by leaders such as Ambedkar and M.C. Rajah.[4] The ideological strand of Gandhism emerged in the 1920s from the thinking of Gandhi on the system of hierarchy among Hindus, inter-caste relationships and method of caste reform; importantly, it shaped the position of the INC on the caste question during the national movement. The early Congress leadership in north India remained passive in their attitude to the need for ameliorating the conditions of the depressed classes, and made a conscious attempt to separate the 'political' and 'social' issues, arguing that the latter would be taken up after Independence.[5] Under Gandhi's leadership, the INC adopted a policy of 'Harijan uddhar' (upliftment of Harijans) rather than opposition to the caste system. Attempts were made to stop both untouchability and begar, and improve their economic condition; a Harijan Sewak Sangh was also established.[6] This model of Harijan uddhar, once established, continued into the post-Independence period. Following Independence, the Gandhian ideology was adopted by the Congress party and remained the basis of its relationship with the SCs, particularly during the Nehruvian period.[7]

This explains the long period of ambivalent accommodation of the SCs within the Congress party; in fact, the post-Independence period up to the late 1970s appears as one of integration, stridently challenged by two short but significant spells of revolt, by the United Provinces Scheduled Caste Federation (UPSCF) in the 1940s and the Republican Party of India (RPI) in the 1960s. They were instrumental in raising political consciousness but were geographically located in western UP, were limited largely to the dominant Jatavs, and proved to be short-lived. Once the Congress party was able to re-establish itself as a dominant party following a brief period of weakness, they disappeared.

Period of Separation: UPSCF and the RPI

In 1944, a small, educated group comprising mainly Jatavs, formed the UPSCF as a branch of the All-India Scheduled Castes Federation established by Ambedkar in 1942. It was the first SC party to be formed in the former United Provinces during a period of growing political awareness among the depressed classes and separatism from caste Hindus and the Congress in the country.[8] Given the political situation, its energies were focused on obtaining separate electorates for SCs in the constitution of independent India. The UPSCF contested the 1945–46 elections with enthusiasm, despite being a young party with limited resources. Ambedkar took great interest in the elections and campaigned actively in Agra and few other towns of the United Provinces. Despite the UPSCF's remarkable performance in the SC primaries or first round of voting[9,10] held in October 1945, in the final elections held in March 1946, the Congress won an impressive victory. The UPSCF, the only opposition party to the Congress, gained 9.9 per cent of the votes. The defeat of the UPSCF was due to its limited social base, lack of an organization and funds, and internal factionalism. Equally important, it was because by the 1940s nationalism proved to be the more dominant sentiment overwhelming the nation, leaving little room for the quest for social equality. Consequently, in the United Provinces the SCs grew divided between the 'Congress Harijans' who supported the Congress, and the 'Ambedkarites' who formed the base of the UPSCF.[11]

The election results strengthened the resolve of the UPSCF to mobilize against the Congress during 1946, demanding separate electorates under the Constitution. Beginning in June 1946, the agitation affected twenty-three districts in Oudh. On 16 July 1946, hundreds of satyagrahis marched to the assembly in Lucknow and courted arrest in large numbers.[12] A second round took place between 26 March and 14 May 1947 but proved to be short-lived and unsuccessful. Despite the AISCF suspending the agitation on 28 July in the United Provinces, protests continued until 15 August, when the assembly adjourned. However, the agitation gradually died down, due to the rapidly changing political situation.[13]

On 28 April 1947, the Constituent Assembly passed a bill abolishing untouchability and making its practice a criminal offence. On 2 July, Ambedkar was nominated to the Constituent Assembly as a Congress candidate from the Bombay Legislative Council, which led to his appointment as the law minister in Jawaharlal Nehru's cabinet. In this situation, prominent SC leaders in the United Provinces such as Pyarelal Kureel,

Nandlal Jaiswar Manik and Shamlal offered their cooperation and services to the Congress. Most of them contested the elections in 1951–52 as official candidates of the Congress and won: Pyarelal from Banda (general and SC) and Manik from Bharatpur (reserved) in Rajasthan were prime examples.[14] Thus, the UPSCF disintegrated at Independence. It had been an important political force during the transitional phase of 1945–47, but with Independence its task was over; it lacked roots in the rural areas to evolve either into a broad social movement of the SCs, or a political party in the presence of the dominant Congress in the United Provinces.

The failure of the UPSCF led to a rapid decline of the Dalit movement in the former United Provinces. Following Independence, from 1950 to 1980 under the Congress party, the Gandhian ideology regarding the caste question defined the dominant mode of subaltern politics for the SCs. Congress leader Jagjivan Ram was the central figure upholding this approach; after the 1980s, it was relegated to the margins.

However, a feeling of disenchantment with the Congress party gradually grew among the SCs during the Nehruvian period. While they accepted that their conditions were improving, they were disappointed at the pace of the change. Recognizing this, when the AISCF failed to make a mark in the 1952 and 1956 general elections, Ambedkar called upon his followers to form a more broad-based party drawing support from both Dalits and other castes and classes. An eminent Dalit activist of the time, Chandrika Prasad Jigyasu, recorded that Ambedkar was keen to form a party that would be not only a Dalit party based on communitarian values, but also on values such as liberty, equality, freedom and fraternity that would be fundamental to good citizenship after Independence. With this in mind, on 30 September 1956, Ambedkar announced the establishment of the RPI but he died before the formation of the party on 6 December 1956.[15] However, his followers and activists took over and at a meeting held in Nagpur on 1 October 1957 in the presence of N. Sivaraj, Yashwant Ambedkar, A.G. Pawar, Datta Katti and Dadasaheb Rupwate,[16] it was decided to establish the party. The RPI was officially founded on 3 October 1957, with a branch in UP. It was a party meant to cater to all sections of the population, but with special emphasis on the needs and desires of the SCs.[17]

Emergence, Decline and Hiatus

The Republican Party of India enjoyed a short period of success when it obtained ten seats and about 4 per cent of the votes in the 1962 and 1967 assembly elections. At the time, the Congress was not doing well and its vote-share had dropped from 47.93 per cent in the 1952 elections to 36.33 per cent in 1962. However, the RPI remained a marginal party in UP, more like a 'flash in the pan' phenomenon. After the 1969 elections, the Dalit movement as a whole lost its identity and entered a phase of long-term decline. An important reason for this was that its leaders were unclear about the kind of party they had formed: a party of the SCs only, or of all the rural poor. Moreover it attempted to combine social and economic issues related to Dalit uplift, together with a cultural aspect seen in the conversion to Buddhism by many SCs in the western, districts which created differences among its leaders.[18] Its regional and social base was limited: it remained confined to the same districts as the UPSCF, it support base primarily comprised the Chamar–Jatavs; the large mass of SCs remained trapped in the larger Hindu identity, unaware of their distinct Dalit identity.[19]

Equally important, the existing power structure in UP, particularly in the rural areas, in the first two decades after Independence, did not allow space for the development of a strong Dalit party. The Congress, based on a single-party dominant system, was a broad-based, aggregative party that had built patron–client relations in each district, and thereby vote-banks of the SCs using the locally dominant proprietary castes of Brahmins, Rajputs and Bhumihars. Its leadership was from the upper castes though its support base included the SCs and the backwards. In the 1960s the Congress also had its own Dalit organization, the Dalit Varg Sangh, which enabled it to gain a chunk of the SC votes. Before the RPI could mobilize itself, improve its vote-share and spread to new areas, the party itself disappeared. By the late 1960s, the RPI split into several groups and a large section of the Dalits moved closer to the Congress. This enabled it to co-opt the party and the Dalit movement as a whole.[20]

From the mid-1960s to the 1980s there was a long hiatus or interval between two periods of separatism, when the Dalits supported the Congress party. However, despite the failure of the RPI, a process of Ambedkarization that had begun under its presence, particularly in western UP, continued.[21] Ambedkarization refers to the multifaceted activities by which Dalits attempted to disseminate the ideas of Ambedkar through discussions, by installing his statue, setting up libraries, establishing schools for SC children, celebrating this birthday with processions and songs, and setting up temples for Valmiki and Ravi Das, as well as everyday forms of assertion against upper-caste oppression. While this process dwindled following the collapse of the RPI, it continued at a subterranean and an individual level in western UP, in which education imparted bya small emerging group of Dalit teachers played an important role. Their efforts helped enhance consciousness of the Dalits' low-caste status and triggered a desire to improve their lot. As a progressive ideology, it attacked the entire caste system and went much beyond what Dalit parties stood for.[22] It formed an important base for the growth of grassroots assertion in UP. It is, in fact, the thread that binds the two periods of assertion in western UP.

New phase of Separatism: the BSP

In the 1980s, the Dalit movement in UP, after many years of fragmentation and co-option by the Congress party, entered into a new phase of separatism and hostility to mainstream parties and the upper-caste Hindu community, leading to the formation of the BSP. The two phases of the RPI and the BSP are distinct from each other. The latter, established after a period of rising Dalit consciousness, had a definite self-identity, strong and assertive leadership and a distinct social base.

The BSP was formed during a period of Congress weakness and collapse in 1984; as mentioned already, the latter had been on the decline from the 1970s onwards, eventually leading to its decay and de-institutionalization.[23] It symbolized the end of Gandhian Dalit politics and leaders like Jagjivan Ram. As our narrative has shown, the BSP became a radical, anti-caste movement from the late 1980s onwards and a dominant party in UP in the 1990s when it formed the government twice under the leadership of Mayawati. However, in the 2000s the party and the Dalit movement in UP entered a phase of rapid decline in which a section of the smaller Dalit sub-castes moved away from the BSP; since 2014, they have supported the BJP. The smaller Dalit sub-castes today identify with the BJP not only for material benefits but also because the party has accorded respect and recognition to their distinctive history, saints, religious and local traditions.[24]

The Dalit movement during its phase of resurgence under the BSP enjoyed a number of advantages in comparison with the period of the RPI. We know the Congress party was going downhill, with little evidence of revival even today. The BJP, though it won the 1991 assembly elections in UP following the destruction of the Babri Masjid in 1992, also then entered a period of decline, enabling the BSP to emerge as the dominant party in the 1990s. This provided Kanshi Ram and Mayawati the time required to build the movement on the ground and establish a Dalit party. These developments coincided with the rise of Dalit assertion and identity politics during the decade, which helped the BSP consolidate all sections of Dalits behind it and come to power. The continuing decline of the then upper caste-centric parties[25] in the early 2000s enabled Mayawati to obtain the support of sections of the upper and backward castes, Muslims and Dalits to gain a majority in 2007. Thus, the phase of resurgence under the BSP has been longer, which enabled the party to build a larger, pan-UP regional and social base, enabling Dalits to challenge upper-caste domination more effectively, and help them gain greater self-respect, dignity, political empowerment and confidence.

Despite these advantages, significant changes led to the rapid decline of the BSP after its defeat in 2012: the waning of identity politics that has led to Dalits aspiring for not only social justice, but also economic advancement, and failures and weaknesses on the part of the BSP leadership, particularly Mayawati. The sarvajan experiment, which enabled the BSP to gain a majority, making it a dominant party for a brief period, contributed to creating divisions within the Dalit community between the better-off and the poorer, smaller, marginalized sections, leading to the unravelling of the social base of the party. The change in policies have been just as critical, the functioning and attitude of Mayawati following the party's defeat in 2012, that have been responsible for the party's poor electoral performance, the breakdown of its organizational structure, the exodus of committed leaders and workers, the loss of Muslim support, leading to a perception within the population, including Dalits, of the BSP as a failed party. The previous chapters have documented these developments that underlie the existential crisis it is facing today.

Despite these developments, it cannot be denied that the revival of the BJP under the leadership of Narendra Modi has dealt a body blow to the BSP. If the 1980s heralded the process of consolidation of Dalit discourse under the banner of the BSP and Ambedkarite ideology, the 2000s under the hegemony of the BJP signify the process of its disintegration. The rise of the BJP as a hegemonic party happened precisely when the BSP faced its worst and ignominious defeat in 2012, leaving it little time to recover. By 2012, the BJP campaign for the 2014 general election—not to forget the Muzaffarnagar riots of 2013—so impacted the party's performance that it won no seats. Subsequently, attempts by the two social justice parties, which came together to defeat the BJP in 1993, did not prove successful; the latter has been able to effectively marginalize the SP and BSP in the society and polity of UP.

Decline under a Hegemonic Hindutva Party

The revival of the BJP under Narendra Modi, with massive subaltern outreach, has once again narrowed the space available for a lower-caste party. However, this phase of decline in the 2000s is significantly different in many ways from the earlier period of Congress rule, following the collapse of the RPI. The decline and disintegration that the Dalit movement is experiencing today runs far deeper and is more complex than that faced by the Dalit movement in the 1970s. Recovering from it will be much more difficult.

The collapse of the BSP has been accompanied by, as our narrative has shown, a caste/class dispersion or scattering of the Dalit movement, which is visible along three interrelated axes: *sub-caste, ideological and sub-regional.* Due to the breakdown of the BSP, sub-caste identities have come to the fore once again. The emergence of sub-caste politics among Dalits is both an outcome and the cause of the fragmentation of Dalit discourse. The BSP has experienced an implosion, leading to the smaller, poorer and more marginalized sub-castes deserting the party.

In the 1960s, many of these smaller sub-castes residing in the more backward regions of the state were not part of the RPI and it disappeared before it could mobilize them. By the 2000s, many were entering the mainstream and experiencing a process of modernization with each sub-caste discovering its own history, heroes, culture and distinct identity. This is the reason why the social and cultural distance that had always existed between them and the Jatavs had widened considerably, leading to each attempting to chart its own social and political journey. Ambivalence and accommodation, once again, as in the period of Congress dominance, characterize the relationship between the smaller Dalits and the BJP. There are, as our study has shown, strong protests against atrocities upon Dalits but preference for the BJP while voting. However, the current phase is more challenging, with large sections of the Dalits being included culturally into the saffron fold, suggesting that it is not just a tactical step, but a move towards ideological conversion.

Our narrative has highlighted that in terms of ideology, the Dalit movement has been divided into Ambedkarites or pro-BSP and Hindutvawadis or pro-BJP, though these divisions intersect each other in more complex ways in politics. The Hindutvawadi Dalits, for example, have embraced the legacy of Ravidas, a Bhakti era religious figure, while the Ambedkarites view Ambedkar as the inheritor of the legacy of the Buddha.[26] The fragmentation in the 2000s is greater as, unlike in the period of Congress dominance, it is not only *political*, that is, it is not just an attempt to gain the support of Dalits to win elections and become a dominant ruling party. Importantly, it is also *cultural*, as the BJP has endeavoured to bring Dalits into the larger Hindu fold, rendering the Muslim as the common 'other'. By looking after their cultural needs and desires, by showing respect to their distinct culture and identity, and by initiating new welfare strategies, the BJP and the RSS have conveyed that Dalits will be an important part of the Hindutva discourse. Thus, political, social and cultural strategies have been deftly combined to create a broad spectrum of the Hindu support base. This ideological conversion is not merely top-down, but permeates society as a whole today. Due to the cultural mobilization of the BJP–RSS, there is greater acceptance of the idea of a Hindutva among large sections of the population, including the Dalits and backward castes.

Moreover, the agenda of social justice, which the BSP under the leadership of Kanshi Ram propagated as its core ideology, has lost much of its importance for the party. Arguably it could be attributed to Dalits aspiring for and moving towards greater material advancement in the 2000s, as well as Mayawati's strategy in 2007 of helping the sarva samaj. It is also due to the new politics of *recognition and redistribution* that the BJP has made the bedrock of its ideology of subaltern Hindutva. The smaller Dalit sub-castes today have earned recognition for their distinct culture, identity and history, and as labhartis[27] they receive welfare measures to satisfy their basic material needs from the BJP, something that they argue was not provided to them by the BSP. Yet, it is undeniable that the idea of social justice—of helping the disadvantaged and poor—is a contribution of the BSP. It will remain a significant ideological legacy of the BSP to transformative democratic politics, which no party can ignore.

Nowhere is the unravelling of the BSP more evident than in the sub-regional disintegration of the Dalit movement in UP since the rise of the BJP. Divisions within the Dalit movement along sub-regional lines have historically been a feature in the state, both due to UP's large size and the existence of different cultural regions. In recent years it has taken two forms: the emergence of new, separate Dalit organizations, and rising differentiation between the smaller sub-castes residing in different sub-regions of UP. The former has been the work of a younger generation unhappy with Mayawati's failure to deal with increasing atrocities by the upper and middle castes, confront the BJP, her lacklustre campaigns in recent years and the consequent rapid downward spiral of the BSP. New organizations have been formed by both the Ambedkarites and the Hindutvawadi Dalits, as well as by different sub-castes, though the large majority is by Jatavs, many of whom are former members of the BSP. These organizations reflect Dalit assertion on the ground and are popular among the younger generation. However, they are yet to build organizational strength and mobilize beyond their limited areas; they also lack the resources to fight elections. Mayawati has not shown a desire to join hands with them to strengthen the BSP. Nor are they willing to join hands with each other to fight the BJP, as each organization would like to replace the BSP on its own and emerge as a strong Dalit party. Thus, at present they lack the capacity to build a strong pan-UP Dalit movement or party.

A second aspect of fragmentation is the emerging social and political divisions between smaller sub-castes residing in different sub-regions of UP, who are rediscovering their own specific sub-regional and cultural identities. Much literature exists which has mapped the shifting terrain of the political choices of the numerically weaker Dalit castes, like the Balmikis in western UP, the Pasis in the Awadh region and the Khatiks in Purvanchal.[28] During the phase of consolidation of Dalit identity in the 1980s, these sub-castes shifted from the Congress to the BSP. However, by the late 1990s, disillusioned with the BSP, they began to respond to the outreach of the non-BSP parties—the SP, the Congress and, subsequently, the BJP.

A common feature that has fuelled this shift is disillusionment with the Jatav-centric politics of the BSP. The Balmiki community's consistent mobilization behind the BJP and Hindutva discourse in western UP is a classic case of how the BJP has been able to fulfil both their material and cultural aspirations. Their electoral and political trajectory in the last decade shows that the community has not responded to overtures by non-BJP parties. In our longitudinal fieldwork in 2015, 2017, 2019 and 2022 in Balmiki localities in western UP, we found the community fully integrated into the saffron discourse. Materially, they felt let down and left out by the BSP and the SP in the 1990s and early 2000s vis-à-vis the Jatavs and Yadavs, respectively. Culturally, they feel they have been shown respect through consistent outreach and positive resonance by the Hindutva outfit.[29]

Similarly, in the Avadh region, while the Pasi Dalits supported the BSP until 2012, they shifted to the SP in the 2012 assembly election. In our field study, conducted between December 2012 and January 2013 in the aftermath of defeat of the BSP and the victory of the SP, the Pasi respondents communicated the sense of being left out and harassed by the police under BSP rule on the charge of manufacturing illicit liquor during 2007–12. They shifted to the BJP in 2014 and since then have been supporting the party. But in the 2022 assembly election, a section of them shifted away and supported the SP, inflation and unemployment being the major reasons for this.[30]

While the Khatiks view the SP and BSP as being exclusionary and catering solely to the Jatavs, Yadavs and Muslims, the shift of this community in the Purvanchal region towards the BJP has taken a different route.[31] The Khatiks alleged that the communal riots during the rule of the SP saw the latter favouring Muslims against them in Mau, Azamgarh and Gorakhpur, among other districts. They also asserted that it was the Hindu Yuva Vahini and other saffron outfits that came to their support. Hence, the community developed an affinity for the Hindutva discourse. Though a majority in the community voted for the BJP in the 2022 assembly election, we found in our fieldwork that a section among them was angry with the saffron party due to issues of inflation and unemployment, which have affected them.[32]

***

The Dalit movement in UP is once again entering a period of decline, or a hiatus, as historical evidence suggests, before the next round of separation. Our discussion raises some significant questions regarding its future in UP. Does the deepening of fault lines along the axes of ideology, sub-caste and sub-regionalities among Dalits indicate a crisis or the emergence of a new sense of confidence among various sections of the community to chart a separate political course in the coming years? Will a new pan-UP Dalit movement arise out of the various regional organizations in the future? How will the competing ideological schism between the Ambedkarite and the Hindutva Dalit discourse shape the future of subaltern politics in the state? Most importantly, what does it mean for the BSP and Mayawati?

The BSP having played its role in providing self-respect, dignity and empowerment to Dalits and challenging upper-caste dominance has entered a period of long-term decline. Mayawati's image as a strong Dalit leader who could unite the Dalit community has diminished. We are witnessing a post-BSP phase in which the party will not disappear like the RPI as it has succeeded in letting down roots, but an autonomous Dalit politics with its own leadership, as in its heyday, will no longer be possible. The BSP could occupy a position similar to the Dalit Panthers—currently celebrating their fiftieth anniversary— who, despite having no strong party or organization and often divided into groups, touched the lives of a section of Dalits and still wield considerable influence in Maharashtra. While the Dalit Panthers based their action on Marxist ideology, writing and poetry, in the case of the BSP it was Ambedkarization that kept the movement alive in an earlier phase. Today, the legacy of the BSP is continuing assertion on the ground and the emergence of new organizations that describe themselves as Ambedkarite and also based on the ideas of Kanshi Ram. At this moment, with the BJP in a hegemonic position in UP and the country, a revival of the Dalit movement in the state seems difficult. However, in the long run, with Dalit assertion remaining strong on the ground and a section which keen to maintain its distinct identity under a new and younger leadership, a regrouping of the scattered organizations seems a possibility.

Epilogue

Assembly Elections 2022 and the Road Ahead

~~~

Social media reported a 'mad melee' in UP on 14 April 2022, Ambedkar Jayanti, to appropriate Baba Saheb's legacy, namely, the BSP's vote-bank, following the party's poor performance in the assembly elections.[1] The BJP organized 'Samrasta Divas' while the SP held wide-ranging programmes at the district level. The Yogi Adityanath government, fresh from its victory, organized functions in all ninety-eight organizational districts in the state. Ministers and BJP leaders participated and apprised the Dalit community about the 'Dalit Mitra' agenda initiated by the government for their welfare. The BSP took out rallies and organized social programmes among the Dalit community. At the same time, Mayawati accused rivals of exploiting the name of Dr Ambedkar. She appealed to her community not to lose hope after the results and to continue to support the BSP.[2]

The programmes to honour Ambedkar were a result of the BSP's dismal performance in the 2022 UP assembly elections compared to 2017. The party obtained only one seat, in Rasara constituency of Ballia district in eastern UP, with 12.9 per cent of the vote, its lowest since 1989 when it had gained only 9.46 percent of the vote but had managed to win thirteen seats. Even in its bastion, Ambedkar Nagar district, it stood third in four of the five seats there. In fact, the BSP got fewer seats than all the other small lower-caste parties such as the Suheldev Bharatiya Samaj Party (6), Nirbal Indian Shoshit Hamara Aam Dal (6), Jansatta Dal Loktantrik (2), and Apna Dal (S) (12). It did, however, manage to get the third highest number of votes in the state.

The BJP returned to power in the key state of UP winning a majority with 255 seats, the first time a sitting chief minister was re-elected since 1985, that is, after thirty-seven years. The SP obtained 112 seats and 32.06 per cent of the vote, emerging as the principal opposition party. The Congress obtained only two seats, down from seven in 2017 with its vote-share slumping from 6.2 per cent to 2.33 per cent, in one of its worst performances despite Priyanka Gandhi Vadra's sustained campaign for over a year. The Congress state chief, Ajay Kumar Lallu, lost his Tamkuhi Raj seat, coming third.

We examine the reasons underlying the victory of the BJP and why the SP leader Akhilesh Yadav, despite a bipolar fight, failed to unseat the Yogi Adityanath government. Against this backdrop of the election results, we analyse the reasons for the BSP's dismal performance and, more importantly, discuss whether the Jatavs, the core support base of the BSP, are, as is being claimed, deserting the party? And what it means for the future of the Dalit movement and Mayawati—aspects that are significant and have ramifications for the 2024 general elections, discussed in the concluding section.

Election 2022

BJP: Renewed Dominance with a Difference

The BJP gained a majority in UP but compared to 2017, it was a renewed dominance with a difference. It obtained 255 seats, down from 312 in 2017, with 41.29 per cent of the vote, an increase of 3 per cent. For the first time since 2014, the SP was able to challenge BJP's hegemonic position in UP, rendering the election bipolar. Compared to 2017 when the SP obtained barely forty-seven seats, it managed to increase its seat tally by sixty-four, and an increase of 12 per cent points; together with its allies, it polled 36.32 per cent of the votes. It was the best ever performance of the SP which could not earlier breach the 30 per cent mark; in 2012 it had formed the government with 29.15 per cent, in 2017 it obtained 21.8 per cent, and in 2019, 17.96 per cent of the vote.[3] But there remained a 7.5 per cent gap between the BJP and the SP. If the Congress and BSP had performed slightly better, the gap between the BJP and the SP would have been narrower. But the election turned so sharply bipolar that the alliances led by the BJP and SP polled over 80 per cent of the votes and shared 398 of the 403 seats amongst them. Despite this, in twenty-nine out of seventy-five districts in UP, the SP could not even open its account—this included its stronghold of Kannauj. Akhilesh Yadav represented the Kannauj Lok Sabha seat thrice, his wife Dimple Yadav twice, and Mulayam Singh Yadav once.[4]

In caste terms, as Table 6 (see Appendix 1) shows, the BJP increased its votes among all caste groups in 2022 compared to

2017, except among the Kewat, Kashyap, Mallah and Nishad groups. It not only increased its vote-share among the upper and backward castes, but also substantially among Jats and, to a lesser extent, even among the Yadavs. It significantly increased its vote-share among the Dalits, which adversely impacted the fortunes of the BSP.

How did the BJP chart this impressive win and obtain the support of large numbers of Dalits and OBCs, despite the fact that the economy was doing badly and there was unhappiness due to poor management of the second wave of the Covid-19 pandemic in March–April 2021, unemployment, inflation, the issue of stray cattle, poor law and order, and atrocities against Dalits and women, leading to anger on the ground as widely reported by many observers? In fact, according to official estimates, the gross state domestic product of UP grew at a compound rate of only 1.95 per cent per annum during 2017–21. In contrast, the growth rate was 6.92 per cent in 2012–17 during the previous SP government and 7.9 per cent during Mayawati's 2007–12 regime. A decelerating rate of growth under the Adityanath government meant that per capita income in UP had increased by merely 0.43 per cent on average over four years.[5]

The media has drawn attention to the communal rhetoric employed by Yogi Adityanath, and later Modi and Amit Shah, during their campaign. For instance, Adityanath used communal terms like 'abbajan' and 'chachajan' and made communal references such as 'those with Ali versus Bajrangbali' and '80 versus 20'.[6] He claimed that Akhilesh Yadav and Asaduddin Owaisi, the chief of All India Majlis-e-Ittehadul Muslimeen, were spreading hatred in a state that had been riot-free during his five years. He also alleged that the Congress planted the 'seeds of terrorism in Kashmir' in the form of Article 370 and the SP 'withdrew cases against terrorists who attacked Ram Janmbhoomi'.[7] On their visits to Kairana in Shamli district, Adityanath and Shah attempted to revive the bogey of 'palayan' or exodus by Hindu families due to so-called 'Muslim terrorism', a claim, it is alleged, helped the BJP win in 2017.[8]

However, in 2022, straightforward communal rhetoric was not as important as in earlier elections. This election was fought on a Hindutva template already in place since 2014. There is far greater acceptance today, of the BJP's cultural agenda among the OBCs and Dalits but it is now communicated in different ways: the inauguration of the Ram Temple, the Kashi Corridor by Modi, and, closer to the election, deputy CM Keshav Maurya's remark regarding the 'unresolved' matter of the Krishna Janmasthan temple assuring voters that it continues to be an important issue for the BJP.[9]

Most of the strategies responsible for the BJP's victory and support among the Dalits and backwards are not new but have been built over time since 2014, enabling it to win successive elections. As journalist Saba Naqvi has pointed out, while majoritarian sentiment is now acceptable and growing incrementally not just in UP, but other parts of the country, 'it would be a lazy analysis to put down the BJP's emphatic win in UP solely to communal polarization'.[10]

As our narrative has shown, in the run-up to the critical 2014 elections, Modi established an ideological and strategic Hindutva template consisting of foundational principles for the party, combining promises of rapid economic development and religious mobilization, which appealed strongly to Dalits, and to which there have been significant additions over time. This multi-layered discourse can be put on a political continuum ranging from promises of development, welfare programmes, cultural inclusion and hyper-nationalism, to religiosity. Each strategy has been used at different points of time, separately or together, to create a Hindu vote-bank but also to obtain lower-caste support; these messages have been deployed in a targeted manner in contexts and geographies where the BJP believed it could benefit from using them, depending on need, both during and between elections. Modi has used a new language in each election, signalling the redefinition and orientation of Hindu nationalism, in an effort to gain Dalit support and to 'other' the Muslim. To effectively employ these strategies, the party has over the years used both personal and digital methods to convey its rhetoric and build a perception effectively through use of social media.

Another important strategy, gradually built up since 2014, which had provided electoral benefits to the BJP earlier, was the targeted use of welfarism, with the labharti (group of beneficiaries) emerging as a major supportive bloc.[11] Many voted for the BJP as they had benefited from central and state welfare schemes and direct benefit transfers: Kisan Samman Nidhi, Ujjwala scheme, PM Aawas Yojna, health insurance scheme, free ration scheme, as well as cash benefits. Almost four in five (80 per cent) households in UP benefitted from the free ration scheme, and three in five from the public distribution scheme which provides rations at subsidized cost. The direct benefit transfer schemes, the Kisan Samman Nidhi (which benefitted 57 per cent of farmer households) and the Ujjwala scheme (46 per cent of households) also reaped benefits for the party. More than half the beneficiaries of these schemes voted for the BJP alliance. Interestingly, the free ration beneficiaries did not help the BJP much; a little over two-fifths amongst them voted for the BJP. The survey pointed to mixed evidence on whether the labhartis voted overcoming their social identity: more of the poor who benefited from the free ration and cash transfer voted for the BJP as compared to the non-beneficiaries. In addition, Dalit beneficiaries who supported the BJP were proportionally higher in number than non-beneficiaries. Three in ten voters also benefitted from the health insurance scheme, and 27 per cent received money in their accounts against welfare schemes. One-fifth of the households also got assistance to build their houses.[12] To ensure that the deliverables were attributed to the Centre and thereby the BJP, the Central bureaucratic machinery was used as much as possible, together with strong and persistent messaging, highlighting the role of the benefactor, particularly Modi.

A Resurgent SP

An analysis of the campaign strategies of the SP is useful given how as it challenged the BJP in the assembly elections. Moreover, it is the only opposition party that is preparing to confront the BJP in 2024. During his campaign, Akhilesh Yadav aggressively highlighted the failures of the Adityanath government and formulated strategies that helped improve the SP's tally. The BSP was facing an existential crisis and the subaltern social coalition of the lower backwards was being perceived as unravelling, with leaders like Swamy Prasad Maurya moving to the SP. Akhilesh made efforts to shed the SP's image of a Muslim–Yadav party by creating an anti-BJP front of smaller OBC and Dalit parties with the Jayant Chaudhary-led Rashtriya Lok Dal in western UP, Om Prakash Rajbhar's Suheldev Bhartiya Samaj Party in eastern UP, Keshav Dev Maurya's Mahan Dal in central UP, the Apna Dal (K) in eastern UP, and Sanjay Chauhan's Janwadi Party (Socialist). He also formed the Baba Sahib Vahini[13] to attract Dalit votes. By positioning himself as the leader of the *'pitchade'* he shifted the election discourse into a battle between Hindutva and social justice.[14]

Another factor, which the SP had hoped would help them win, was the expansion of the Mandal[15] forces in the 2000s to the smaller OBCs—the Kushwahas, Kurmis, Patels, Nishads and others having become politically conscious and demanding. The attempt by the BJP to include them in the government raised their aspirations. But a section alleged that their interests were neglected once the BJP won, and therefore they preferred the SP.[16] However, this development did not help the SP defeat the BJP. A major reason was—as in earlier elections—that the fear of Yadav dominance was greater, it seems, than Thakurwad (domination of Thakurs) in Adityanath's regime. In addition, the RLD in western UP was not able to sufficiently consolidate its Jat vote, a majority of whom (54 per cent) voted for the BJP (see Table 6, Appendix 1). The expected Jat–Muslim combine did not materialize, at least not across western UP; it was confined more to the region's northern part. Moreover, if the vote-share of 80 per cent of the Hindu community is taken into account, the BJP secured a little over half the Hindu votes (54 per cent) across UP, while the SP polled one-fourth (26 per cent).[17] At the same time, the SP secured over three-fourths of the Muslim vote which was responsible for the counter mobilization and consolidation of Hindus behind the BJP.[18]

Yet, the SP did make considerable gains in number of seats and vote-share; it managed to dent the western UP citadel of the BJP. SP–RLD candidates defeated BJP leaders such as Suresh Rana, Sangeet Som and Umesh Malik who had been active in the Muzaffarnagar riots. Rana, the minister for sugarcane development, lost to Ashraf Ali Khan of the RLD from the Thana Bhawan seat by a margin of 10,806 votes; this constituency lies in the communally charged Shamli district. The RLD won Shamli and three Jat-dominated seats in Muzaffarnagar district—Puraqazi (SC), Bhudhana and Meerapur, with a section of Jats and Muslim supporting them. The SP–RLD alliance benefited from Muslim support; thirty-six Muslim candidates won, up from twenty-four in 2017. The farmer's movement was primarily concentrated in four Jat-dominated districts—Muzaffarnagar, Shamli, Baghpat and Meerut. Of the nineteen seats in these districts, the BJP won only six, all largely urban; in Baghpat the BJP beat the RLD by a narrow margin. Table 6 (see Appendix) points to a close competition between the BJP and the SP for the votes of the politically ambitious and upwardly mobile Kurmi, Koeri, Maurya, Kushwaha, Saini and other OBCs, with other parties receiving hardly any from them.

Historical weaknesses also contributed to the SP's inability to defeat the BJP.[19] In the 2022 elections, we saw for the first time since 2014 a challenge to Hindutva by the forces of Mandal.[20] In the early 1990s, both the Mandal and the Ram Mandir projects were initiated and though the BJP gained a majority in 1991, it lost in 1993 to the SP–BSP combine. But by that time, the Rath Yatra led by Lal Krishna Advani had taken place and the foundation of the Hindu project laid, particularly among the OBCs. The destruction of the Babri Masjid led to a decline of the BJP in UP. However, the SP under Mulayam Singh failed to unite the backwards as it favoured the Yadavs, ignoring the lower OBCs, and began to be viewed as a Yadav–Muslim party. Mandal and Kamandal[21] divided the BCs and upper caste Hindus as Mulayam Singh mobilized a section of the backwards and Muslims against the BJP. As a result, he lost Hindu upper-caste support; his being described as 'Maulana Mulayam' led to further consolidation of the Hindu vote behind the BJP. Akhilesh succeeded to some extent in 2012 in widening the party base by gaining support across castes.[22] Using a heightened communal agenda combined with generous welfarism under Modi, the Hindutva forces succeeded in gaining the support of large sections of non-Yadav OBCs and Dalits who see the SP as a Muslim–Yadav party.

More immediately, despite these tremendous challenges, the SP began its electoral campaign for 2022 only in October 2021, too late to take advantage of the palpable anger on the ground and the unhappiness among OBCs and Dalits. Moreover, SP leaders were not visible during the Covid-19 pandemic nor were they active in the farmers' movement. The efforts to mobilize farmers outside of western UP were made much too late, only after the Lakhimpur Kheri incident on 3 October 2021.[23]

2022: BSP and the Future of Dalit Politics

The major battle in UP in 2022 was fought between the BJP and the SP; the BSP was further marginalized, its already low fortunes dipping further. Despite this, Mayawati maintained a low profile during the campaign and held few rallies, kicking off as late as 1 February from Agra, a city where the party had performed well in the past. The BJP candidate, Baby Rani Maurya, also from the same Jatav sub-caste as Mayawati, had defeated the BSP here in 2017. At the Agra rally, Mayawati dismissed the charge that she was 'invisible' and 'not in the race' for the UP polls, arguing that she was working silently to strengthen her party's prospects in the elections. In her hour-long address, she attacked the BJP, the SP and the Congress and signalled to her cadre to 'only vote for BSP'.[24] The BJP, she pointed out, did not help Dalits despite gaining their support, it was responsible for creating communal disharmony and, during its rule, Dalits and women had not been safe. Her reference to the custodial death of Arun Valmiki in Agra was welcomed with huge cheers from the audience.[25] But it was observed that Mayawati was 'mild' in her attacks against the BJP and severe against the Congress and the SP.[26]

She accused the BJP and the RSS of spreading the false propaganda that she would be 'made the President' if the saffron party won. Mayawati responded angrily: 'How can I accept such a post when we know that it will be the end of our party. So, I want to make it clear to every BSP office-bearer that in the interest of our party and movement, I will not accept any offer for the President's post from the BJP or other parties and they should never be misled in future.'[27]

Targeting the Congress, Mayawati said the party had been vocal on atrocities against Dalits only when horrendous incidents occurred, as in Hathras. It was only after Priyanka Gandhi Vadra took charge of UP in 2019 that the party had tried to win over Dalits, particularly women, with visits to the homes of victims in Sonbhadra, Hathras and Unnao, among others. Further, the Congress had never recognized the great contribution of Bhim Rao Ambedkar and had insulted Kanshi Ram by not declaring national mourning upon his death in 2006.[28] Also, the Congress had ended reservation in government contracts. Attacking the SP, Mayawati reminded her followers that the 2013 Muzaffarnagar riots had taken place due to poor handling by the SP government. At a rally in Aligarh, she promised to restore the names of districts, formerly named by her after personalities held in high regard by the Dalits. Claiming that the BSP would come back to power in the 2022 polls, Mayawati warned journalists: 'Don't repeat your mistake of ignoring the BSP as you did in 2007.'[29]

More than Mayawati, it was Satish Chandra Mishra, the Brahmin face and general secretary of the party and Rajya Sabha member, who was active from July to October 2021, holding rallies based on the sarvajan strategy. Under his leadership, the BSP organized a number of conferences to woo Brahmins, across seventy-five districts in UP. However, towards the end of the campaign, the BSP seems to have given up its upper-caste outreach policy, realizing that while on the one hand it could not reap dividends as the Brahmins were consolidating in favour of the BJP, on the other, its pro-Brahmin policy had cost it Dalit votes in 2019. Confident of creating Dalit–Muslim social engineering, Mayawati gave one-in-three tickets to Muslim candidates and most of the remaining to OBC and Dalit candidates.[30]

However, these strategies did not help the BSP. Its late and lacklustre campaign, organizational breakdown at the district and lower levels, and exodus of senior and prominent faces like Lalji Verma, Ram Achal Rajbhar, Indrajit Saroj, Swami Prasad Maurya and Naseemuddin Siddiqui over the years to other parties, had already dented its image, including among Dalits and Muslims. Moreover, the media portrayal of Mayawati as not stepping out to campaign aggressively for fear of being investigated by the ED and the CBI for unaccounted assets, also worked against her.

Consequently, the data provided in Table 6 (see Appendix) shows that the BSP was the biggest loser among all caste groups, getting no votes from the Brahmins who had supported it in 2007, signalling the end of the sarvajan strategy, and very little from all sections of the backwards, whose support was crucial for its victories in the late 1990s and early 2000s vis-à-vis the SP. The results also point to the end of the Dalit–Muslim alliance which, as our narrative has shown, had been gradually breaking down since 2014, particularly after the Muzaffarnagar riots. The minority community no longer had faith in the BSP's ability to challenge the BJP.

As table 6 (Appendix) shows, the BJP made significant gains among both Jatavs and non-Jatavs. It won over two-fifth of the support of non-Jatavs, as opposed to one third the last time. More important, it made some of its most impressive inroads among Jatavs, the community that had supported Mayawati in the past, securing nearly a fifth of their votes, more than double that obtained in 2017. The BSP's vote-share among Jatavs came down drastically from 87 per cent to just 65 per cent. Among non-Jatavs too, who had already started moving away from the party since the last few elections, the BSP's vote-share reduced considerably. With the decline in performance of the BSP in 2022, the SP (including the RLD) increased its vote-share among all sections of Dalits. However, the increase was only slightly more than that of the BJP in the case of the other SCs, and less than the BJP in the case of Jatavs; the BJP increased its vote-share among Jatavs by 13 per cent, the SP gained just 6 per cent more. Dalit voters, who shifted from the BSP to the BJP in 2017, again voted for the BJP (see Table 6). Many of them could have gone to the BSP if they had found the party to be a strong contender for power. Also, despite giving tickets to 87 Muslim candidates, much more than the SP which fielded only fifty-nine Muslim candidates, the BSP could not get much Muslim support. It was the SP, which had remained mute on the issues of minorities to avert polarization, that witnessed a consolidation of Muslims in its favour.

However, our extensive fieldwork across large parts of western and eastern UP suggests[31] that the BSP with a total vote-share of 12.9 per cent (Table 6) was able to hold onto most of its Jatav votes. The party's vote-share fell, we argue, due to loss of votes from the other SC groups (from 44 to just 27 per cent) but equally due to the strong consolidation of the Muslim vote behind the SP. As our narrative has shown, the BSP vote-share among Muslims had been falling over elections; it fell from 19 per cent in 2017 to just 6 per cent in 2022 (Table 6). In the backdrop of intense bipolarity and the fight for the Hindu votes between the BJP and the SP which led to the polarization of Muslim votes towards the latter, the BSP was the loser.

Following the poor performance of the BSP in the election, Mayawati has begun an exercise to rebuild the entire party organization, dissolving party units and retaining only the district and state unit presidents.[32] The first prominent change after announcement of the 2022 results was in the Lok Sabha, where the party has ten members. However, in the past three years, the BSP has changed its leader in the Lok Sabha five times. After the 2019 elections, the BSP had appointed the MP from Nagina, Girish Chandra Jatav, to lead in the Lok Sabha. After a long time Mayawati chose a Dalit MP for this post, earlier upper caste or OBC leaders were assigned this responsibility. But a few days later, just before the first session of the 17th Lok Sabha, she replaced him with Danish Ali, MP from Amroha. A few weeks later, Mayawati replaced Ali with Shyam Singh Yadav, an OBC MP from Jaunpur, saying the move was aimed at making a balance in 'sarva samaj'. Three months later, Mayawati re-nominated Danish Ali to the post and Yadav was given organizational responsibility. In January 2020, Ritesh Pandey, a Brahmin MP from Ambedkar Nagar district, considered a stronghold of the party, was made leader of the BSP in the Lok Sabha.[33] However, on 14 March 2022, after the declaration of the election results, Mayawati decided to replace Ritesh Pandey, the party's Brahmin face in the Lok Sabha with Girish Chand Jatav.[34] 'The party will assign Ritesh Pandey some other responsibilities in view of 2024 Lok Sabha polls,' said a BSP spokesperson following the announcement. This shift was made because unlike in the 2017 election, when despite a strong electoral wave for the BJP, the

BSP had won three seats in Ambedkar Nagar district—Katehri, Jalalpur and Akbarpur. In 2022, the SP won all five seats in the district. It was also decided that while Ram Shiromani Verma, the party's Shrawasti MP, would continue as deputy leader of the party in the House, Sangeeta Azad, BSP's MP from Lalganj (SC reserved seat), would be the new chief whip.[35]

Mayawati has been successful in bringing back to the party fold the estranged party leader, Shah Alam alias Guddu Jamali, a BSP legislator in the previous UP assembly. After quitting the BSP, Jamali had contested a recently held assembly poll from Azamgarh on the ticket of Owaisi's AIMIM. Mayawati has decided to field Jamali for the by-election of the Azamgarh parliamentary seat which fell vacant after its MP, Akhilesh Yadav resigned, preferring to keep his MLA seat.[36]

Mayawati has assigned important positions in the party to close family members. In order to neutralize forces like the Bhim Army and its leader Chandrashekar Azad, Mayawati had, in 2017 itself, entrusted her nephew Akash Anand, then in his early thirties and holding an MBA degree from London, to bring youth, especially from the SC community, to the party fold. Widely viewed as her heir apparent, Akash heads a team of around 150 youngsters who manage the party's digital and social media outreach and accompanied Mayawati to her rallies during the 2019 general elections. In March 2022, he was appointed the national coordinator of the party.[37] Akash's father, who is Mayawati's younger brother Anand, was also brought in around the same time. Initially working as a clerk in Noida he later switched over to the real estate business and came under the income tax department's scanner for accumulating wealth in excess of his known sources of income during 2007–12 when Mayawati was in power. Anand now manages the party's finances while coordinating with zonal committees.[38]

At a review meeting, called after the declaration of the election results, Mayawati pointed out that voters from her caste within the Dalit community had stood firmly behind her. The BSP's loss was due to the return of the BJP, for which the SP and the Muslim community were to blame, she said.[39] The Hindu community voted for the BJP as they did not want the SP to return to power, fearing a return to mafia and *goonda* rule, while the Muslims deserted the BSP, preferring the SP. According to a senior BSP leader, the party is mulling over a review of its Muslim outreach policy to make it more convincing and robust. Mayawati held that till the 2024 Lok Sabha elections, every effort should be made to convince the Muslim community that the BJP can be stopped only if the Dalits and Muslims join hands. She has also said that for the BSP to regain its erstwhile dominant position, the party needs to mobilize upper-caste votes alongside those of the most backward and Dalits, as well as Muslims, just as the BSP had managed to do prior to the 2007 elections.[40]

The revamp of the party by Mayawati so far does not signal any radical change. The new appointments in important party positions point to Mayawati reposing greater faith in Jatav leaders and her own family members. Little effort has been made to reach out to leaders of the smaller Dalit groups and OBCs who earlier supported the party or bring younger Dalits or Muslims into the party organization.

BSP and Dalit Politics Ahead

Against this backdrop a number of scenarios emerge for the Lok Sabha elections in 2024. The future of the BSP depends on the ability of its leadership to rebuild its once-strong, social base and organizational structure. As discussed earlier, the

BSP has, since 2012, been unravelling due to the loss of large sections of its traditional support base made up of the OBCs, a section of Brahmins, Muslims, non-Jatav Dalits and, more recently, Jatavs. Given the ascendancy of the BJP in UP, the possibility of the Brahmins and the OBCs, who were attracted to the BSP in 2007, returning to it is remote. This leaves its core constituency of Dalits and Muslims: if they decide to support the BSP it could revive the party.

In the 2022 elections, the BJP was able to attract a large chunk of Dalit votes, including a section of the Jatav vote. If the BJP is able to further consolidate its gain among Dalits, particularly the Jatavs, that would further weaken the BSP and Mayawati's position as a Dalit leader. There is also a possibility of a section of the Dalits, particularly the Pasis and Khatiks, exercising the choice they made in 2012 and again in 2022, of moving towards the SP, which would further deplete the BSP. However, given the efforts being made by Mayawati post-2022 to bring Dalits back into the BSP fold, there is a possibility of the Jatavs remaining loyal to the party and its leader, going by their historical attachment to the Bahujan ideology and Mayawati,

Equally important will be the electoral choice of the Muslims in 2024 in light of the gradual breakdown since 2012 of the Dalit–Muslim understanding nurtured by Kanshi Ram and Mayawati in the 1990s. In UP, since the decline of the Congress party, Muslims have voted strategically, identifying the party in each constituency most likely to defeat the BJP. Hence, the Muslim vote remained divided between the Congress, the SP and the BSP. Muslims never rallied behind one single party, a scenario which changed significantly for the first time in 2022 when they moved away in large numbers from the BSP to the SP. Rebuilding the trust and support of the Muslim community will not be easy.

Much also depends on Mayawati's efforts to rebuild the party's organizational structure at the zonal, district and lower levels. This would require appointing honest, dedicated and capable leaders at various levels, rather than selecting persons with deep pockets. It remains to be seen if she can reach out to and bring back trusted leaders who helped build the party under Kanshi Ram, and who had either been thrown out by her, or had defected. These seem difficult tasks given Mayawati's personality and reclusive behaviour of late.

The 2022 assembly election once again showed that the electoral competition that the BSP faces is primarily from the BJP and the SP rather than the emerging Ambedkarite fragments and the new-generation Dalit leaders like Azad and Nirala. As argued in previous chapters, this new crop of leaders is electorally insignificant but extremely successful in acting as watchdogs for Dalit interests by flagging relevant Dalit issues and mobilizing community members. Given the ground sentiment among the larger Jatav community as seen in our recent fieldwork, it would be desirable for the BSP and Mayawati to reach out to these new leaders and bring them into the party's fold. Hitherto, Mayawati has been hostile to Ambedkarite leaders from her community who tried to carve out a space outside the BSP. However, rethinking on this issue, on her part, is warranted for three reasons. One, it is the popular sentiment of the Jatavs to see greater unity between Mayawati and these leaders. Two, it will create a positive perception about a larger Dalit unity behind the BSP at a time when the party is in tatters. Three, there is a possibility that such a measure would galvanize a section of non-Jatav Dalits too, particularly the youth, who in 2022 drifted away from the BJP to the SP. In politics, winning the war of perception is indispensable. In the last two assembly elections, the party lost the perception battle even before the actual elections took place. This led to the party being perceived as electorally irrelevant, particularly by the Muslims and a section of the OBCs. Creating a buzz around the possible unity of Dalit leaders across generations, if that were that to happen, would act as an incentive to a section of Muslims and others to rally behind the party.

The Road to 2024

Given the political scenario in UP, can opposition parties, individually or collectively, challenge the BJP in 2024? The decision by Akhilesh Yadav to give up his Lok Sabha seat and retain his membership of the UP legislative assembly (from the Karhal constituency)indicates that he has decided to fight the BJP in 2024, a decision that suggests the emergence of a 'new leader'.[41] When he was made chief minister in 2012, he remained in the shadow of his father, Mulayam Singh, and his troublesome uncle Shivpal Yadav. The electoral campaign for the 2022 elections showed a more determined Akhilesh who was able to draw large crowds and emerge as a possible alternative to the BJP.

Akhilesh's decision is significant as UP is a key state in the fight against the BJP. A study pointing to 'the regional limits of the BJP's success'[42] argues that there are social and geographical limits to Hindutva; it is strong in some regions in the country and weak in others. The Hindutva ideology has struck deep roots in UP and in the Hindi heartland compared to the rest of the country. It has not found much resonance in the southern states of Kerala, Andhra, Telangana and particularly Tamil Nadu, where Dalits have been hostile to it. The defeat of the BJP in West Bengal and Punjab and the entrenched position of the Biju Janata Dal (BJD) in Odisha indicate that it has not been successful in these states either. It is UP, the 'heartland' of India,[43] with the conservative outlook of its upper caste, particularly the Brahmins, who also form the elite in control of its backward economy, which seems to be the mainstay of this ideology. As successive elections have shown, the fight in 2024 will be not only on political or economic, but also cultural grounds as the BJP has successfully managed to spread its subaltern Hindutva ideology among the lower castes/classes. The opposition parties will have to develop an alternative set of ideas that appeal to the people. Thus, what Akhilesh brings to the table in 2024 will be of great importance.

The improved performance of the SP and the marginally lower numbers of the BJP in UP could encourage the opposition parties to join hands against the latter in 2024. A difficult question is which party will form the fulcrum of such an alliance, if it is attempted? Each party and its leaders are ambitious and this could come in the way of a concerted, organized attempt, to form a coalition. The SP at present seems to be the only party that could lead the alliance but the BSP and the Congress may not be open to accepting its leadership. On the other hand, the BJP has a strong leadership and a formidable organization and electoral machinery on the ground in UP. Despite the momentum building up behind the SP, the BJP can only be challenged by a united opposition, which is nowhere in sight.

As the 2024 general elections approach, it is noteworthy that the Congress is the largest opposition party in the country with a national image; it gained fifty-two seats and 19.5 per cent of the vote in 2019. Without a revived and improved Congress, mounting a challenge to the BJP in 2024 appears impossible, whether in UP or elsewhere in the country. Ten states go to the polls in the next two years before the general elections— Himachal Pradesh, Karnataka, Chhattisgarh, Madhya Pradesh,

Rajasthan, Telangana, Tripura, Meghalaya, Nagaland, and Mizoram that, together, account for 146 Lok Sabha seats; the BJP holds 121 of these. The only party challenging the BJP in each of these states is the Congress.[44] But in UP it has shrunk and is perceived by the other opposition parties as weak, faction-ridden, with little organizational strength and is undergoing a serious crisis of leadership, organization and ideology. With most regional parties not having a significant presence nationally, the Opposition cannot expect to dent the BJP's fortunes in many states without a solid performance from the Congress. In fact, it is the abject failure of the Congress in these states, as well as in UP, that has been one of the key factors behind the BJP's successive victories in general elections.

On the other hand, the BJP has already begun its efforts to further strengthen the party in UP. The Yogi Adityanath government in March 2022 was considering extending many of its welfare schemes—particularly the free ration programme for 15 crore people from the economically weaker sections, as promised during the campaign for the 2022 elections—up to the 2024 elections. Started in the state during the second wave of Covid-19, the scheme proved popular and it was believed to have helped the BJP win in 2022, despite the dismal condition of the economy.[45]

Similarly, the new UP cabinet has been formed keeping 2024 in mind.[46] An effort was made to balance regional, caste, and geographical issues: two ministers were selected from the Apna Dal, one leader from the Nishad Party and from other smaller caste groups in other parts of the state. Care was taken not to induct tainted individuals, and leaders responsible for the party's victory through their hard work were rewarded, such as Swantantra Dev Singh. Two former bureaucrats, Asim Arun and Rajeshwar Singh, who won, and Jitin Prasada the former

Congress leader, were also included. The party rewarded those who had won in difficult constituencies, such as Baby Rani in Agra in 2017, and Anjula Mahour in Hathras and Pratibha Shukla in Akbarpur–in 2022; four other women were also included. BJP MLA Brijesh Singh from Deoband constituency, Rajeev Singh alias Babbu Bhaiya from Dataganj constituency, both of whom retained their seats, and Rajesh Chaudhary, from the Mant assembly constituency in Mathura district who defeated seven-time MLA, Shyam Sundar Sharma, were also included.[47]

After the victory, the UP BJP unit decided to make major changes in top positions, including the posts of president and general secretary.[48] This is being done keeping in mind the differences within the party prior to the elections. The RSS leadership, which is involved in this endeavour together with Amit Shah, has shifted senior leader Sunil Bansal from Uttar Pradesh to the organization in-charge of West Bengal, Telangana and Odisha. Sticking to the policy of 'one man, one post', the party is looking for a new state president. Along with the appointment of new faces in these top posts, a new executive committee of the UP BJP will also be formed. With these changes, the RSS aims to strengthen the party prior to the 2024 elections.[49]

In this situation, a senior BSP leader and former spokesperson for the BSP pointed out after the 2022 elections, opposition parties in UP and elsewhere should take a leaf out of the strategy of 'non-Congressism' adopted by the opposition parties in the 1970s.[50] Based on this common ideological platform when the state of Emergency was lifted by Indira Gandhi and elections were held in 1977, an amalgam of opposition parties with differing ideologies such as the Congress (O), Bharatiya Jana Sangh, Bharatiya Lok Dal as well as defectors from the Indian

National Congress, joined hands. They formed the collaborative Janata Party which won a sweeping majority defeating the Congress and thereby restoring democracy in the country, even though the Janata Party broke up soon after. Bhadoria said he was disappointed that Mayawati, the tallest Dalit leader in the country, had failed to play a role in putting together such an alliance that would have sent a positive message to the people in 2022.

However, the situation today is not comparable on several counts. In the absence of a charismatic anchor like Jayaprakash Narayan, political parties in UP are unable to come together due to differences among themselves. The BJP has managed to form a social coalition of the upper and backward castes and Dalits, attract important leaders from other parties and form alliances with smaller parties such as the Apna Dal, thereby making it a strong force. In the past, smaller alliances such as the SP–Congress alliance in 2017 or the mahagathbandhan between SP–BSP in 2019 could not make even a dent in the hegemonic position of the BJP whose vote-share in 2019 crossed 50 per cent. Rather, the BSP and SP, dominant parties in the 1990s and early 2000s, by their opportunistic politics provided space to the BJP, which has entrenched itself in UP and become difficult to dislodge.

In light of the weaknesses of the opposition parties and their leaders, their inability to resonate with the larger electorate and lack of alternative strategies, the prognosis for 2024 appears grim for them. More specifically for the BSP and Mayawati, both the political situation in UP and its own internal weaknesses constitute a serious challenge. With the BJP and their sister Hindutva organisations employing a massive Dalit outreach strategy which combines the material and cultural aspirations of the community, the BSP now faces a herculean challenge to prevent the possibility of its core support base, the Jatavs, and particularly the youth, from rallying behind the saffron party. The fact that an overwhelming majority of Dalits need state support perpetually for their everyday survival makes them prone to respond to the ruling party of the day. Thus, the BJP's ascendency and the BSP's electoral decline paints a gloomy scenario for the latter in future. With its party organization having broken down, its social base unravelled, its ideology no longer attractive to the electorate, including the Dalits, and whose leadership does not step out to mobilize as in the past, the BSP is a pale shadow of what was once a dominant Dalit party.

Besides the external challenge from the BJP, Mayawati is also facing an internal crisis wherein she seems to have lost the support of the younger generation of Dalits, many of whom who are flocking to the new Dalit organizations emerging in various parts of UP. Having played a significant historical role in providing self-respect, confidence and political empowerment to the weaker sections for over a decade, the BSP has succeeded in catapulting the Dalit question as a central normative presence across the political spectrum so much so that all parties today compete to prove their better credentials on this plank. However, in the new grammar of politics, it seems the BSP is fast losing the plot. The space vacated by the party is rapidly being filled by the BJP and new players. While it may not be the end of the road for the BSP, it is certainly the end of Dalit discourse as we have known it since the 1980s.

Acknowledgments

～～

Our book draws on many years of writing and research on the Dalit movement in the Hindi heartland and in Uttar Pradesh in particular. Little attention has been paid in recent years to the BSP and the changing trajectory of the Dalit movement since 2000. On the other hand, there is proliferating literature on the BJP since its revival under Narendra Modi. While we have covered most of the academic data available on the BSP, as the book is a narrative for the general reader, we have made extensive use of interviews, discussions, our field work, as well media reports.

While writing this book we have received encouragement and support from a number of persons only some of whom we can acknowledge here. This book would not have been written without Mimi Choudhury's initiative. Mimi spoke to us in 2019 about a possible book on Dalit politics to be published in time for the UP elections. We were unsure at that time. In 2021, we reconnected with her to discuss our plans, and she was instrumental in the finalization of the proposal and its preparation for publication. We are grateful to Vidhu Verma and Niraja Gopal Jayal who were kind enough to read parts of the manuscript and provide valuable suggestions. Nilanjan Mukhopadhyay with his extensive knowledge of national politics, particularly the BJP/RSS, provided us with valuable information.

While we interviewed a number of public intellectuals, journalists, and political leaders, Swapan Dasgupta, Sudheendra Kulkarni, Nilanjan Mukhopadhyay, Harish Khare, Harish Damodaran, Sudhindhra Bhadoria, Chandrashekhar Azad, and Jayant Choudhry spared a considerable amount of their time, and our discussions with them helped shape our ideas. BSP leaders Satish Chandra Mishra, Nasimuddin Siddiqui, Shrawan Kumar Nirala, Daddu Prasad and others on the ground provided significant information on the working of the BSP and sharpened our understanding of the reasons for its dominance and decline. Sanjay Kumar and his team at the CSDS deserve a special mention for providing us Election and Caste-based voting Data for the National and Uttar Pradesh Assembly elections. Thank you to the endorsers too.

We would like to thank our publishers Siddhesh Inamdar and Swati Chopra, and editors Suchismita Ukhil and Shatarupa Ghoshal at Harper Collins for their efficient, timely, and friendly handling of the book.

Sudha Pai
Sajjan Kumar

Appendix

Table 1

Seats and votes won by parties in the UP general and assembly elections

Party	2014 General Election	2019 General Election	2007 Assembly Election	2012 Assembly Election	2017 Assembly Election	2022 Assembly Election
	Seats won/ Votes (%)	Seats won/ Votes (%)	Seats won/ Votes (%)	Seats won/ Votes (%)	Seats won/ Votes (%)	Seats won/ Votes (%)
BJP	71/42.3	62/49.4	51/16.97	47/15	312/39.67	255/41.29
Congress	2/7.5	1/6.31	22/8.6	28/11.63	7/6.25	2/2.33
SP	5/22.20	5/17.96	97/25.4	224/29.15	47/21.82	112/32.06
BSP	0/19.60	10/19.26	206/30.43	80/25.91	19/22.23	1/12.9
RLD	0	0	10/3.70	9/2.33	1/1.78	8/2.85
AD#	1/1.0	2/1.0	0/1.06	1/0.90	9/0.98	12/1.62
Independents	1/1.8	1/6.73	9/6.97	1/1.78	3/2.57	0/1.11
Total	80/100	80/100	403	403	403	403

#Apna Dal

Source: Compiled from the reports of the Election Commission of India

Table 2

Social basis of voting for four major parties in UP assembly elections 2007 and 2012 (Figures in Percentage)

Caste/Community	BSP 2007–2012 (%)		SP 2007–2012 (%)		BJP 2007–2012 (%)		Congress 2007–2012 (%)	
Brahmin	16	19	10	19	44	38	19	13
Rajput	12	4	20	26	46	29	9	13
Vaishya	14	15	12	12	52	42	10	21
Other upper castes	15	17	17	15	41	17	12	13
Jats	10	16	8	7	18	7	2	11
Yadav	7	11	72	66	5	9	4	4
Kurmi/Koeri	16	19	17	35	42	20	6	13
Other OBC	30	19	20	26	17	17	9	12
Jatav	86	62	4	15	3	5	2	5
Balmiki	71	42	2	9	11	3	4	12
Pasi/Pano	53	57	16	24	12	4	7	7

Caste/Community	BSP 2007–2012 (%)		SP 2007–2012 (%)		BJP 2007–2012 (%)		Congress 2007–2012 (%)	
Other SC	58	45	16	18	9	11	4	17
Muslim	17	20	45	39	3	7	14	18
Class								
Upper	14	21	25	27	30	17	12	16
Middle	24	15	28	33	24	15	10	9
Lower	33	26	25	28	15	15	10	12
Poor	41	33	23	28	12	12	5	10
Others	30	23	23	32	14	16	12	9

Source: 'Special Statistics 2012: Sixteenth Assembly Elections In Uttar Pradesh', *Economic and Political Weekly*, 7 April 2012, Vol. 47, No.14, Compiled from Table 3, p.83.

Table 3

Support Base of various political parties across castes in 2017 assembly elections (Figures in Percentage)

Caste community	Congress	BJP	BSP	SP	RLD	Others
Overall	6.3	39.7	22.2	21.8	1.8	8.2
Upper caste	3	66	7	12	4	8
Yadav	11	10	6	63	--	10
Kurmi/Koeri	3	55	17	17	--	8
Other OBCs	4	58	14	14	1	9
Jatav	1	8	86	3	--	2
Other Dalits	3	37	39	11	1	9
Muslims	17	9	21	42	1	10
Others	8	40	24	17	1	10

Source: CSDS Uttar Pradesh Post Poll 2017

Table 4

Support base of various political parties across castes in 2014 and 2019 general elections (Figures in Percentage)

Caste/Community	Congress		BJP		BSP		SP	
	2014+RLD (%)	2019 (%)	2014 +AD (%)	2019 (%)	2014 (%)	2019 MGB* (%)	2014 (%)	2019 (%)
Brahmin	11	6	72	82	5	6	5	—
Rajput	7	5	77	89	5	7	8	—
Vaishya	—	13	—	70	—	4	—	—
Other upper castes	9	5	76	84	3	10	7	—
Yadav	8	5	27	23	3	60	53	—
Kurmi/Koeri	16	5	53	80	4	14	17	—
Other OBCs	8	5	60	72	11	18	13	—
Jatav	2	1	18	17	68	75	4	—
Other Dalits	4	7	45	48	29	42	10	—

Caste/ Community	Congress		BJP		BSP		SP	
	2014+ RLD (%)	2019 (%)	2014 +AD (%)	2019 (%)	2014 (%)	2019 MGB* (%)	2014 (%)	2019 (%)
Muslim	11	14	10	8	18	73	58	—
Others	10	1	51	50	20	35	17	—

Source: CSDS-Lokniti Post-poll survey,*The Hindu*,26 May 2019,https://www.thehindu.com/elections/lok-sabha-2019/post-poll-survey-why-uttar-pradeshs-mahagathbandhan-failed/article27249310.ece?homepage=true

**mahagathbandhan*: BSP, SP and RLD contested the 2019 Lok Sabha election in alliance.

Note: Figures may not add up to 100 due to rounding off.

Table 5

Budget expenditure in selected sectors by the BSP government during 2007–12

Sectors	2007–08	2008–09	2009–10	2010–11	2011–12
			Figures in thousands		
Housing department	87,30,748	1,57,34,396	1,03,53,409	1,35,86,474	1,16,34,862
Industry (all types)	63,19,354	47,39,849	54,65,687	78,20,729	58,57,314
Sugarcane development	55,62,464	73,96,294	71,31,019	19,84,077	55,06,732
Energy	7,28,63,146	7,66,89,276	7,57,54,466	7,66,02,938	8,22,34,678
Agriculture	5,78,36,787	6,96,29,976	7,74,45,597	9,72,90,854	3,53,70,306
Health	3,96,65,341	4,52,05,569	5,56,57,775	6,61,91,366	6,96,46,313
Urban development	1,23,70,203	3,04,44,330	1,16,33,629	2,34,24,310	3,20,80,187
Public works dept (only buildings)	5,26,72,935	6,20,06,894	6,06,29,861	6,68,52,160	9,20,000

Sectors	2007-08	2008-09	2009-10	2010-11	2011-12
		Figures in thousands			
Education	12,42,947 12,27,99,210	10,81,620 13,35,39,835 22,36,61,611	4,42,836 16,83,06,968 28,27,07,408	6,09,376	NA
Social welfare	7,50,69,709	10,67,38,126	11,80,62,292	14, 10, 46, 230	1,51,29,361
Handicapped and backward class welfare	1,03,44,465	1,49,02,021	1,53,72,244	1,51,86,599	—*
SC welfare	1,76,30,962	2,38,07,459	2,72,75,323	3,17,27,598	3,45,78,143
ST welfare	2,26,298	2,79,009	3,10,547	8,15,072	10,96,227
SC SCP**	4,68,67,984	6,77,49,637	7,51,04,178	9,33,16,961	11,61,29,857
Minority welfare	26,40,406	48,08,170	55,99,802	1,22,10,192	1,11,44,823

Sectors	2007–08	2008–09	2009–10	2010–11	2011–12
			Figures in thousands		
Women and child welfare	1,79,94,482	2,06,07,549	2,97,23,087	3,50,59,473	4,01,91767

Source: Provided by the chief minister's secretariat, Lucknow, on 10 August 2011 during fieldwork conducted to obtain the figures. Figures for 2011–12 were provided later.

*In 2011–12 the expenditure on social welfare and handicapped and backward class welfare has been given together.

**SCP: Unavailable

Note: Table 5 is taken from Sudha Pai, unpublished paper, 'Building caste–class alliances: The BSP experiment in Uttar Pradesh', presented at a workshop on Political Economy of Caste–Class Alliances in India, JNU, 2015. For this paper, a few days' fieldwork was undertaken in Lucknow in August 2011. Senior officials of the chief minister's secretariat, who did not wish to be named, provided the figures.

Table 6

How castes and communities voted in 2022 versus how they voted in 2017

	BJP+ 2017	BJP+ 2022	SP+ 2017	SP+ 2022	BSP 2017	BSP 2022	INC 2017	INC 2022
Brahmin (7%)	83	89	7	6	2	--	1	1
Rajput/Thakur (7%)	70	87	11	7	9	2	3	1
Vaishya (2%)	71	83	11	12	3	1	--	1
Other upper castes (2%)	70	78	15	17	5	1	2	2
Jat (2%)	38	54	57	33	3	12	1	--
Yadav (11%)	10	12	68	83	2	2	14	1
Kurmi (5%)	63	66	16	25	7	3	5	4
Koeri, Maurya, Kushwaha, Saini (4%)	56	64	18	22	22	4	--	2
Kewat, Kashyap, Mallah, Nishad (4%)	74	63	7	26	15	7	1	2
Other OBC (16%)	62	66	15	23	11	4	4	3
Jatav (12%)	8	21	3	9	87	65	<1	1
Other SC (8%)	32	41	11	23	44	27	2	4
Muslim (19%)	6	8	46	79	19	6	19	3

Figures are %; the rest voted for other parties; the 2017 figures for SP+ are based on the 2022 alliance with RLD; the Congress, which had an alliance with the SP in 2017 but not this time, is shown separately in the table. The composition of these communities as a proportion of the population is shown in brackets

Notes

Prologue

1   Sajjan Kumar, involved in fieldwork prior to the 2017 election, was present during this discussion at Jatav Nagar on 26 March 2017 at the residence of Surendra Boudh, a BSP cadre.

2   Census of India, UP 2011 District Census Handbook, Series 10 Part XII - A, Primary Census Abstract.

3   Sajjan Kumar, involved in fieldwork prior to the 2017 election, was present during this discussion at Jatav Nagar on 26 March 2017 at the residence of Surendra Boudh, a BSP cadre.

4   Angana P. Chatterji, Thomas Blom Hansen and Christophe Jaffrelot (eds), *Majoritarian State: How Hindu Nationalism Is Changing India* (New Delhi: Harper Collins, 2019).

5   Milan Vaishnav (ed.), *Religious Nationalism and India's Future* (Carnegie Endowment for International Peace: 2019).

6   Suhas Palshikar, 'Towards Hegemony: BJP Beyond Electoral Dominance,' *Economic and Political Weekly* No. 33 (18 August 2018): 36–42.

229

7   See particularly the articles on UP in Paul Wallace (ed.), *India's 2014 Elections A Modi-led Sweep* (New Delhi: Sage Publications, 2015) and Paul Wallace (ed.), *India's 2019 Elections The Hindutva Wave and Indian Nationalism* (New Delhi: Sage Publications, 2019).

8   Prashant Jha, *How the BJP Wins: Inside India's Greatest Election Machine* (New Delhi: Juggernaut Books, 2017).

9   Christophe Jaffrelot, 'Class and Caste in the 2019 Indian Election–Why Have So Many Poor Started Voting for Modi?' *Studies in Indian Politics* (2019):1-19. DOI: 10.1177/2321023019874890.

10   Oliver Heath and Sanjay Kumar, 'Why Did Dalits Desert the BSP in UP', *Economic and Political Weekly,* Vol. 47, No. 28 (14 July 2012): 44.

11   Shivam Vij, 'The Mayawati era is over. Bye Bye Behenji',*The Print* (27 January 30,2020). For a different view see Suryakant Waghmore, 'The Competing Armies of Bhim', *India Today* (22 September 2018).

12   S.K. Thorat, 'Social discrimination and socioeconomic realities add to disadvantages faced by Scheduled Castes in the labour market', *Hindustan Times* (7 September 2018).

13   Anand Teltumbde, 'Onslaughts on Dalits in the Time of Hindtuva', in Niraja Gopal Jayal (eds.), *Re-Forming India: The Nation Today* (New Delhi: Penguin Random House, 2020), pp.363–82

14   Sujata Patel (ed.), *Neoliberalism, Urbanisation and Aspirations in Contemporary India* (OUP, 2021). Also see Sudha Pai, *Developmental State and the Dalit Question in Madhya Pradesh: Congress Response* (New Delhi: Routledge, 2011).

15   Sudha Pai and Sajjan Kumar, *Everyday Communalism: Riots in Contemporary Uttar Pradesh* (New Delhi: Oxford University Press, 2018).

16   Badri Narayan, *Fascinating Hindutva Saffron Politics and Dalit Mobilization,* (New Delhi: Sage, 2009).

17   Badri Narayan, *Republic of Hindutva: How the Sangh is Reshaping Indian Democracy,* (New Delhi: Penguin Viking, 2021).

18   Together with the existing body of scholarly and journalist studies, our narrative draws on contacts, fieldwork and interviews conducted earlier during the research for our volume *Everyday Communalism: Riots in Contemporary UP* (New Delhi: OUP, 2019). Also, numerous interviews of prominent BSP,

BJP and Bhim Army leaders, journalists, writers, commentators and scholars on the subject, during 2021-22. Fresh fieldwork was also conducted in 2021 and immediately prior to the 2022 assembly elections.

19   Gail Omvedt, 'Kanshi Ram and the BSP' in *Caste and Class in India*, ed. K.L. Sharma, Jaipur: Rawat Publications, 1994), pp.153–57.

20   Sudha Pai, 'Changing Political Preferences Among Dalits in Uttar Pradesh in the 2000s: Shift from Social Justice to Aspiration', *Journal of Social Inclusion* (19 July 2019), https://doi.org/10.1177%2F2394481119852190.

21   Oliver Heath and Sanjay Kumar, 2012.

22   We use the terms Chamar and Jatav to describe the dominant sections among the Scheduled Castes in UP. In UP, according to the Census, there are 66 sub-castes or jatis, identified as those standing below the line of pollution, which in the ritual hierarchy separates the upper caste 'clean' from the 'unclean' castes considered untouchable. There is, at the same time, considerable differentiation among those placed below the line of pollution. (See, Louis Dumont, *Homo Hierarchicus: The Caste System and Its Implications*, University of Chicago Press, 1970). Among them the Jatavs constitute a distinct section of the Chamars found in western UP, who have a strong sense of pride in their low-caste identity. Though they experimented with Sanskritization and attempted upward mobility in the caste system in the colonial period, compared to the smaller Dalit sub-castes, the process of Hinduization did not have much of an impact on them. Owen Lynch's study on Agra shows they prospered due to the leather industry started by the British after 1857, creating not just a new identity of *Jatav-Kshatriya* for themselves but also a legend to prove it, and emulating customs used by Kshatriyas (Owen Lynch, *Politics of Untouchability: Social Mobility and Change in a City of India*, Columbia University Press, 1969). They put pressure on the British government to recognize them as *Jatav-Kshatriya* in the 1931 Census and hoped the caste Hindus would accept this step; however, this did not happen.

Another reason for their dominant position in western UP was the construction of canals and early commercialization of agriculture in the colonial period, due to which almost all agricultural development took place in this region. The Jatavs received a share in the prosperity of their landlords. Mohinder

Singh's study, based in the 1940s, shows that the Jatavs of western UP were more prosperous, better fed, housed and clad, and closer to their Punjabi neighbours than the Chamars of eastern UP and Bundelkhand who lived in extreme poverty, and often performed *begari* for their landlords (Mohinder Singh, *The Depressed Classes: Their Economic and Social Condition*, Bombay: Hindi Kitabh, 1947, pp. 32-33). Historically, the Jatavs have been at the forefront of all social movements in north India, including in the formation of the BSP. As Mayawati belongs to the Jatav community, they are loyal to her and a large section has remained with her, despite the decline of the BSP.

23   Sudha Pai, 'From Social Justice to Aspiration: Transformation of Lower Caste Politics in Uttar Pradesh in the 2000s', in Sujata Patel (ed.), *Neoliberalism, Urbanisation and Aspirations in Contemporary India*, (New Delhi: OUP, 2021).

24   Hugo Gorringe, *Untouchable Citizens: The Dalit Panthers and Democratisation in Tamil Nadu* (New Delhi: Sage, 2005).

25   Ibid.

26   Kanshi Ram conceptualized that the Dalit movement would pass through two stages. The first was capturing power through mobilization and electoral victory from the Brahmins. It was in the second stage, with the use of state power, that the revolution could, under the leadership of the BSP, penetrate into society, transforming it. Kanshi Ram, *Era of the Stooges*, 1982.

27   In the national elections of 2014 and 2019, the BJP received over 40 per cent of the votes of smaller Dalit sub-cast and around 17 per cent of the votes of the Jatavs; in the 2017 assembly election it received 37 per cent and 8 per cent respectively. See tables 3 and 4 in Appendix.

28   Amit Ahuja, *Mobilizing the Marginalized: Ethnic Parties without Ethnic Movements* (New Delhi: OUP, 2019).

29   Ibid.

30   Nilanjan Mukhopadhyay in our extended interaction with him on Zoom on 9 January 2022.

31   Ibid.

32   Karishma Mehrotra, 'How BJP marketed to a new voting bloc: the 22 crore beneficiaries', *The Indian Express*, (23 May 2019), https://indianexpress.com/article/india/how-bjp-marketed-to-a-new-voting-bloc-the-22-crore-beneficiaries-5745514/

1: *The Sarvajan Experiment*

1   The two slogans reflect the changing electoral strategy of the BSP,
from a Dalit party to one that attempted to gain the support
of all sections of society and to work for them. The first slogan
was used in the late 1980s/early 1990s by the BSP under Kanshi
Ram to challenge the upper castes. The *tilak* or caste mark
denoted the Brahmin, *tarazu* or weighing scales the Vaishya or
trader, and *talwar* or sword, the Kshatriya or warrior. The BSP
exhorted Dalits to throw shoes at them. Kanshi Ram argued
that this was to introduce confidence among Dalits so that they
could challenge the so-called twice-born castes, rather than an
expression of abuse. Ian Duncan, in 'Dalits and politics in rural
North India: Bahujan Samaj party in Uttar Pradesh', *The Journal
of Peasant Studies* 27(1) (1999): 35-60, has given an interesting
reason for the use of such slogans. He points out that the D-S4,
(Dalit Shoshit Samaj Sangharsh Samiti) formed by Kanshi Ram
in 1981, and the BSP, inherited the tradition of shouting slogans
during demonstrations and processions from the Republican
Party of India (RPI), the main vehicle for Ambedkarite politics
in the 1960s. Some of the election campaigns of the RPI were
contested in court, particularly the Allahabad High Court, on the
charge that campaigners were seeking to win votes on the basis of
caste and religion. One of the slogans used was *Thakur, Brahman
aur Lala/Kardo inka muh kala* (Thakur, Brahmin and Bania,
blacken their faces). While the slogan was intended to disgrace
the Hindu upper castes, it also meant the *Jatavs* did not like the
upper castes calling them black. This is seen in the attempt to
rhyme Lala/kala, where kala means black and Lala is a Hindi
word for Bania.

The second slogan was used during the campaign for the 2007
assembly election. Literally it meant that Behenji (Mayawati) was
entering the election fray for the uplift of the entire society and
not just Dalits. It reflected the shift towards the sarvajan strategy
of the BSP by which the party attempted to gain the support of
the upper castes in order to obtain a majority. Sudha Pai, 'From
Dalit to Savarna: The Search for a New Social Constituency by
the Bahujan Samaj Party in Uttar Pradesh' in Sudha Pai (ed.),
*Political Process in Uttar Pradesh: Identity, Economic Reforms
and Governance* (New Delhi: Pearson Longman, 2007).

2   An edited volume by Sudha Pai published prior to the 2007 elections, in which a number of scholars discussed the Sarvajan strategy and the possibilities of its success, was greeted with much skepticism and incredulity by journalists and scholars. But following the elections, the same book was used to explain how the victory was made possible. See review of the book by Harish Khare, 'Political churning in U.P.', *The Hindu*, 22 May 2007. Sudha Pai (ed.), *Political Process in Uttar Pradesh: Identity, Economic Reforms and Governance*, (New Delhi: Pearson Longman, 2007).

3   No major political commentator or psephologist predicted the BSP winning a full majority, including those at Star News, the Indian Express, CNN, IBN7, NDTV, India TV or Sahara TV. Instead, each of them foresaw a hung assembly suggesting that the BSP would get between 103 and 168 seats. While many put the BSP and the SP in the same range, the SP eventually wound up with less than half of the BSP's seats.

4   Farzan Ahmed, Ashok K. Damodaran, 'Mayawati rules Uttar Pradesh', *India Today*, 21 May 2007, https://www.indiatoday.in/magazine/cover-story/story/20070521-bsp-pride-mayawati-748519-2007-05-21

5   On this slogan and reasons for its use see endnote 1.

6   The Editors, *Himal Southasian*, 1 June 2007, https://www.himalmag.com/king-mayawati/

7   New Delhi: *The Times of India*, 12 May 2007.

8   Vivek Kumar, 'Bahujan Samaj Party: Some Issues of Democracy and Governance' in Sudha Pai (ed.), *Political Process in Uttar Pradesh: Identity, Economic Reforms and Governance* (New Delhi: Pearson Longman, 2007).

9   Lalmani Verma, 'Explained: Why is Mayawati wooing Brahmins again ahead of 2022 assembly elections?' *Indian Express*, 12 August 2020, https://indianexpress.com/article/explained/explained-why-mayawati-is-wooing-the-brahmins-again-ahead-of-2022-assembly-elections-6550437/

10   The term is derived from the name of the legendary author Manu who composed the law code, the Manu-smriti (Laws of Manu), which upholds the caste system. Hence, the use of the term 'Manuvadi' for upper-caste parties.

11   For the meaning of these two slogans, and detailed reasons for their use by the BSP in the 1990s, see endnote 1.

12   A.R. Akela, *Kanshi Ram Saahab ke sakshatkaar* (Interviews with Kanshi Ram), (Aligarh: Anand Sahitya Sadan, 2006).

13   This was 22 per cent within the undivided state of UP, but following the formation of the state of Uttarakhand, the percentage of Dalits is now 21 per cent.

14   *Patrika* April 1992, https://m.patrika.com/newsdog/etawah-news/untold-story-of-bsp-leader-slogan-writer-khadin-abbas-4448800/?fromNewsdog=1&utm_source=NewsDog&utm_medium=referral

15   In the Lok Sabha by-polls in Gorakhpur and Phulpur in eastern UP in March 2018, and in Kairana in June 2018 in western UP, the BJP was defeated by an alliance of the SP-BSP and SP-BSP-RLD respectively, see chapter 3.

   Sudha Pai, 'Changing Political Preferences Among Dalits in Uttar Pradesh in the 2000s: Shift from Social Justice to Aspiration,' *Journal of Social Inclusion Studies* 5(1) (2019): 33–43. DOI: 10.1177/2394481119852190.

16   Personal interview with Naseemuddin Siddiqui on 22 September 2021, at his residence at Lucknow.

17   Raghav Khattri, 'Meerabai Guest House Horror: When a BJP MLA Saved Mayawati from SP Goons', *Politics*, (19 January 2019).

18   *Madam Chief Minister* is a 2021 Hindi-language political drama film, directed by Subhash Kapoor with actor Richa Chadda in the lead role of Mayawati. The film's official announcement was made by Chadda on 12 February 2020. It portrays a Dalit politician taken under the wing of a powerful entity rising to become Chief Minister. Subhash Kapoor's film has borrowed generously from Mayawati's life. *The Times of India*, (22 January 2021).

19   Pradeep Kumar, 'Dalits and the BSP in UP Issues and Challenges', *Economic and Political Weekly*, Vol. 34, No. 14, 3 April 1999, pp. 822–6.

20   Sudha Pai, *Dalit Assertion and the Unfinished Democratic Revolution: The Bahujan Samaj Party in Uttar Pradesh* (New Delhi: Sage Publications), 2002, p. 169.

21   Abhay Kumar Dubey, 'Anatomy of a Dalit Player: A Study of Kanshi Ram' in Ghanshyam Shah (ed.), *Dalit Identity and Politics* (New Delhi: Sage Publications, 2001), pp. 289–310.

22   Sudha Pai, 'Pradhanis in the New Panchayats: Field Notes From Meerut', *Economic and Political Weekly*, 2 May 1998.

23   For Mayawati's policies, see Department of Information and Public Relations, Government of Uttar Pradesh, Report Issued on 20 September 1997: 'Sushri Mayawati Ke Gatisheel Netritwa Mein Uttar Pradesh Sarkar Ke Pramukh Nirnay Awam Thos Uplabdhiya' (in Hindi), Lucknow.

24   In the 1996 assembly elections, the BSP gave Dalits 28 per cent, OBCs 24 per cent, Muslims 18 per cent, and upper-caste candidates 16.6 per cent seat share. But in 1998 the share of Dalits fell to 25 per cent, the BCs were given 41 per cent, an increase of more than 10 per cent since the 1996 assembly elections. Among them, it was the MBCs who received 66 per cent of the total tickets given to the backwards.

25   The BSP allotted 20 seats to the Dalits, 38 to the BCs, and 10 to the upper castes (5 Brahmins and 5 Thakurs).

26   'Industrialist-politician Jayant Malhotra conveys Kanshi Ram's message to PM Rao over dinner', *India Today*, 15 November 1993, https://www.indiatoday.in/magazine/indiascope/story/19931115-industrialist-politician-jayant-malhotra-conveys-kanshi-ram-message-to-pm-rao-over-dinner-811783-1993-11-15

27   Sambiah Gundameda, 'The Bahujan Samaj Party: Between Social Justice and Political Practice', *Social Change* 44(1): 2014, pp. 21–38.

28   Swati Mathur, 'Jatavs on top of SC population in UP', *The Times of India*, 4 July 2015, https://timesofindia.indiatimes.com/city/lucknow/jatavs-on-top-of-sc-population-in-up/articleshow/47931787.cms

29   See Part 2, Chapter 1.

30   After Sone Lal Patel's death in a road accident in 2009, his wife Krishna Patel became National President of Apna Dal. His daughter Anupriya Patel was elected to Lok Sabha in 2014 from Mirzapur Lok Sabha constituency. When the party split, Anupriya Patel named her party Apna Dal (Sonelal) and won from Mirzapur again in 2019 in partnership with the BJP. In the recent 2022 elections her party won 12 seats.

31   Sharad Pradhan, 'Kanshi Ram declares Mayawati as his successor', Rediff.com, 15 December 2001. https://www.rediff.com/news/2001/dec/15bsp.htm

32 In the early 1990s the BJP under the leadership of Lal Krishna Advani, then president of the BJP, had undertaken a Rath Yatra from September to October 1990 across the country to Ayodhya. The purpose of the yatra was to support the agitation, led by the Vishwa Hindu Parishad (VHP) and its affiliates in the Sangh Parivar, to erect a temple to the Hindu deity Rama on the site of the Babri Masjid. Sudha Pai, 'From Dalit to Savarna: The Search for a New Constituency by the Bahujan Samaj Party in Uttar Pradesh', in Sudha Pai (ed.), *Political Process in Uttar Pradesh: Identity, Economic Reforms and Governance* (New Delhi: Pearson/Longman), pp. 221–240.

33 In the assembly elections, the BJP gained 88 seats and 20.08 per cent of the votes, while the Congress dropped to a historic low of 25 seats with 8.96 per cent votes (Pai 2002: p. 237). In the by-elections to two Lok Sabha and 16 assembly seats, the BJP won only one seat; in seven of the 16 assembly seats, it got less than 5 per cent of the valid votes polled, and in only two of the 18 elections did its vote share cross even 25 per cent. (*The Times of India*, New Delhi, 11 June 2005).

34 *The Times of India*, 17 May 2002.

35 In 2007, the Supreme Court disqualified 13 of the 37 MLAs of the BSP for breaking away from the parent party and merging with the SP in UP in August 2003. The case of the 24 other BSP MLAs who had also defected was referred back to the speaker of the state. This disqualification of the 13 MLAs declared the split in the BSP void and illegal. However, Mulayam Singh called for a floor test and mustered the support of 223 MLAs in the 402-member assembly.

36 Interview with Siddiqui on 22September 2021 at his residence in Lucknow.

37 Sambiah Gundameda, 'The Bahujan Samaj Party: Between Social Justice and Political Practice,' *Social Change* 44(1): 2014, pp. 21–38.

38 Ibid.

39 As related by Siddiqui during our interaction with him on 22 September 2021 at his residence in Lucknow.

40 These are ground-level committees that were constituted with the aim to promote amity between communities. The word 'bhai-chara' means brotherhood, and in this case, inter-caste brotherhood.

41 Panna means page, so 'panna pramukh' is a person in charge of
    ensuring that all voters are registered, their names are put on the
    voter list, they go to the polling booth and they vote. They are
    also expected to persuade people to vote for the BJP.
42 As related by Siddiqui during our interaction with him on 22
    September 2021 at his residence in Lucknow.
43 Dipankar Gupta and Yogesh Kumar, 'When the Caste Calculus
    Fails: Analysing BSP's Victory in UP', *Economic and Political
    Weekly*, 18 August 2007, Special article, pp. 3383–96.
44 'The saga of Mayawati's Banda trio in BSP, once trusted and now
    banished', *India Today* Web Desk, 15 May 2017, https://www.
    indiatoday.in/india/story/naseemuddin-siddiqui-mayawati-bsp-
    babu-singh-kushwaha-nrhm-scam-976782-2017-05-12
45 Online interaction with Satish Chandra Mishra on 12 July 2021.
46 Satish Mishra has served on many committees in the Rajya Sabha
    such as External Affairs, Parliament Local Area Development
    Scheme, Business Advisory Committee, Wakf committee and
    Forum on Youth.
47 'The saga of Mayawati's Banda trio in BSP, once trusted and now
    banished', *India Today* Web Desk, 15 May 2017, https://www.
    indiatoday.in/india/story/naseemuddin-siddiqui-mayawati-bsp-
    babu-singh-kushwaha-nrhm-scam-976782-2017-05-12
48 Ibid.
49 Anil K. Verma, 'BSP's Strategy in Uttar Pradesh: Wooing the
    Brahmins for a New Alliance', *Economic and Political Weekly*,
    25 June 2005, pp. 2647–48.
50 *The Hindu*, 10 June 2005.
51 *The Times of India*, New Delhi, 18 June 2005.
52 *The Hindu*, 10 June 2005.
53 Anil K. Verma, 'BSP's Strategy in Uttar Pradesh: Wooing the
    Brahmins for a New Alliance', *Economic and Political Weekly*,
    25 June 2005, pp. 2647–48.
54 *The Times of India*, New Delhi, 18 June 2005.
55 Anil K. Verma, 'BSP's Strategy in Uttar Pradesh: Wooing the
    Brahmins for a New Alliance', *Economic and Political Weekly*,
    25 June 2005, p. 2647.
56 Smita Gupta, 'The Rise and Fall of Hindutva in Uttar Pradesh,
    1989-2004', in Sudha Pai (ed.), *Political Process in Uttar
    Pradesh: Identity, Economic Reforms and Governance* (New
    Delhi: Pearson Longman), 2007.

57   *The Hindustan Times*, New Delhi, 2 May 1999.

58   Ibid.

59   *The Times of India*, New Delhi, 16 July 2005.

60   See Table 1 in Appendix.

61   Anil K. Verma, 'BSP's Strategy in Uttar Pradesh: Wooing the Brahmins for a New Alliance', *Economic and Political Weekly*, 25 June 2005, pp. 2647-8.

62   Ibid.

63   Dipankar Gupta and Yogesh Kumar, 'When the Caste Calculus Fails: Analysing BSP's Victory in UP', *Economic and Political Weekly* (18 August 2007), Special article, pp. 3383–96.

64   Ibid.

65   Ibid.

66   Ibid.

67   Anil K. Verma, 'BSP's Strategy in Uttar Pradesh: Wooing the Brahmins for a New Alliance', *Economic and Political Weekly*, 25 June 2005, pp. 2647–48.

68   Ibid.

69   In the 1996 Lok Sabha election, upper-caste support gained by the BSP was quite insignificant (4.1 per cent) when calculated as part of the total upper-caste votes. In the 2002 assembly and the 2004 Lok Sabha elections, the BSP gained only 6 and 5 per cent of the Brahmin vote, respectively. Much of the widening of its base in the 1990s was because of greater support from the MBCs (most backward classes) rather than from the upper-castes. Pradeep Kumar, 'Dalits and the BSP in UP: Issues and Challenges', *Economic and Political Weekly*, Vol. 34, Issue No. 14, 3 April 1999, p. 823.

70   For 2007, see Table 2 in Appendix.

2: Sarvajan in Practice

1   Venkitesh Ramakrishnan, 'Dalit power', *Frontline* (1 June 2007), https://frontline.thehindu.com/cover-2

2   Santosh Mehrotra, 'As Uttar Pradesh heads to polls, how does the Yogi govt's economic performance hold up?' *The Wire* (20 December 2021).

3   Ibid.

4   Ashish Tripathi, 'How dalits have actually fared in Uttar Pradesh', *The Economic Times*, 1 November 2011, https://economictimes. indiatimes.com/news/politics-and-nation/how-dalits-have-actually-fared-in-uttar-pradesh/articleshow/10562987. cms?from=mdr

5   Venkitesh Ramakrishnan, 'Dalit power', *Frontline* (1 June 2007), https://frontline.thehindu.com/cover-6

6   Ibid.

7   Ibid.

8   Rajbhar said: 'They have grown up with the BSP from the state of being nobodies, who could not even exercise their franchise, to the point of getting a Chief Minister on the strength of their own party. Clearly, their social, political and cultural standing has improved and they know this will improve further in due course.' *Frontline* (1 June 2007): 7.

9   Man Mohan Rai, 'Maya, 49 ministers sworn in', *The Economic Times*, 14 May 2007, https://economictimes.indiatimes. com/news/politics-and-nation/maya-49-ministers-sworn-in/ articleshow/2042080.cms?from=mdr

10   HT Correspondent Lucknow 'Satish Misra to quit government, Mayawati' *Hindustan Times*, 27 June 2007, https://www. hindustantimes.com/lucknow/satish-misra-to-quit-government-mayawati/story-wrPqapuHqdrhuE8gePtVqL.html

11   Ibid.

12   Sudha Pai, 'Populism and Economic Reform: The BJP Experiment in Uttar Pradesh' in Jos Mooij (ed.), *Politics of Economic Reform in India* (New Delhi: Sage Publications, 2005), p. 101.

13   *Frontline* (24 May 2002): 20.

14   Lalmani Verma 'Mayawati memorials cost Rs 5,919 cr, says LDA' *Indian Express* 21 May, 2012 http://archive.indianexpress.com/ news/mayawati-memorials-cost-rs-5919-cr-says-lda/951755/

15   Ibid.

16   The state's annual growth declined from 3.1 per cent in the period 1990–92 to 2.4per cent during 1992–96. While total government expenditure as a proportion of state domestic product (SDP) increased from 19.82 per cent in 1996–97 to 26.96 per cent in 1998–99, revenue receipts stagnated at around 13.3 per cent of the SDP. Consequently, by the end of the 1990s, total indebtedness of the state government was nearly two-fifths of UP's income. The fiscal and revenue deficits touched about 7.9 per cent and 5.7

per cent respectively of the SDP by 1998–99.Ajit K. Singh,'The Economy of Uttar Pradesh since the 1990s' in Sudha Pai (ed.), *Political Process in Uttar Pradesh Identity, Economic Reforms and Governance* (New Delhi: Pearson Longman), pp. 273–294.

17   National Human Development Report (2001):140-41.

18   Venkitesh Ramakrishnan,'Dalit Power', *Frontline* (1 June 2007): 8.

19   'Mayawati wants Rs 80,000 crore to change the face of UP', *The Indian Express*, 21 July 2007.

20   Ibid.

21   Ibid.

22   Siddharth Kalhans,'Mayawati has new proposal: socio-economic engineering', *The Indian Express*, New Delhi, 11 August 2007.

23   'Maya gets her way, PM clears Rs 80,000 crore', *The Indian Express*, New Delhi, 19 February 2008.

24   Ibid.

25   Table 5 is taken from Sudha Pai (unpublished paper), 'Building Caste-Class alliances: The BSP experiment in Uttar Pradesh' presented at a workshop on Political Economy of Caste Class Alliances in India, JNU, 2015. For this paper, a few days' fieldwork was undertaken in Lucknow in August 2011. Senior officials of the CM's secretariat, who did not wish to be named, provided the figures.

26   For detailed expenditure on other areas see Table 5 in Appendix.

27   A list is provided in Rahil, 'List of top, major achievements of Mayawati as UP's Chief Minister', *The IndianWire*, 5 September 2018, https://www.theindianwire.com/politics/achievements-of-mayawati-as-up-cm-71637/

28   A study by Shyam Singh of some key policies of the BSP government in its first three years in office enables us to evaluate its performance: 'Three years of BSP government in UP', *Economic and Political Weekly*, 18 September 2010. Also see, 'Mayawati launches welfare scheme for the poor', *The Hindu*, New Delhi, 2 November 2010.

29   Ibid.

30   Shyam Singh, 'Three years of BSP government in UP', *Economic and Political Weekly*, 18 September 2010, pp. 77–81.

31   Ibid.

32   Lalmani Verma, 'Housing for urban poor: govt issues fresh guidelines', *The Indian Express*, 5 December 2009, https://

indianexpress.com/article/cities/lucknow/housing-for-urban-poor-govt-issues-fresh-guidelines/

33   Shyam Singh, 'Three years of BSP government in UP', *Economic and Political Weekly*, 18 September 2010, pp. 77–81.

34   Ibid.

35   Rahil, 'List of top, major achievements of Mayawati as UP's Chief Minister', *The Indian Wire*, 5 September 2018, https://www.theindianwire.com/politics/achievements-of-mayawati-as-up-cm-71637/

36   C.S. Verma, 'Maternal health services in Uttar Pradesh: Has JSY delivered?' *International Journal of Social Science and Development Policy*, Vol. 2 No. 1 (January-June 2016): 49–61.

37   'Mayawati ki Sarkar ke chhe mahki uplabhdiya is bath ki sacshi he', Information and Publicity Department, Government of UP, Lucknow. Advt in *The Times of India*, New Delhi, 13 November 2007.

38   The UP government established an anti-terror squad (ATS) in 2007 to deal with terrorist activities in the state. *About Us ATS* website of the Uttar Pradesh police, https://uppolice.gov.in/pages/en/topmenu/police-units/anti-terrorist-squad-(ats)/en-about-us-ats September 21, 2022.

39   'Mayawati works in 2007 to 2012', Voice of Dalits, YouTube. This YouTube video showcases the achievements of the Mayawati government https://www.youtube.com/watch?v=7NN_Mb_u6as

40   '18 companies bid for Ganga Expressway', *The Hindu*, 7 December 2007.

41   Masoodul Hasan, 'UP CM announces Ganga Expressway', *Hindustan Times*, Lucknow, 5 September 2007, https://www.hindustantimes.com/lucknow/up-cm-announces-ganga-expressway/story-Ka6R9yZjN7HYlhsj5yUzxN.html

42   S.K. Ramachandran, 'Mayawati hails Delhi Metro's maiden journey into Noida,' *The Hindu*, 12 November 2009, https://www.thehindu.com/news/cities/Delhi/Mayawati-hails-Delhi-Metrorsquos-maiden-journey-into-Noida/article16891717.ece

43   Much before the central government, or any of the industrialized states of India, on 8 September 2002, the Mayawati government had passed a UP SEZ Act to provide for the constitution of an Authority for the development of certain areas in the state into industrial and urban economic zones, and enable land acquisition for SEZs. The earlier Act was amended in 2007 and detailed rules

provided to enable industrial houses to acquire land and build industry. Sudha Pai and Avinash Kumar, 2014, 'Land Acquisition for SEZs: Contrasting Cases from the National Capital Region', in Rob Jenkins, Lorraine Kennedy and Partha Mukhopadhayay (eds), *Power Policy and Protest: The Politics of India's Special Economic Zones* (New Delhi: OUP).

44   'NTPC, UP ink MoU for 1,320-Mw plant', *Business Standard*, 5 February 2013. The eight plants expected to add capacity were Paricha (500 MW), Harduaganj (500 MW), Anpara D (500 MW) and Obra (1,000 MW) in the public sector; Anpara C (1,200 MW), Roja (1,200 MW), Bara (1,980 MW) and Karchana (1,320 MW) were given to the private sector.

45   Built by EMC, a Kolkata-based company in collaboration with the UP Power Corporation Ltd and the Poorvanjal Vidyut Vitran Nigam Ltd. The estimated cost of this project was Rs 800 crore and the project took 7 years to complete. The total number of solar modules used is 21,300, which would continue to produce electricity even during overcast weather.

46   *The Indian Express*, November 2013.

47   'OPD at Kanshiram hospital in Greater Noida starts', Times News, 3 April 2013.

48   Purusharth Aradhak, 'Noida to have India's best child medical institute: UP chief secretary', *The Times of India*, 2 September 2013.

49   Aniruddha Ghosal 'Dream run for Mayawati's govt schools', *The Times of India*, 1 June 2013, https://timesofindia.indiatimes. com/city/noida/dream-run-for-mayawatis-govt-schools/ articleshow/20375167.cms

50   Maulshree Seth, 'State hires pvt firm to run its Nivesh Mitra in top gear', *The Indian Express*, 23 February 2011, https:// indianexpress.com/article/lucknow/state-hires-pvt-firm-to-run-its-nivesh-mitra-in-top-gear/

51   'Maya gifts Asia's largest sewage plant to Lucknow', *The Times of India*, New Delhi, 16 January 2011, https://timesofindia. indiatimes.com/city/lucknow/maya-gifts-asias-largest-sewage-plant-tolucknow/articleshow/7294611.cms. It was a partial relief for the heavily polluted river Gomti, as 290 million litres per day (mld) of sewage was pumped into the 342 mld STP at Bharwaha close to the state capital.

52 'Formula One in India', *The Hindu* Editorial, https://www.
    thehindu.com/opinion/editorial/formula-one-in-india/
    article2589379.ece
53 Ibid.
54 Shilpa Kannan, 'Why India's Formula 1 Grand Prix is under
    threat', BBC News (New Delhi), 25 October 2013, https://www.
    bbc.com/news/business-24659690
55 The Ambedkar Village programme originally begun by Mulayam
    Singh in 1991 during the centenary celebration of B.R. Ambedkar
    was taken forward on a larger scale by Mayawati. During
    her 1995 and 1997 regimes, villages in UP with a majority of
    Dalits were identified and were provided funds for one year for
    infrastructure development such as roadbuilding, bricklaying,
    drinking water schemes, building drains, etc. These projects
    were taken up by the panchayats. Loans were also given to buy
    buffaloes, build houses, and engage in dairying and poultry, bee-
    hiving and other small businesses. It improved the infrastructure
    and conditions of these villages; however, since these two tenures
    of Mayawati's regime were short, only some villages benefitted.
    For details, see Sudha Pai, *Dalit Assertion and the Unfinished
    Democratic Revolution: The Bahujan Samaj Party in Uttar
    Pradesh* (New Delhi: Sage Publications, 2002), Chapter 3.
56 'Mayawati to develop gram sabhas', *The Hindu*, Reuters, 14
    September 2007.
57 Ibid.
58 'Mayawati ki Sarkar ke chhemahki uplabhdiya is bath kisacshi
    he', Information and Publicity Department, Government of UP,
    Lucknow. Advt in *The Times of India*, New Delhi, 13 November
    2007.
59 'Mayawati gives landholding to Dalits', *The Economic Times*,
    New Delhi, 11 June 2010.
60 'Demolished stadium left a void hard to fill', Express News
    Service, Lucknow, 14 August 2010, http://archive.indianexpress.
    com/news/demolished-stadium-left-a-void-hard-to-fill/660075/
61 Ibid.
62 The ten most important were Dr Bhimrao Ambedkar Samajik
    Parivartan Sthal, Manyawar Kanshi Ram Memorial, Kanshi Ram
    Museum, Kanshi Ram Bahujan Nayak Park, Ramabai Ambedkar
    Rally Maidan, Kanshi Ram Sanskritik Sthal, Dr Bhimrao
    Ambedkar Samajik Parivartan Prateek Sthal, Manyawar Kanshi

Ram Yaadgar Vishram Sthal, Buddha Sthal and Sharda Canal Front Development. Lalmani Verma, 'Maya's Memorials', *The Indian Express*, New Delhi, 28 December 2008.

63 'Eco-friendly' Mayawati gifts Rs 834 cr park', *The Times of India,* Times News Network, 4 March 2011, https://timesofindia. indiatimes.com/city/lucknow/eco-friendly-mayawati-gifts-₹-834-cr-park/articleshow/7623582.cms

64 Lalmani Verma, 'Maya's Memorials', *The Indian Express*, New Delhi, 28 December 2008, http://archive.indianexpress.com/news/mayas-memorials/403670/0

65 Ibid.

66 Ajoy Bose, *Behenji: A Political Biography of Mayawati* (New Delhi: Penguin Books, 2009).

67 *Hindustan Times*, Lucknow, 14 April 2008.

68 'Maya warns of "consequences" if Dalit leaders' statues are demolished', Expressindia.com, 17 September 2009.

69 Anant Zanane, 'Mayawati inaugurates Rs685-crore memorial park in Noida India', *Kashish*, Updated: 14 October 2011, NDTV, https://www.ndtv.com/india-news/mayawati-inaugurates-₹-685-crore-memorial-park-in-noida-572902

70 'Defiant India leader gets new rupee garland', BBC News, 17 March 2010. http://news.bbc.co.uk/2/hi/south_asia/8571983.stm

71 'Garland made of Rs 1000 notes presented to Mayawati', *The Times of India*, 15 March 2010, http://articles.timesofindia. indiatimes.com/2010-03-15/india/28115473_1_bsp-rally-memorials-and-parks-statues

72 Interaction with Sudhindhra Bhadoria on 1 November 2021 at his office in Vasant Kunj, New Delhi.

73 'BSP's regime better than SP, Digvijaya says', *The Times of India*, Press Trust of India, 8 September 2013.

74 'Sonia praises Mayawati, calls her symbol of women's empowerment', *The Times of India*/TNN, 19 March 2011.

75 '"Dalit dominant" BSP better than "Goonda Raj" SP: Beni Prasad Verma', ANI News, 16 May 2016.

76 'Maulana Ahmed Bukhari praises Mayawati, says she only knows how to rule', *The Economic Times*/PTI, 22 April 2013.

77 Ashish Tripathi, 'How Dalits have actually fared in Uttar Pradesh', *The Economic Times*, 1 November 2011, https://economictimes. indiatimes.com/news/politics-and-nation/how-dalits-have-

actually-fared-in-uttar-pradesh/articleshow/10562987.
cms?from=mdr

78 Ibid.

79 Seminar at the Observer Research Foundation, New Delhi, on 23–24 May 2008. The papers presented have been published in *Uttar Pradesh: The Road Ahead*, ed. Venkitesh Ramakrishnan, (New Delhi: Academic Foundation,2009).

80 V. Ravi Shankar, 'Development of Uttar Pradesh Performance and Prospects', in Venkitesh Ramakrishnan (ed.), *Uttar Pradesh: The Road Ahead* (New Delhi: Academic Foundation, 2009), pp. 85–88.

81 Anand Swarup, 'Governance of Uttar Pradesh: A Case Study for Effective Restructuring in Venkitesh Ramakrishnan (ed.), *Uttar Pradesh: The Road Ahead* (New Delhi: Academic Foundation, 2009), pp. 121–134.

82 Hari Singh Tyagi, 'New Social Consensus in UP: Problems and Possibilities' in Venkitesh Ramakrishnan (ed.), *Uttar Pradesh: The Road Ahead* (New Delhi: Academic Foundation, 2009), pp. 47–54.

83 *Patta* is a legal document in the name of the actual owner of a particular plot of land.

84 Venkitesh Ramakrishnan, 'The New Consensus Needs a Socio-political Ideology', in Venkitesh Ramakrishnan (ed.), *Uttar Pradesh: The Road Ahead* (New Delhi: Academic Foundation 2009), pp. 61–65.

85 Ashish Tripathi, 'CAG reports tabled in UP assembly reveal financial irregular of over ₹10,000 crore in Mayawaiti's rule', *The Times of India* (30 May 2012), https://timesofindia. indiatimes.com/india/cag-reports-tabled-in-up-assembly-reveal-financial-irregularities-of-over-₹-10000-crore-in-mayawaitis-rule/articleshow/13676599.cms

86 Ibid.

87 Melia Belli, 'Monumental pride: Mayawati's memorials in Lucknow', *Ars Orientalis*, Vol. 44, https://quod.lib.umich. edu/a/ars/13441566.0044.006/--monumental-pride-mayawatis-memorials-in-lucknow?rgn=main;view=fulltext

88 Ibid.

89 'Thousands throng Ambedkar Memorial', *The Indian Express*, 7 December 2009, http://www.indianexpress.com/news/thousands-throng-ambedkar-memorial/550767/.

90 Jason Burke, 'Mayawati – the untouchable idol of India's most populous state', *The Guardian* Profile, 7 February 2012.
91 Ibid.
92 Ashish Tripathi, 'How Dalits have actually fared in Uttar Pradesh', *The Economic Times*, 1 November 2011, https://economictimes. indiatimes.com/news/politics-and-nation/how-dalits-have-actually-fared-in-uttar-pradesh/articleshow/10562987. cms?from=mdr
93 Omar Rashid, 'Talking statues at the Ambedkar Park in Lucknow', *The Hindu*, Lucknow, 10 February 2019, https://www.thehindu. com/news/national/talking-statues-at-the-ambedkar-park-in-lucknow/article26231160.ece
94 Ibid.
95 Sanjay Singh, 'Operation damage control', *The Indian Express*, New Delhi, 27 May 2010.
96 Subodh Ghildiyal, 'Maya has opp. on mat as BSP sweeps UP bypolls', *The Times of India*, New Delhi, 17 April 2008. The BSP government had announced that political parties, in keeping with constitutional provisions, could not participate in the elections. Hence all parties put up their candidates as 'independents' and supported them.
97 Ibid.
98 Amita Verma, 'UP BSP wins the panchayat poll', *Deccan Chronicle*, 1 November 2010, http://www.deccanchronicle.com/national
99 Table 2 (see appendix), compiled from 'Special Statistics, Sixteenth Assembly Elections', *Economic and Political Weekly*, 2012, p. 83.
100 See Chapter 2.
101 Oliver Heath and Sanjay Kumar, 'Why Did Dalits Desert the Bahujan Samaj Party in Uttar Pradesh?', *Economic and Political Weekly*, 14 July 2021, p. 44.

3: Disillusionment, Decline, Existential Crisis

1 Shivam Vij, 'Why Mayawati's defeat is the BSP's victory', rediff. com March, 6 March 2012, https://www.rediff.com/news/column/why-mayawatis-defeat-is-the-bsps-victory/20120306. htm
2 Ibid.

3   S. Prasannarajan, 'Mayawati manages to preserve her social core', *India Today*, 10 March 2012.

4   Oliver Heath and Sanjay Kumar, 'Why Did Dalits Desert the Bahujan Samaj Party in Uttar Pradesh?', *Economic and Political Weekly*, 14 July 2012. Following delimitation, the number of seats reserved for Dalits declined from 89 to 85.

5   See Table 1 in the Appendix.

6   Census 2001: 3.

7   Oliver Heath and Sanjay Kumar, 'Why Did Dalits Desert the Bahujan Samaj Party in Uttar Pradesh?', *Economic and Political Weekly*, 14 July 2012.

8   Shivam Vij, 'Why Mayawati's defeat is the BSP's Victory', 7 March 2012, https://kafila.online/2012/03/07/why-mayawatis-defeat-is-the-bsps-victory/

9   Shivam Vij, 'The Mayawati era is over. Bye Bye Behenji', *The Print*, 27 January 2020.

10 Rehanamol Raveedran, 'Bhim Army and Azad Samaj Party mark a new phase of Dalit assertion', *The Indian Express,* 18 March 2020.

11 Suryakant Waghmore, 'The competing armies of Bhim', *India Today*, 22 September 2018.

12 The survey is provided in detail in Oliver Heath and Sanjay Kumar, 2012.

13 Ibid. Table 7: 17.

14 Ibid. Table 5: 14.

15 Ibid. 13.

16 Ibid.

17 Ibid. 23.

18 Mulayam literally meant he had a strategy or plan of action to remove Mayawati from power. He used the instance of the overthrow of Hosni Mubarak of Egypt in February 2011 during the Egyptian Revolution, to say he would similarly throw out Mayawati from power and recapture the state of UP.

19 Sudha Pai, 'Mulayam Singh, man with a plan', *The Indian Express*, New Delhi, 12 March 2011, https://indianexpress.com/article/opinion/columns/mulayam-singh-man-with-a-plan/

20 Pervez Iqbal, 'Mayawati regime doing better on law and order than Mulayam's?' *The Economic Times*, 28 June 2011.

21 To strengthen democracy two special institutional commands, namely, 'Lokpal' and 'Lokayukta 'were recommended by the First

Administrative Reforms Commission (ARC) of India (1966-1970) to redress citizens' grievances against the administration. Dr L.M. Singhvi in 1963 coined the terms Lokpal and Lokayukta. Meant to check corruption, the idea had been discussed for some time. It finally took shape with the passing of the Lokpal and Lokayukta Bill, 2013, in the Lok Sabha with the support of all major political parties, but only after a countrywide protest led by India Against Corruption, a civil society movement of activist Anna Hazare. The Lokpal and Lokayukta Act, 2013 aims to establish the institution of the Lokpal at the Central level and Lokayukta at the state level. K. Deepalakshmi, 'The long wait for a Lokpal', *The Hindu*, 27 April 2017.

22 Details provided in Chapter 2.

23 Swati Mathur, 'CAG raps Maya statues worth Rs 288 crore', TNN, 7 August 2011.

24 Teena Thacker, 'Behind UP doctors' killings, multi-crore health fraud', *The Indian Express*, 18 July 2011, http://www.indianexpress.com/story-print/818963/

25 Piyush Srivastava, 'Mayawati government spends on parks, ignores healthcare, education and infrastructure', *India Today*, 11 August 2011, https://www.indiatoday.in/india/north/story/mayawati-government-uttar-pradesh-luxury-statue-citizens-neglected-139133-2011-08-11

26 Ibid.

27 'Mayawati speaks on Muzaffarnagar violence: Highlights', NDTV.com, 9 September 2013, https://www.ndtv.com/india-news/mayawati-speaks-on-muzaffarnagar-violence-highlights-534061

28 Sanjay Pandey, 'Riot-accused BSP MP to face wife in Muzaffarnagar seat', *Deccan Herald*, 19 March 2014, https://www.deccanherald.com/content/393221/riot-accused-bsp-mp-face.html

29 Sudha Pai, 'Caste in the same mould', *The Indian Express*, 15 April 2014.

30 Ibid.

31 At the Idea Exchange interaction of *The Indian Express* on 13 May 2014 after voting in the Lok Sabha elections concluded, Amit Shah claimed that the BJP would win 50–55 seats and the BSP would emerge as the second largest party in Uttar Pradesh. http://indianexpress.com/article/india/politics/50-55-for-bjp-bsp-second-in-up-amit-shah/).

32 Sudha Pai and Avinash Kumar, 'Understanding the BJP's Victory in Uttar Pradesh,' in Paul Wallace (ed.), *India's 2014 Elections: A Modi-led BJP Sweep* (New Delhi: Sage Publications, 2014), pp. 119-138.

33 Ibid.

34 Sajjan Kumar, 'Dalits solidly behind BSP in Uttar Pradesh', *The New Indian Express*, 11 January 2017, https://www.newindianexpress.com/nation/2017/jan/11/dalits-solidly-behind-bsp-in-uttar-pradesh-1558335.html

35 Ibid.

36 Ibid.

37 Sudha Pai, 'Will Mayawati succeed in uniting Dalits and Muslims ahead of the UP elections?' *The Wire*, 26 August 2016, https://thewire.in/politics/will-mayawati-succeed-in-uniting-dalits-and-muslims-ahead-of-the-up-elections

38 Ashutosh Bharadwaj, 'Searching for Dalits: A yatra by Buddhist monks taking BJP to Dalits across UP', *The Indian Express*, 31 July 2016.

39 Diksha, literally meaning 'preparation or consecration for a religious ceremony', is giving of a mantra or an initiation by a guru into Indian religions such as Hinduism, Buddhism and Jainism. In this instance, the reference is to the conversion by Dr Ambedkar to Buddhism at Nagpur on 4 October 1956. This place is now referred to as Dikshabhumi and is a place for pilgrimage by Buddhists 'Nagpur's Diksha Bhoomi Now an "A" Class Tourist Destination', *Loksatta*, 8 March 2016.

40 Ibid.

41 Ibid.

42 Ritika Chopra, 'Rohith Vemula was not a Dalit, says probe panel set up by HRD Ministry', *The Indian Express*, 6 October 2016.

43 Sanjay Singh, 'BJP's Tiranga Yatra on Independence Day: Propaganda or national unity?' *Firstpost*, 20 July 2016, https://www.firstpost.com/india/bjps-tiranga-yatra-on-independence-day-propaganda-or-national-unity-2903672.html

44 'Boost for Mayawati as 4 Muslim MLAs join BSP', *The Hindu*, 11 August 2016, https://www.thehindu.com/news/national/other-states/Boost-for-Mayawati-as-4-Muslim-MLAs-join-BSP/article14562543.ece

45 Sudha Pai, 'Will Mayawati succeed in uniting Dalits and Muslims ahead of the UP elections?', *The Wire*, 26 August 2016.

46   Ibid.
47   See Table 1 in Appendix.
48   See Table 3 in Appendix.
49   Extended interaction with Harish Damodaran on 2 February 2022.
50   The All India Backward and Minority Communities Employees Federation (BAMCEF) was formed in 1971. It attempted to unite educated SC, ST and minority government employees who were expected to donate a portion of their salary. It was a think-tank and fund-raising organization that prepared the ground for the formation of the BSP in 1984.

The Dalit Shoshit Samaj Sangharsh Samiti (DS-4), formed in 1981, was the agitational arm of the Bahujan movement. Before the formation of the BSP, DS-4 entered local elections in Delhi and Haryana in the name of 'Limited Political Action'. Later on, Kanshi Ram dissolved DS-4 and formed the BSP as a completely political wing.
51   Damodaran in our interaction with him.
52   Interview by Sajjan Kumar of Shrawan Kumar Nirala at Gorakhpur on 24 January 2022.
53   The complete interview of his career and the formation of a Dalit organization by him is given in Chapter 7.
54   Long list of BSP leaders sacked by Mayawati, TOI/TNN, 23 June 2016.
55   'Mayawati expels old loyalist Daddu Prasad', *The Times of India*, 29 January 2015, https://timesofindia.indiatimes.com/city/lucknow/maya-expels-old-loyalist-daddu-prasad/articleshow/46047744.cms
56   Lalmani Verma, 'Dara Singh Chauhan: UP OBC leader's stint was "uneasy" with BJP, journey started from BSP', *The Indian Express*, 12 January 2022.
57   Ramendra Singh, 'Swami Prasad Maurya's exit: BSP loses OBC face, Mayawati's voice before the media', *The Indian Express*, 23 July 2016.
58   'After Maurya, another BSP rebel plans "grand rally",' TOI/PTI, 11 July 2016, https://timesofindia.indiatimes.com/city/lucknow/after-maurya-another-bsp-rebel-plans-grand-rally/articleshow/53155395.cms
59   'After Swamy Prasad Maurya, RK Chaudhry, Mayawati's aide Brajesh Pathak jumps ship, joins BJP', *Firstpost*, 22 August 2016,

https://www.firstpost.com/politics/after-swamy-prasad-maurya-rk-chaudhry-mayawatis-close-aide-brijesh-pathak-jumps-ship-joins-bjp-2970440.html. Brajesh Pathak became an important leader in the BJP in UP and has been made a minister in the new Yogi Adityanth cabinet following the victory in 2022. Mayawati lost an important organization man; he has worked hard for the BJP. Some of the success of the 2022 elections is attributed to him.

60 'The saga of Mayawati's Banda trio in BSP, once trusted and now banished', *India Today* web desk, 15 May 2017, https://www.indiatoday.in/india/story/naseemuddin-siddiqui-mayawati-bsp-babu-singh-kushwaha-nrhm-scam-976782-2017-05-12

61 Ibid.

62 Interview by Sajjan Kumar on 2 September 2021 at his residence in Lucknow. Siddiqui spent over two hours with him and was very forthcoming on many issues.

63 'Dayashankar Singh compares Mayawati to prostitute: Comments by UP leaders embarrassed BJP', *The Indian Express* web desk, 21 July 2016, https://indianexpress.com/article/india/india-news-india/prostitute-mayawati-dayashankar-singh-haramzada-bjp-bsp-yogi-adityanath-sakshi-maharaj-sadhvi/

64 'Expelled Leader Siddiqui says Mayawati made objectionable comments against Muslims', *Hindustan Times*/PTI, Lucknow, 10 May 2017.

65 Ibid.

66 On this, also see 'The saga of Mayawati's Banda trio in BSP, once trusted and now banished', *India Today* web desk, 15 May 2017, https://www.indiatoday.in/india/story/naseemuddin-siddiqui-mayawati-bsp-babu-singh-kushwaha-nrhm-scam-976782-2017-05-12

67 Ibid.

68 Interview with Sudhindra Bhadoria, 1 November 2021, at his residence in Vasant Kunj, New Delhi.

69 'Nasimuddin Siddiqui, former BSP stalwart, joins Congress', India.com, 22 February 2018, https://www.india.com/news/india/nasimuddin-siddiqui-former-bsp-stalwart-joins-congress-2908748/

70 Ramendra Singh, 'Naseemuddin Siddiqui, BSP leader who enjoyed Mayawati's trust for decades', *The Indian Express*, 11 May 2017.

71 'Naseemuddin Siddiqui expelled from BSP, hits back at Mayawati', *Mint*/PTI, 10 May 2017, https://www.livemint.com/Politics/BeJbD7r7kvyo18vxNYYIPL/Naseemuddin-Siddiqui-expelled-from-BSP-hits-back-at-Mayawat.html

72 As told by Sudhindhra Bhadoria during our interaction with him on 1 November 2021, at his residence in Vasant Kunj, New Delhi.

73 'Mayawati quits Rajya Sabha, says she was muzzled', *The Hindu*, 18 July 2017.

74 Ramendra Singh, 'UP election results 2017: SP, BSP lose strongholds too', *The Indian Express*, 12 March 2017, https://indianexpress.com/elections/uttar-pradesh-assembly-elections-2017/uttar-pradesh-assembly-election-results-2017-bjp-sp-samajwadi-party-bsp-bahujan-samaj-party-lose-strongholds-too-4565984/

75 Sudha Pai, 'Changing political preferences among Dalits in Uttar Pradesh in the 2000s: Shift from social justice to aspiration', *Journal of Social Inclusion Studies* (19 July 2019), https://doi.org/10.1177/2394481119852190

76 Ibid.

77 Manoj Singh, 'Has the SP-BSP alliance for the Gorakhpur and Phulpur by-polls rattled the BJP in UP?' *The Wire*, 11 March 2018 https://thewire.in/politics/sp-bsp-alliance-gorakhpur-phulpur-by-polls-bjp-up

78 Ibid. For details of the Gorakhnath temple close to Gorakhpur, see Sudha Pai and Sajjan Kumar, *Everyday Communalism: Riots in Contemporary Uttar Pradesh* (New Delhi: OUP, 2018), pp. 118–122.

79 Sudha Pai and Sajjan Kumar, *Everyday Communalism: Riots in Contemporary Uttar Pradesh* (New Delhi: OUP, 2018).

80 Sudha Pai, 'Changing political preferences among Dalits in Uttar Pradesh in the 2000s: Shift from social justice to aspiration', *Journal of Social Inclusion Studies*, 19 July 2019, https://doi.org/10.1177/2394481119852190

81 Gyan Verma and Anuja, 'SP and BSP tie up for Uttar Pradesh ahead of 2019 polls', *Mint*, 12 January 2019, https://www.livemint.com/Politics/LYio0BWCxrTZ3sdsMjnEZI/SP-and-BSP-join-hand-for-Uttar-Pradesh-ahead-of-2019-polls.html

82 Ankur Bharadwaj, 'Elections 2019: Will SP-BSP alliance maths trump Modi's chemistry in UP?' *Business Standard*, 2 January 2019, https://www.business-standard.com/article/politics/elections-

2019-will-sp-bsp-alliance-maths-trump-modi-s-chemistry-in-up-119010200312_1.html

83 Rajesh Kumar Singh and Pankaj Jaiswal, 'Lok Sabha Elections 2019: How SP-BSP aim to repeat 1993 BJP defeat', *Hindustan Times*, 12 March 2019, https://www.hindustantimes.com/lok-sabha-elections/lok-sabha-elections-2019-how-sp-bsp-aim-to-repeat-1993-bjp-defeat/story-FUG4PljzkNByrnz5rrDjiK.html

84 Kumar Anshuman, 'SP, BSP and RLD begin campaign to prevent vote split', *The Economic Times,* 19 May 2019, https://m.economictimes.com/news/elections/lok-sabha/uttar-pradesh/sp-bsp-rld-begin-campaign-to-prevent-vote-split/articleshow/68474164.cms

85 See Table 1 in Appendix.

86 'Lok Sabha verdict 2019: BJP wins 62 seats in Uttar Pradesh, SP BSP Alliance gets 15', *The Times of India*/PTI, 24 May 2019, https://timesofindia.indiatimes.com/city/lucknow/lok-sabha-verdict-2019-bjp-wins-62-seats-in-uttar-pradesh-sp-bsp-alliance-gets-15/articleshow/69478766.cms

87 The CSDS tables refer to the smaller non-Jatav Dalits as 'Other Dalits', see Table 2 in Appendix.

88 Table 4 in Appendix.

4: BJP's Politics of Dalit Inclusion

1 *Daily News and Analysis* (DNA), Diligent Media Corporation, 30 April 2014.

2 http://www.india272.com/2013/11/08/modi-charms-baharaich-vijayshankhnadrally/

3 'The idea behind BJP's campaign song, *Ache Din Aane Wale Hain*', Zee News, July 2014.

4 See Table 1 in Appendix.

5 Ibid.

6 'UP Election Results 2017: Modi wave sweeps BJP to 312 seats; landslide win stuns Akhilesh, Mayawati, Congress', *Firstpost*, 12 March 2017.

7 See Table 4 in Appendix.

8 Vidhi Choudhary, Gyan Varma and Makarand Gadgil, 'The ad agencies behind BJP's successful campaign', *Mint,* 9 October 2014.

9   Sudha Pai and Sajjan Kumar, 'War of Perception, Brand Modi and Voters' Choice', in Paul Wallace (ed.), *India's 2019 Elections: The Hindutva Wave and Indian Nationalism* (New Delhi: Sage Publications, 2020).

10   Literally, discussion over tea. In the 2014 campaign Modi, addressing voters from a tea stall in Gujarat, called upon them to hold '*chai pe charcha*' sessions as this was the place people congregated and talked. He said, 'Tea stall is like a "Footpath Parliament", all topics under the sun are discussed.' He added, 'I have myself learnt a lot while selling tea'. The programme was relayed at 1,000 tea stall locations identified by the BJP in 300 cities across the country, including 61 locations in 22 cities and towns in Gujarat, via video conferencing. See 'Narendra Modi kicks off BJP's "Chai Pe Charcha" campaign; says tea stalls are like Footpath Parliament',agencies,https:// economictimes.indiatimes.com/news/politics-and-nation/ narendra-modi-kicks-off-bjps-chai-pe-charcha-campaign-says- tea-stalls-are-like-footpath-parliament/articleshow/30290418. cms?from=mdr

11   Edward S. Herman and Noam Chomsky, *Manufacturing Consent: The Political Economy of the Mass Media* (New York: Pantheon Books, 1988).

12   Vidhi Choudhary, Gyan Varma and Makarand Gadgil, 'The ad agencies behind BJP's successful campaign', *Mint*, 9 October 2014.

13   Rajdeep Sardesai, *2014: The Election That Changed India* (UK: Penguin, 2015).

14   On this see Swati Chaturvedi, *I Am a Troll* (Delhi: Rupa Publications, 2016).

15   Karishma Mehrotra, 'After 2014 digital debut, 2019 push came from BJP cadre', *The Indian Express*, 24 May 2019, https://indianexpress.com/elections/lok-sabha-elections-2019- results-after-2014-digital-debut-2019-push-came-from-bjp- cadre-5745537/

16   Sudha Pai and Avinash Kumar, 'Understanding the BJP's Victory in Uttar Pradesh', in Paul Wallace (ed.), *India's 2014 Elections: A Modi-led BJP Sweep* (New Delhi: Sage publications, 2014), pp. 119–38.

17   Sudha Pai and Sajjan Kumar, *Everyday Communalism: Riots in Contemporary Uttar Pradesh* (New Delhi: OUP, 2018).

18 Extensive online interaction with Swapan Dasgupta on 12 January 2022 on various aspects of the BJP's ideology.

19 Nilanjan Mukhopadhyay (interaction on 9 January 2022) and Sudhindra Kulkarni (interaction on 22 December 2021) also agreed that the mobilization of the Dalits is more recent, the latter describing it as a 'centerpiece' of Modi's politics.

20 Ibid.

21 Sudha Pai and Sajjan Kumar, *Everyday Communalism: Riots in Contemporary Uttar Pradesh* (New Delhi: OUP, 2018).

22 Badri Narayan, *Fascinating Hindutva: Saffron Politics and Dalit Mobilization* (New Delhi:Sage Publications, 2009), p. ix.

23 Ibid.:10.

24 Ibid.: 30.

25 Ibid.: 94.

26 For details see Sudha Pai and Sajjan Kumar, 2018.

27 Ibid.

28 Vijayendra Rao and Michael Walton (eds.), *Culture and Public Action* (New Delhi: Permanent Black), 2004.

29 Eric Hobsbawm and Terence Ranger (eds.), *The Invention of Tradition* (Cambridge: Cambridge University Press, 1983).

30 Paul Brass, *Ethnicity and Nationalism: Theory and Comparison* (New Delhi: Sage Publications, 1991), p. 75.

31 Ibid.

32 S. Bhatt, 'Why Modi had to get rid of Harin Pathak', *India Abroad*, 4 April 2014.

33 Walter Anderson, 'The BJP: A Victory for Narendra Modi', in Paul Wallace (ed.), *India's 2014 Elections: A Modi-led BJP Sweep* (New Delhi: Sage Publications, 2015), pp. 46–64.

34 A political sobriquet which literally means 'Monarch of the Hindu Hearts' or crusader of Hindutva. Many politicians have used it—Bal Thackeray, Kalyan Singh and Yogi Adityanath—but Modi has been able to use it for high electoral gain and social engineering to absorb Dalits into the larger Hindu identity. First used in Gujarat for Modi, it was later used in national elections. Though 'Vikas Purush or 'Development Man' was used in 2014 and subsequently, in recent years, particularly after 2019, with emphasis on religiosity witnessed in the building of the Ram Temple, the term has re-surfaced and been used again. 'Tracking Hindu Hriday Samrat as a Political Slogan', *The Madras Mail*,

15 February 2022, https://madrascourier.com/opinion/tracking-hindu-hriday-samrat-as-a-political-slogan/

35 Sudha Pai and Avinash Kumar, 2015.

36 Modi used the controversial Gujarat Model during the 2014 election campaign claiming it underlay the growth of 10 per cent over the past ten years in the state, above the national average at 7.71 per cent. The Congress party decried it as crony capitalism and pointed to the large number of poor in Gujarat, but it caught the imagination of the poor and migrant voters in UP and elsewhere. Jerin Mathew, 'India elections 2014: Can Narenda Modi make his Gujarat model work?' *International Business Times*, 16 May 2014, https://www.ibtimes.co.uk/india-elections-2014-can-narenda-modi-make-his-gujarat-model-work-1448844

37 R.B. Bhagat and S. Mohanty, 2009 'Emerging Pattern of Urbanization and the Contribution of Migration in Urban Growth in India', *Asian Population* Studies, Vol. 5, No. 1, 2009, pp. 5–20.

38 Sudha Pai,'Economic Backwardness and Migratory Patterns in Uttar Pradesh in the 2000s: A Research Note', unpublished paper, February 2021, written in the context of the crisis of reverse migration during the Covid pandemic in 2020.

39 Bharatiya Janata Party, *Manifesto 2014*, www.bjp.org/manifesto2014

40 Mahapanchayats refers to the larger panchayats consisting of villagers from many villages held during the Muzaffarnagar riots to discuss future course of action on the part of Dalits. See Sudha Pai and Sajjan Kumar, *Everyday Communalism: Riots in Contemporary Uttar Pradesh* (New Delhi: OUP, 2018).

41 Appu Esthose Suresh, 'Express investigation part-I: Over 600 "communal incidents" in UP since LS results, 60 per cent near bypoll seats', *The Indian Express*, 9 August 2014, https://indianexpress.com/article/india/uttar-pradesh/express-investigation-part-iii-dalit-muslim-divide-deepens-goes-rural/

42 Ibid.

43 A longitudinal fieldwork done by Sajjan Kumar in western Uttar Pradesh, Meerut, Muzaffarnagar, Shamli and Saharanpur districts during December 2012–January 2013, February 2014, October 2016–June 2017, March 2019 and October-2021 through February 2022.

44 Appu Esthose Suresh, 'Express investigation part-III: Dalit-Muslim divide deepens, goes rural,' *The Indian Express*, 9 August 2014, https://indianexpress.com/article/india/uttar-pradesh/express-investigation-part-iii-dalit-muslim-divide-deepens-goes-rural/.

45 Ibid.

46 Shikar Jiwrajkar, 'Exclusive: All you want to know about the Saharanpur riots in Uttar Pradesh', India.com, 27 July 2014.

47 Mihir Shah, 'View: India's economy is ailing from more than Covid-19', *The Economic Times*, 26 June 2020, https://economictimes.indiatimes.com/news/economy/indicators/view-indias-economy-is-ailing-from-more-than-covid-19/articleshow/76637162.cms

48 Ibid.

49 'India's unemployment rate rises to 27.11 per cent amid COVID-19 crisis: CMIE', *The Hindu-BusinessLine*/PTI, 5 May 2020.

50 Maitreesh Ghatak and Udayan Mukherjee, 'The Mirage of Modinomics', *The India Forum*, 8 March 2018.

51 Abhishek Anand, Vikas Dimble and Arvind Subramanian, 'New Welfarism of Modi govt represents distinctive approach to redistribution and inclusion', *The Indian Express*, 22 December 2020.

52 Ibid.

53 Ibid.

54 Karishma Mehrotra, 'How BJP marketed to a new voting bloc: the 22 crore beneficiaries', *The Indian Express*, 23 May 2019, https://indianexpress.com/article/india/how-bjp-marketed-to-a-new-voting-bloc-the-22-crore-beneficiaries-5745514/

55 Ibid.

56 Ibid.

57 Interaction with Swapan Dasgupta on 12 January 2022.

58 The field study done by Sajjan Kumar was supported by Peoples Pulse, a Hyderabad-based research institution and Asiaville Media outlet.

59 Punjab, with army personnel of 89,088, accounts for 7.7 per cent of the army's rank and file, even though its share of the national population is 2.3 per cent. Maharashtra, with 87,835 soldiers, occupies the third slot followed by Rajasthan, with 79,481 soldiers.

60 Sudha Pai and Sajjan Kumar, 'Phase-2 not easy turf for the Mahagathbandhan in Uttar Pradesh', *The Wire*, 18 April 2019, https://thewire.in/politics/elections-2019-uttar-pradesh-phase-2

61 Ibid.

62 'An overwhelming majority of non-Yadav, non-Jatav, non-Muslim respondents in our field study, selected on the basis of purposive sampling in every Lok Sabha constituency, shared the perception that a Modi-led BJP was the need of the hour on account of his bold and decisive leadership image—something that helped BJP overcome its poor developmental record.

63 B. Ravichandran, 'By washing feet, PM Narendra Modi was honouring himself not safai karamcharis', *The Print*, 26 February 2019.

64 Kapil Dikshit, 'PM Narendra Modi washes feet of sanitary workers', *The Times of India*, 25 February 2019.

65 Table 1 in Appendix.

66 Sudha Pai, 'Other Aspirational Class', *The Economic Times*, New Delhi, 24 May 2009.

67 Table 4 in Appendix.

5: Dalit Preference and Protest

1 Ritwika Mitra, 'Anti-Dalit violence: Victims, families feel it is still a long way to justice', *The New Indian Express*, 5 October 2020, https://www.newindianexpress.com/nation/2020/oct/05/uttar-pradesh-records-highest-number-of-atrocities-against-dalits-accounts-for-over-25oftotal-ca-2205992.html

2 For details on this framework see, Sajjan Kumar, 'Political Dynamism and Electoral Determinism', unpublished PhD thesis, *Hindutva, Mandal and State Security Discourses: Reconstitution of Muslim Identity Since the 1980s,* Centre for Political Studies, Jawaharlal Nehru University, 2016.

3 Ritwika Mitra, 'Anti-Dalit violence: Victims, families feel it is still a long way to justice', *The New Indian Express*, 5 October 2020.

4 Devyani Srivastav, *IndiaSpend*, 9 October 2020.

5 Ritwika Mitra, 'Anti-Dalit violence: Victims, families feel it is still a long way to justice', *The New Indian Express*, 5 October 2020.

6 See chapter 4 for more on this aspect.

7   Field work for this chapter was conducted by Sajjan Kumar during September 2021 and again in February 2022 in western and eastern UP.

8   Interview on 22 December 2021 at India International Centre, New Delhi.

9   Ibid.

10   Ibid.

11   Sudha Pai, 'From social justice to aspiration: Transformation of lower caste politics in Uttar Pradesh in the 2000s' in Sujata Patel (ed.), *Neoliberalism, Urbanization and Aspirations in Contemporary India* (New Delhi: OUP, 2021).

12   There are other smaller organizations, formed more recently in UP, which are active on the ground particularly when atrocities take place. They are discussed in chapter 8.

13   Sudha Pai, 'The BJP is losing the support of the Dalits in the Hindi heartland', *The Wire*, 4 April 2018.

14   Pawan Dixit, 'Living in fear: Dalits still at receiving end of caste atrocities in Uttar Pradesh', *Hindustan Times*, 31 January 2017.

15   Piyush Srivastava, '3 Dalit girls gangraped and murdered in UP village', *India Today*, 22 March 2015.

16   CSDS National Election Study, UP Post Poll 2017.

17   UP accounted for 43 per cent of the total number of cases registered of harassment against minorities and SCs in 2018-19. Mukesh Rawat, 'With 43% share in hate crimes, UP still most unsafe for minorities, Dalits', *India Today*, 19 July 2019.

18   Sudha Pai and Sajjan Kumar, 'Saharanpur protests herald new phase in Dalit politics', *The Wire*, 24 May 2017.

19   Ibid.

20   Field work by Sajjan Kumar in May and June 2017 following the violent incidents at Saharanpur.

21   Saharanpur Nagar Assembly constituency is one of the 403 constituencies of the Uttar Pradesh Legislative Assembly. It is a part of the Saharanpur district and one of the five assembly constituencies in the Saharanpur Lok Sabha constituency.

22   Ibid.

23   'In Saharanpur, another youth shot at, UP govt suspends DM and SSP,' *The Indian Express*, New Delhi, 25 May 2017.

24   Abhishek Angad, 'On the run, Bhim Army founder at Jantar Mantar: stage set for struggle', *The Indian Express*, New Delhi, 22 May 2017.

25 'Bhima-Koregaon violence: FIR against Jignesh Mevani, Umar Khalid for "provocative" speeches in Pune"', *The Indian Express,* 4 January 2018, https://indianexpress.com/article/cities/pune/fir-registered-against-jignesh-mevani-umar-khaid-for-provocative-speeches-in-pune-bhima-koregaon-5010950/

26 Sudha Pai,'The BJP is losing the support of Dalits in the Hindi heartland', *The Wire,* 4 April 2018.

27 Ibid.

28 'Parliament passes bill to restore original SC/ST atrocity law', *The Times of India,* 9 August 2018. Retrieved from https://timesofindia.indiatimes.com/india/parliament-okays-bill-to-restore-original-sc/st-atrocity-law/articleshow/65340768.cms

29 'As Bharat bandh gains steam, upper caste Hindus in rural UP take to the streets to protest SC/ST amendment Act', *Firstpost,* 12 September 2018. Retrieved from https://www.firstpost.com/videos/india/as-bharat-bandh-gains-steam-upper-caste-hindus-in-rural-up-take-to-the-streets-to-protest-scst-amendment-act-5168661.html

30 Rajasthan, Telangana, Chhattisgarh, Mizoram, MP election results 2018: Highlights, TimesofIndia.com, 12 December 2018.

31 Sudha Pai, 'Changing political preferences among Dalits in Uttar Pradesh in the 2000s: Shift from social justice to aspiration', *Journal of Social Inclusion,* 19 July 2019, https://doi.org/10.1177/2394481119852190

32 Ibid.

33 Kumar Abhishek, 'UP government orders early release of Bhim Army Chief Chandrashekhar', *India Today,* 13 September 2018.

34 'Bhim Army chief released after confidential report, not for Dalit votes: UP law minister', *Outlook,* 23 September 2018.

35 Ibid.

36 The RLD won no seat in its stronghold of western UP, the BSP and SP won three each; in eastern UP the BSP won seven seats, the SP gained only one. In Rohilkhand, the alliance had expected a number of seats due to the demographic preponderance of Yadavs and Muslims in combination with Jatav Dalits, but the SP gained only one seat.

37 Sudha Pai, 'Other aspirational class', *The Economic Times,* New Delhi, 24 May 2019.

38 Ravish Tiwari, 'BSP's heartland surge flattens identity politics in UP, Bihar', *The Indian Express,* 24 May 2019, https://

indianexpress.com/article/explained/lok-sabah-elections-results-bjps-heartland-surge-flattens-identity-politics-in-up-bihar-5745501/

39 Unnati Sharma, 'Before Hathras and Balrampur, UP reported at least 6 rape-murders in August', *The Print*, 2 October 2020.

40 Kumar Abhishek, 'Minor girl gang-raped, strangled in UP's Lakhimpur Kheri; cops deny family's "eyes gouged, tongue slit" claim', *India Today*, 16 August 2020.

41 'Uttar Pradesh horror: Dalit woman gang-raped by two in Balrampur, dies', *Business Standard*, 1 October 2020.

42 'Balrampur: Anger grows after new India "gang rape" death', BBC News, October 2020.

43 In 1980, the Balmiki Dalits were attacked by the locally dominant Jats. For details see, Vijay Joshi, 'Caste conflict in Hathras', *Economic and Political Weekly*, Vol. 15, No. 29, 19 July 1980, p. 1211.

44 'Allahabad HC takes suo motu cognisance of Hathras gang-rape', https://timesofindia.indiatimes.com/city/lucknow/allahabad-hc-takes-suo-motu-cognisance-of-hathras-gang-rape-case/articleshow/78432852.cms, accessed on 26 December 2021.

45 Kumar Abhishek, 'Minor girl gang-raped, strangled in UP's Lakhimpur Kheri; cops deny family's "eyes gouged, tongue slit" claim', *India Today*, 15 August 2020, https://www.indiatoday.in/crime/story/minor-dalit-girl-gang-raped-strangled-uttar-pradesh-lakhimpur-kheri-eyes-gouged-tongue-slit-1711717-2020-08-16

46 Omar Rashid and Vijita Singh, 'Four farmers killed as car in Union Minister's convoy runs amok in Uttar Pradesh', *The Hindu*, 3 October 2021, https://www.thehindu.com/news/national/other-states/farmers-killed-as-car-in-union-ministers-convoy-runs-amok/article36807735.ece

47 BJP's Harvinder Sahani won the Palia constituency of Lakhimpur Kheri district by 38,129 votes, Shashank Verma the Nighasan seat by 41,009 votes, Yogesh Verma the Lakhimpur seat by 3,537, Saurabh Singh the Kasta seat by 13,817, Lokendra Singh the Mohammadi seat by by 4,871 votes, Arvind Giri theGola Gokranath constituency by 29,294 votes, Manju Tyagi the Sri Nagar constituency by 15,159 votes, Vinod Shankar the Dhaurahra seat by 24, 610 votes; 'UP elections: BJP wins all eight seats in Lakhimpur Kheri district', *Scroll*, 10 March 2022.

48 'How BJP micro-managed Lakhimpur Kheri and adjoining areas in UP', *Business Standard*/IANS, 18 March 2022.

49 'Stay in your house, notice to Bhim army chief over UP rape protest. Cops deny', https://www.hindustantimes.com/india-news/stay-in-your-house-notice-to-bhim-army-chief-over-up-rape-protest-cops-deny/story-7Qd0Us3jXsEHRxUAaYfZJM. html, accessed on 26 December 2021.

50 'Hathras case: FIR registered against Chandrashekhar Azad for violating Section 144', https://www.hindustantimes.com/india-news/hathras-case-fir-registered-against-chandrashekhar-azad-for-violating-section-144/story-kTfXMKi6LraiyYuEt5I0JI.html, accessed on 26 December 2021.

51 'Hathras incident: BSP defends absence of workers on ground', https://timesofindia.indiatimes.com/city/lucknow/hathras-incident-bsp-defends-absence-of-workers-on-ground/articleshow/78524361.cms, accessed on 26 December 2021.

52 'Dalits in Agra burn Mayawati's effigy over her silence on Hathras gang-rape case', https://www.news18.com/news/politics/dalits-in-agra-burn-mayawatis-effigy-over-her-silence-on-hathrasgang-rape-case-2951249.html, accessed on 26 December 2021.

6: Dalit Shift: Tactical-Instrumental or Ideological

1 Sudheendra Kulkarni in our extended interaction with him at the India International Centre on 22 December 2021.

2 Most studies, as our narrative has shown in chapter 1 Part II, focus on the methods used by the BJP under the leadership of Modi, such as promises of rapid development, welfare, use of social media, nationalism and cultural mobilization that have succeeded in attracting a section of Dalit voters. Others point to an ideological shift, a new form of 'ethno-political majoritarianism, but delinked from religious Hindu nationalism which has been the key to the party's ability to attract new voters'. Pradeep Chibber and Rahul Verma, 'The rise of the second dominant party system in India: BJP's new social coalition', *Studies in Indian Politics*, Vol. 7, No. 2, 2019, pp.131–148. Another view is that the BJP succeeded because of its ability to spread its message of majoritarianism, and attributes 'the increase in the majoritarian sentiment to the systematic matching of the BJP's ideology to the demand side of political culture'. The narrative of victimhood and dominance creates a craving for 'leadership' which, since 2014, the BJP has resoundingly met with Modi leading the

campaign. Suhas Palshikar, 'Towards hegemony: BJP beyond electoral dominance', *Economic and Political Weekly*, Vol. 53, Issue No. 33, 18 August 2018. Still others suggest an 'interactive theory of social identity' arguing that consolidation of Hindu nationalism among all castes/classes is being authored not only by parties or the state, but also by middle-class Indians, leading to its spread in micro-public spheres in times of apparent peace between elections. Aseema Sinha and Manisha Priyam, 'Willing ethnic-nationalists, diffusion, and resentment in India: A micro-foundational account', unpublished paper. A survey of public opinion across 23 states in India, between elections, shows how it is shaped by social attitudes, inter-community relationships and governance patterns and how these variables in turn shape voting behaviour in the next round of elections. It shows that Hindu Dalits, swayed by cultural nationalism, particularly in the Hindi heartland, tend to support a majoritarian position. Siddharth Swaminathan and Suhas Palshikar, *Politics and Society Between Elections Public Opinion in the Indian States* (South Asia: Routledge, 2021).

3   Two eminent commentators, Nilanjan Mukhopadhyay and Sudheendra Kulkarni, with whom we held extended discussions on the subject, gave importance to both the immediate shifts in the 2000s and the historical process of Hinduization. They linked it with the present, arguing that the process has intensified since the revival of the BJP.

4   Nilanjan Mukhopadhyay in an extended interaction on Zoom, 9 January 2022.

5   Ibid.

6   Many saw it as a big step to gain power. See Vivek Kumar, 'Bahujan Samaj Party: Some Issues of Democracy and Dominance', in Sudha Pai (ed.), *Political Process in Uttar Pradesh: Identity, Economic Reforms and Governance* (New Delhi: Pearson Longman, 2007), pp. 241–272.

7   Anand Teltumbde, 'A Mayawi revolution', *Economic and Political Weekly*, Vol. 42 Issue No. 23, 9 June 2007.

8   Eminent journalist Harish Khare in our discussion with him on 20 January 2022.

9   Professor Ravi Kant, faculty at Hindi department, Lucknow University, in a discussion on the state of BSP and Dalits, on 25 September 2021, at his university office.

10 Sudheendra Kulkarni in our interaction with him on 22 December 2021.

11 Ibid.

12 The DMK is the major party in Tamil Nadu; it arose out of the non-Brahmin movement in the colonial period and has since stood for social justice to the backward castes in the state. Today it is in power under M.K. Stalin, son of Karunanidhi, the protégée of Annadurai who formed the party in 1949. For the DMK, see Hugo Gorringe, 2005.

13 Ibid.

14 Nilanajan Mukhopadhyay in our interaction with him 9 January 2022.

15 On new welfarism and labharti, see Chapter 4. The impact of labharti in the 2022 assembly elections is also described in the Epilogue.

16 Mukhopadhyay mentioned in our interaction with him that he had occasion to see the excel sheets of labhartis with their names, addresses and other details maintained by BJP workers.

17 A recent example is the mention in a speech during the campaign for the 2022 assembly election by Modi, that as soon as the BJP returned to power in UP on 10 March, provision would be immediately made to deal with stray cattle that was eating farm crops, creating massive losses for farmers across the state.

18 Vivek Gupta, 'Punjab: "Don't get distracted, vote for jobs, education," say youth from Kanshi Ram's village', *The Wire*, 18 February 2022.

19 Sudheendra Kulkarni in our interaction with him on 22 December 2021.

20 Ibid.

21 Ibid.

22 Ibid.

23 Mark Jurgensmeyer, *Religious Rebels in the Punjab: The Social Vision of the Untouchables* (New Delhi: Ajanta Publications, 1988), p. 163. Ambedkar visited Agra in 1936 which had an impact on the Chamar-Jatavs of the region. Owen Lynch describes it as a 'turning point'. Owen Lynch, *Politics of Untouchability Social Change and Mobility in a City of India* (Columbia: Columbia University Press), 1969, pp. 86–87.

24 Sudheendra Kulkarni in our interaction with him.

25 The line of pollution refers to the line in the caste system above which are the clean castes, i.e. Brahmin, Kshatriya, Vaishya and Shudra. Those standing below this line are the 'polluted' or (former) untouchable castes today referred to as scheduled castes.

26 On this see Sudha Pai, *Dalit Assertion and the Unfinished Democratic Revolution: The BSP in Uttar Pradesh* (New Delhi: Sage Publications, 2002).

27 G.W. Briggs, *The Chamars* (London: 1920).

28 Owen Lynch, 1969.

29 Gulshan Swarup Saxena, *Arya Samaj Movement in India 1857-1947* (New Delhi: Commonwealth Publishers, 1990).

30 Gail Omvedt, 'Kanshi Ram and the BSP' in K.L. Sharma (ed.), *Caste and Class in India* (Jaipur: Rawat Publications, 1994), p. 160.

31 Owen Lynch, 1969: 72.

32 Mohinder Singh, *The Depressed Classes: Their Economic and Social Condition* (Bombay: Hindi Kitabh, 1947), pp. 32–33.

33 Sudheendra Kulkarni in our interaction with him on 22 December 2021.

34 Rajiv Atwal, 'Finding Balmikis', *Economic and Political Weekly*, Vol. 54, No. 14, 12 October 2019, pp. 43–50.

35 Nicolas Jaoul, 'Casting the Sweepers: Local Politics of Sanskritization, Caste and Labour', in D. Bertie, N. Jaoul and Pralay Kanungo (eds), *Cultural Entrenchment of Hindutva: Local Mediations and Forms of Convergence* (Routledge, 2011), pp. 273–306.

36 S.K. Gupta, *The Scheduled Castes in Modern Indian Politics: The Emergence as a Political Power* (Munshiram Manoharlal Pvt. Ltd, 1985).

37 Rajiv Atwal, 'Finding Balmikis', Economic and Political Weekly, Vol. 54, No. 14, 12 October 2019, pp. 43–50. Mukhopadhyay also drew our attention to the role of these organizations.

38 Joel Lee, *Deceptive Majority Dalits, Hinduism, and Underground Religion* (UK: Cambridge University Press, 2021).

39 V. Prasad, 'The Killing of Bala Shah and the Birth of Valmiki: Hinduisation and the Politics of Religion', *The Indian Economic and Social History Review*, Vol. 32, No. 3, 1995, pp. 287–325.

40 V. Prasad, *Untouchable Freedom: A Social History of a Dalit Community* (New Delhi: Oxford University Press, 2000).

41 The Constitution {Scheduled Castes} Order, 1950: 163, quoted in Atwal, 2019: 49.

42 Nandini Gooptu, 'Caste and Labour: Untouchable Social Movements in Urban UP in the Early Twentieth Century,' in Peter Robb (ed.), *Dalit Movement and the Meanings of Labour in India* (New Delhi: Oxford University Press, 1993), pp. 280–298.

43 Ibid.: 292.

44 Bhagwan Das, *Balmiki Jayanti aur Bhangi Jatiyan*, Delhi: Gautam Book Centre, 1981.

45 Nandini Gooptu, 'Caste and Labour: Untouchable Social Movements in Urban UP in the Early Twentieth Century,' in Peter Robb (ed.), *Dalit Movement and the Meanings of Labour in India* (New Delhi: Oxford University Press), 1993, p. 193.

46 Ibid.: 190.

47 Sudheendra Kulkarni in our interaction with him on 22 December 2021.

48 See Nilanjan Mukhopadhyay, *The RSS: Icons of the Indian Right* (New Delhi: Tranquebar Press, 2019).

49 Mukhopadhyay and Kulkarni also mentioned the role of the RSS in our interaction and linked it to present-day politics.

50 Christophe Jaffrelot quoted in Mukhopadhyay, 2019: 259. Sudheendra Kulkarni also mentioned in our interaction with him on 22 December 2021.

51 Ibid.

52 'This series of lectures was begun by Justice M.G. Ranade in 1875 along with Bal Gangadhar Tilak and were aimed at reviving intellectual discourse in society and provided a platform for speakers to exchange views on various topics. The RSS began to use this platform to address its *swayamsevaks* and to put forward new ideas and methods of reforming Hindu society. Nilanjan Mukhopadhyay, *The RSS: Icons of the Indian Right* (New Delhi: Tranquebar Press, 2019), p. 284.

53 Ibid.

54 Mukhopadhyay in our interaction with him on 9 January 2022.

55 Ibid.

56 Ibid.

57 Ibid.

58 See Chapter 1, part II.

59 'Eying Dalits and backwards, RSS plans nationwide campaign for Hindu unity', *The Economic Times*/PTI, 11 December 2015.

60 In our interaction, Swapan Dasgupta mentioned that while Modi personally was not very keen on playing out his OBC identity, the party prevailed over him.

61   Sudheendra Kulkarni in our interaction with him on 22 December 2021.
62   Badri Narayan, 'In Narendra Modi's model village, development has a caste', Catch News, 13 February 2017, http://www. catchnews.com/india-news/in-narendra-modi-s-model-village-development-has-a-caste-1445878063.html

7: Azad, Bhim Army and Other Ambedkarite Fragments

1   The organizations in Meerut city in the 1990s were of two types: cultural and political. The former consisted of caste panchayats or mahasabhas that met whenever there was a common problem facing the community or an atrocity against Dalits. The second, formed by educated leaders – lawyers or teachers– good examples in 1994 being the Samyukta Dalit Morcha, the Akhil Bharatiya Jan Kalyan Ambedkar Samiti, the Dr Ambedkar Suddhar Samiti, the Dalit Shiksha Andolan, etc. For details see Sudha Pai, *Dalit Assertion and the Unfinished Democratic Revolution: The BSP in Uttar Pradesh* (New Delhi: Sage Publications, 2002), p. 202.
2   Sudha Pai, *Dalit Assertion and the Unfinished Democratic Revolution: The BSP in Uttar Pradesh* (New Delhi: Sage Publications, 2002).
3   Nicolas Jaoul, 'Political and "Non-Political" Means in the Dalit Movement', in Sudha Pai (ed.), *Political Process in Uttar Pradesh: Identity, Economic Reform and Governance* (New Delhi: Pearson Longman, 2007), pp.191–220.
4   Sudha Pai, *Dalit Assertion*, 2002, see Chapter 5.
5   Kanshi Ram, *Chamcha Yug* (Aligarh: Anand Sahitya Sadan, 2016).
6   G.W. Briggs, *The Chamars* (London: 1920).
7   Badri Narayan, 'Scattered and Invisible', *The Times of India*, 15 December 2016.
8   'Dalit group recalls its 1857 martyr Uda Devi', *The Times of India*, 16 November 2015.
9   This section draws on Sudha Pai, 'New Phase in Dalit Politics: Crisis or Regeneration', in K. Raju (ed.), *The Dalit Truth The Battles for Realizing Ambedkar's Vision* (New Delhi: Penguin Random House, 2022), and our interview with Azad on 10 August 2021 at the BA office in Gurgaon, unless otherwise stated.

10   A. Sethi, 'Ambedkar's army: A Dalit force fights caste atrocities
     in Uttar Pradesh', *The Quint*, Video, 2016, https://www.thequint.
     com/quintlab/ambedkar-dalit-army-fights-caste-atrocities-in-
     uttar-pradesh/

11   Hugo Gorringe and Suryakant Waghmore, 'Go write on the walls
     that you are the rulers of this nation: Dalit mobilization and the
     BJP', *Indian Politics and Policy*, Vol. 2, Issue No. 1, April 2019.

12   There are a large number of videos on YouTube of these rallies
     which have gone viral within the Dalit community.

13   A. Sethi, 2016.

14   Ibid.

15   Ibid. Azad described this incident in detail to us, as he considered
     it a major victory of the Dalits of the village.

16   'Ambedkarite 2.0: Saharanpur's Bhim Army signals the rise of a
     new, aggressive Dalit politics', *Scroll*, 8 February 2020.

17   A. Sethi, 2016.

18   Anand Teltumbde, 'Onslaughts on Dalits in the Time of Hindutva'
     in Niraja Gopal Jayal (ed.), *Re-Forming India: The Nation Today*
     (New Delhi: Penguin Random House, 2020), pp. 363–82.

19   Shalini Rajvanshi, 'What is the Bhim Army?' *The Indian Express*,
     New Delhi, 18 May 2018.

20   Sudha Pai and Sajjan Kumar, 'Saharanpur protests herald new
     phase in Dalit politics', *The Wire*, 24 May 2017.

21   Field work by Sajjan Kumar in May–June 2017, soon after the
     violent incidents in Saharanpur reported in Sudha Pai and Sajjan
     Kumar, 'Saharanpur protests herald new phase in Dalit politics',
     The Wire, 24 May 2017.

22   Ibid.

23   Rehnamol Raveedran, 'Bhim Army and Azad Samaj Party mark a
     new phase of Dalit assertion', *The Indian Express*, 18 March 2020.

24   Discussion with a person close to the BA who did not wish to be
     named, 8 June 2020.

25   Field work by Sajjan Kumar in May-June 2017, soon after the
     violent incidents in Saharanpur reported in Sudha Pai and Sajjan
     Kumar, 'Saharanpur protests herald new phase in Dalit politics',
     The Wire, 24 May 2017.

26   'Won't tie-up with SP even for 100 seats now, says Chandrashekhar
     Azad', *Business Standard*/PTI, 18 January 2022.

27   'Bhim Army's Chandrashekhar Azad loses to Yogi in Gorakhpur,
     forfeits deposit', hindustantimes.com, 11 March 2022.

28   Rehnamol Raveedran, 'Bhim Army and Azad Samaj Party mark a new phase of Dalit assertion', *The Indian Express*, 18 March 2020.

29   'CAA: Bhim Army chief Chandrashekhar Azad denied permission for Delhi protest march', *India Today* web desk, 20 December 2019, https://www.indiatoday.in/india/story/caa-protests-chandra shekhar-azad-denied-permission-protest-march-jama-masjid-jantar-mantar-1629941-2019-12-20

30   'EWS is the section of the society in India that belongs to the unreserved category and has an annual family income of less than 8 lakh rupees. This category includes people that do not belong to the caste categories of ST/SC/OBC who already enjoy the benefits of reservation. The Government of India through a constitutional amendment on 8 January 2019 introduced a 10% reservation to this category of people who are not included in the ST/SC/OBC category but belong to the unreserved category and fulfill the economically weaker section criteria.' In 'In-depth: Who is eligible for the new reservation quota for general category?' *BusinessToday*, 8 January 2019.

31   Interview with Shravan Kumar Nirala in Gorakhpur on 23–24 January 2022 and once again in Delhi on 15 April 2022.

32   Telephonic interview with Daddu Prasad on 3 April 2022. We were also told about him at length by Nirala as they had both been part of the BSP.

33   'Mayawati used to sell party tickets: Expelled BSP leader', *The Economic Times*/PTI, 29 January 2015.

34   'Aur Daddu Prasad ne banali "Bahujan Mukti Party"', ABP live, 25 December 2016, https://www.abplive.com/news/states/ex-bsp-leader-daddu-prasad-524723

35   Pankaj Shah, 'Rebel BSP leader Daddu Prasad rejoins party', *The Times of India*, 31 March 2017.

8: *Fragmentation of the Dalit Movement in UP*

1   Sudha Pai, *Dalit Assertion and the Unfinished Democratic Revolution: The BSP in Uttar Pradesh* (New Delhi: Sage Publications, 2002), p. 27.

2   Ibid.

3   Walter Neale, *Economic Change in Rural India Land Tenures and Reform in UP 1800–1955* (New Haven: Yale University Press, 1962).

4   M.C. Rajah or Mylai Chinna Thambi Pillai Rajah was a politician, educationist, social and political activist belonging to Tamil Nadu. A senior leader in the Justice Party, he was the Secretary of the Adi Dravida Mahajan Society in Madras province and had established himself as the leader of the depressed classes by the time Dr Ambedkar returned to India in 1917.

5   Gyanendra Pandey, *The Ascendancy of the Congress in UP 1926–34: A Study in Imperfect Mobilization* (New Delhi: OUP, 1978), p. 206.

6   Gopinath Srivastava, *When Congress Ruled 1937-38* (Lucknow: Upper India Book House).

7   Badri Narayan, *The Making of the Dalit Public in North India: Uttar Pradesh, 1950–Present* (New Delhi: OUP, 2011).

8   Ian R. Duncan, *Levels, the Communication of Programmes and Sectional Strategies in Indian Politics with Special Reference to the BKD and the RPI in UP State and Aligarh District*, Unpublished thesis, University of Sussex, 1979.

9   Peter Reeves, 'Changing Pattern of Political Alignments in the GEs to the UP Legislative Assembly, 1937 and 1946', *Modern Asian Studies*, Vol. 5, No. 2, 1971, pp. 111–142. The election was held under a system of double-member constituencies as per the Poona Pact of 1932, which had granted representation to the Depressed classes. The elections were held in two stages for the reserved seats. In the first stage only the SCs voted for the SC candidates, the second round was not obligatory except when more than four candidates were in the fray. The Congress usually put up one candidate, but the UPSCF usually put up more than four candidates to force a contest. Accordingly, in the second stage the seat became a general seat because the caste Hindus also voted. In these double-member constituencies the voter had two votes, with an option to use them to vote for two general candidates or the two SC candidates, or one each. Both the SCs and Hindus had two votes each. In this situation, the latter played an important role in the election of a SC candidate. They, who were also larger in number, tended to vote for the candidate of the Congress, rather than of the SC party. Thus, despite the SCs being granted reserved seats and enjoying support of their own community, the Congress had a clear advantage (Reeves, 1971: 116).

10 Sekhar Bandhopadhyay, 'Transfer of Power and the Crisis of Dalit Politics in India, 1945–47', *Modern Asian Studies*, Vol. 34, No. 4, 2000, pp. 893–942.

11   Ram Narayan, *The Making of the Scheduled Caste Community in Uttar Pradesh: A Study of the SCF and Dalit Politics 1946-48*, M.Phil Thesis, Department of History, Delhi University, 1996, p. 64.

12   Ibid.

13   Ibid.: p. 121.

14   Ian R. Duncan, *Levels, the Communication of Programmes and Sectional Strategies in Indian Politics with Special Reference to the BKD and the RPI in UP State and Aligarh District*, Unpublished thesis, University of Sussex, 1979.

15   Yashwant Ambedkar (12 December 1912–17 September 1977), one of the founder members of the RPI also known as Bhaiyasaheb Ambedkar, was the first and only surviving child of Ramabai Ambedkar and B.R. Ambedkar. The others were all founder members of the RPI and had been associates of Ambedkar.

16   Ibid.: p. 229.

19   Ibid.: p. 245.

20   Paul Brass, *Caste, Faction and Party in Indian Politics Vol. 2: Election Studies* (New Delhi: Chanakya Publication, 1985).

21   Ibid.

22   Jagpal Singh, 'Ambedkarisation and assertion of Dalit identity: Socio-cultural protest in Meerut district of western Uttar Pradesh', *Economic and Political Weekly*, Vol. 32, No. 4, 3 October 1998, pp. 2611–18.

23   Ibid.

24   Brewer Stone, 'Institutionalized Decay and Traditionalization of Politics: The UP Congress Party', *Asian Survey*, Vol. 27, No. 10, October 1998, p. 1018.

25   A recent example is the visit by the Prime Minister to the Ravidas Vishram Dham Mandir in Karol Bagh area of Delhi on 16 February 2022 on the occasion of Ravidas Jayanti, where he participated in the *kirtan* (prayers) organized by locals. 'PM Modi participates in "shabad kirtan" at Ravidas Temple; sparks meme-fest on Twitter', BusinessToday.in, 16 February 2022.

26   By the early 1990s, the top leadership profile of both the Congress and the BJP was dominated by the upper castes, though the BJP started witnessing the emergence of popular OBC leaders like Kalyan Singh, Uma Bharti, Vinay Katiyar, among others.

27   For instance, in multiple visits between January and June 2017 during Sajjan Kumar's field study at Jatav Nagar, a Dalit locality

in Saharanpur, the politics of cultural symbolism informed the Jatav households. The BJP and Hindutva minded Jatav Dalits displayed pictures of Ravidas, Ambedkar and, in many cases, Kanshi Ram along with the images of Hindu gods and deities, while BSP supporters' households contained images of Buddha, Ambedkar, Kanshi Ram, Mayawati and icons like Phule and Periyar, with the complete absence of pictures of any Hindu gods.

28 See Chapter 4.

29 There is a spatial pattern of different Dalit castes residing significantly in different sub-regions of Uttar Pradesh. Various Census reports highlight this pattern. Also see Badri Narayan, *The Making of the Dalit Public in North India: Uttar Pradesh, 1950-Present* (New Delhi: OUP, 2011); *Fascinating Hindutva: Saffron Politics and Dalit Mobilisation* (New Delhi: Sage Publications, 2011); and *Republic of Hindutva: How the Sangh Is Reshaping Indian Democracy* (New Delhi: Penguin, 2021).

　　Also see books by Vijay Sonkar Shashtri, a Khatik Dalit and leader of the BJP in UP, *Hindu Charmakar Jati* (New Delhi: Prabhat Prakashan, 2014); *Hindu Valmiki Jati* (New Delhi: Prabhat Prakashan, 2014); *Hindu Khatik Jati* (New Delhi: Prabhat Prakashan, 2014); *Dalit–Muslim Rajneetik Gathjod* (New Delhi: Prabhat Prakashan, 2019).

30 These field studies were undertaken by Sajjan Kumar to map the political shifts in Uttar Pradesh as part of Peoples Pulse, a Hyderabad-based research organization.

31 Ibid.

32 From the fieldwork conducted by Sajjan Kumar in Purvanchal region in August 2015.

33 Fieldwork conducted by Sajjan Kumar in Purvanchal during 9–22 January 2022.

Epilogue

1 Ashish Mehta, 'In UP a mad melee to appropriate Ambedkar's legacy, the BSP's vote bank', News9, 14 April 2022.

2 Ibid.

3 Syed Kamran, 'Even a best ever vote share couldn't bring SP to power. What can it do to improve?' *The Wire*, 1 April 2022.

4 Ibid.

5   Santosh Mehrotra, 'As Uttar Pradesh heads to polls, how does
    the Yogi govt's economic performance hold up?' *The Wire*, 20
    December 2021.
6   Though this remark was made to polarize Hindus and Muslims,
    Adityanath argued that he meant 80 per cent support to the
    BJP, while 20 per cent always oppose; it was not about caste
    or religion. '80 vs 20 remark not in context of religion: Yogi
    Adityanath', *The Indian Express*, 14 February 2022.
7   'Chunav Manch 2022: Yogi Adityanath tears into Akhilesh, SP;
    calls alliance with RLD opportunism | Highlights', IndiaTV, 29
    January 2022.
8   Sudha Pai, 'From Lucknow to Delhi: The stakes in UP's assembly
    elections', The India Forum, 22 December 2021, https://www.
    theindiaforum.in/article/lucknow-today-india-tomorrow
9   '"Mathura next": Keshav Prasad Maurya's big remark ahead of
    UP polls', IndiaTV, 1 December 2021.
10 Saba Naqvi, 'Five Muslim candidates: Winners and losers beyond
    the polarisation analysis', substack.com (Unsaid Truth), 11
    March 2022.
11 Jyoti Mishra, 'The labharti factor', *The Hindu*, 12 March
    2022,https://www.thehindu.com/elections/uttar-pradesh-
    assembly/the-labharthi-factor/article65215837.ece.
12 For details, see the tables in Jyoti Mishra, 'The labharti factor',
    The Hindu, 12 March 2022, https://www.thehindu.com/elections/
    uttar-pradesh-assembly/the-labharthi-factor/article65215837.ece
13 During the election campaign Akhiliesh Yadav formed a new
    wing of his party the Baba Sahib Vahini, based on the ideals of
    Baba Saheb Ambedkar. Mithai Lal Bharti who had left the BSP
    to join the SP, was made the President. It had a state level office
    and branches in all districts. With the BSP in decline, by invoking
    Ambedkar, Yadav hoped to obtain the votes of the Dalits. Dinesh
    Rathore, 'Akhilesh Yadav created a new wing of the party! The
    leader who came from the BSP to SP was made the President',
    Hindustan, 17 October 2021.
14 Aditi Phadnis, 'BJP likely to win Uttar Pradesh but with smaller
    mandate, says Sudha Pai', *Business Standard*, 20 January 2021.
15 The Mandal Commission was set up in 1979 to determine the
    criteria to identify the socially and educationally backward
    classes in India and recommend steps to be taken for their
    advancement. The report of the Commission was accepted and

implemented by PM V.P. Singh on 7 August 1990. Based on its rationale that other backward classes identified on the basis of caste, social, economic indicators made up 52 per cent of India's population, the commission's report recommended that members of other backward classes (OBC) be granted reservations to 27 per cent of jobs under the Central government and public sector undertakings. As a consequence, by the 2000s the OBCs, particularly the smaller caste groups, had become politically conscious and economically aspirational. Prior to the 2022 UP assembly elections, although the BJP had mobilized and catered to their demands, there were murmurs of discontent among groups such as the Patels, Nishads etc. It was this expansion of the Mandal groups to the smaller, upwardly mobile group, who were unhappy with the BJP, that led Akhilesh Yadav to try and gain the support of the smaller groups. 'Sunday Story: Mandal Commission report, 25 years later', *The Indian Express News Service*, 1 September 2015.

16 Ibid.
17 Sandeep Shastri, 'The Hindu Religious polarisation and electoral choices', *The Hindu*, 12 March 2022.
18 Ibid.
19 Sudha Pai, 'How Mandir triumphed over Mandal', *The Indian Express*, 17 March 2022.
20 On Mandal see endnote 15. The term 'forces of Mandal' refers to the politically conscious and volatile OBCs who in the 1990s had largely supported the SP or BSP. In the 2000s, the BJP had managed to mobilize large sections, but as they expressed their dissatisfaction with the party prior to the 2022 election, particularly the smaller, newly empowered groups, the SP under Akhilesh hoped to regain their support and thereby defeat the BJP. See, Sudha Pai, 'Mulayam Singh Yadav's politics of secularism, socialism and social justice remains relevant today', *The Indian Express*, 14 October 2022.
21 Kamandal or kamandalam is an oblong water pot, made of a dry gourd (pumpkin) or coconut shell, metal, wood of the Kamandalataru tree, or from clay, usually with a handle and sometimes with a spout. The water-filled kamandal, which is carried by ascetics, is stated to represent a simple and self-contained life. The use of religion-based mobilization and ideology of Hindutva of the BJP has led to it being described

as the forces of Kamandal as opposed to the forces of Mandal represented by parties such as the SP. On kamandal see, Eva Rudy Jansen, *The Book of Hindu Imagery: The Gods and their Symbols* (Binkey Kok Publications, 2004).

22 Ibid.

23 Ibid.

24 Sreya Chatterjee, 'UP polls: "Only vote for BSP," says Mayawati as she kicks-off election campaign in Agra', *India Today*, 2 Feburary 2022.

25 Ibid.

26 Prabhash K. Dutta, 'Curious case of Mayawati's campaign in Uttar Pradesh Assembly election', *India Today*, 4 February 2022.

27 Aryan Prakash, 'President Mayawati? What BSP chief said on rumours about offer from BJP', *Hindustan Times*, 27 March 2022.

28 Ibid.

29 Hemendra Chaturvedi, 'Mayawati promises to restore names of districts after Dalit personalities', *Hindustan Times*, 7 February 2022.

30 Prabhash K. Dutta, 'Curious case of Mayawati's campaign in Uttar Pradesh Assembly election', *India Today*, 4 February 2022.

31 The fieldwork was done in two rounds, from 15 to 16 October 2021 in West UP and from 28 January to 5 February 2022 in Purvanchal. We talked to the Dalit villagers in their localities and to a wide range of Dalit intellectuals, journalists and academics in universities.

32 Namita Bajpai, 'Mayawati brings sweeping changes to party after poll drubbing, reposes faith in kin, caste', *The Indian Express*, 23 March 2022.

33 Ibid.

34 Lalmani Verma, 'Mayawati makes a Jatav Dalit MP the leader of BSP in Lok Sabha', *The Indian Express*, 16 March 2022.

35 Ibid.

36 Ibid.

37 Namita Bajpai, 'Mayawati brings sweeping changes to party after poll drubbing, reposes faith in kin, caste', *The Indian Express*, 23 March 2022.

38 Ibid.

39 Rashmi Sharma, 'Uttar Pradesh: Mayawati blames SP and Muslims for poll debacle, makes major changes in party',The Free Press, 27 March 2022.

40 Ibid.

41 Harish Khare, 'By quitting as MP, Akhilesh shows the fightback against Modi must begin from Lucknow', *The Wire*, 25 March 2022.

42 Partha Chatterjee, 'Populism Plus', *The India Forum*, 30 May 2019.

43 Gyanesh Kudaisya, *Region, Nation, 'Heartland': Uttar Pradesh in India's Body Politic* (New Delhi: Sage Publications, 2006).

44 Kaushik Deka, 'Why Arvind Kejriwal cannot hope to fight Narendra Modi without Congress', *India Today*, 10 March 2022.

45 Namita Bajpai, 'Free ration scheme for 15 crore people in UP may be extended till 2024 Lok Sabha polls', *The New Indian Express*, 16 March 2022.

46 Vikas Bhandari, 'New UP cabinet: Poor performing ministers from Yogi govt first term to not get berth | Check probable list', ABP Live, 17 March 2022.

47 Ibid.

48 Himanshu Jha, 'BJP in preparation for big changes in Uttar Pradesh, Sunil Bansal, close to Amit Shah, will also be transferred', *Hindustan*, 8 May 2022.

49 Ibid.

50 Sudhindhra Bhadoria, telephonic discussion on 12 March 2022.

Bibliography

Reports and Unpublished Thesis

Census of India. UP 2011. District Census Handbook, Series 10 Part XII - A. Primary Census Abstract.

Centre for the Study of Developing Societies (CSDS) National Election Study, UP Post Poll Election Data and Caste-based voting Data: 2014, 2019 Lok Sabha and 2007, 2012, 2017, 2022 Assembly Elections.

Reports of the Election Commission of India: 2014 and 2019 Lok Sabha and 2007, 2012 and 2022 UP Assembly.

Bharatiya Janata Party 'Manifesto 2014' n.d. www.bjp.org/ manifesto 2014

Duncan, Ian R. 1979. *Levels, the Communication of Programmes and Sectional Strategies in Indian Politics with special reference to the BKD and the RPI in UP State and Aligarh District.* Unpublished thesis, University of Sussex.

Narayan, Ram. 1996. *The Making of the Scheduled Caste Community in Uttar Pradesh: A Study of the SCF and Dalit Politics 1946–48*: p. 64. MPhil Thesis, Department of History, Delhi University.

Kumar, Sajjan. 'Political Dynamism and Electoral Determinism', unpublished PhD thesis, *Hindutva, Mandal and State Security Discourses: Reconstitution of Muslim Identity Since the 1980s,* Centre for Political Studies, Jawaharlal Nehru University, 2016.

Books

Ahuja, Amit. *Mobilizing the Marginalized: Ethnic Parties without Ethnic Movements.* Modern South Asia, Oxford University Press, USA 2019.

Akela A.R. *Kanshi Ram Saahab Ke Sakshat Kaar* (Interviews with Kanshi Ram). Aligarh: Anand Sahitya Sadan, 2006.

Andersen, Walter. 'The BJP: A Victory for Narendra Modi'. In *India's 2014 Elections: A Modi-led Sweep,* edited by Paul Wallace, pp. 46–64. New Delhi: Sage Publications, 2015.

Berti, Daniela, Nicolas Jaoul, and Pralay Kanungo (eds). *Cultural Entrenchment of Hindutva: Local Mediations and Forms of Convergence.* New Delhi: Taylor & Francis, 2011.

Bose, Ajoy. *Behenji: A Political Biography of Mayawati.* New Delhi: Penguin Random House, 2017.

Brass, Paul R. *Caste, Faction and Party in Indian Politics. Vol. 2, Election Studies.* Delhi: Chanakya Publications, Delhi, 1985.

Brass, Paul R. *Ethnicity and Nationalism: Theory and Comparison.* CA: Sage Publications, 1991.

Briggs, George Weston. *The Chamārs. Vol. 3.* Calcutta: Association Press, 1920.

Chatterji, Angana P., Thomas Blom Hansen and Christophe Jaffrelot (eds). *Majoritarian State: How Hindu nationalism is changing India.* New Delhi: Oxford University Press, 2019.

Chaturvedi, Swati. *I am a Troll: Inside the Secret World of the BJP's Digital Army.* New Delhi: Juggernaut Books, 2016.

Das, Bhagvan. *Balmiki Jayanti aur Bhangi Jatiyan.* Delhi: Gautam Book Centre, 1981.

Dubey, Abhay Kumar. 'Anatomy of a Dalit Player: A Study of Kanshi Ram'. In *Dalit Identity and Politics,* edited by Ghanshyam Shah, pp. 289–310. New Delhi: Sage Publications, 2001.

Dumont, Louis. *Homo Hierarchicus: The Caste System and its Implications.* Chicago: University of Chicago Press, 1970.

Gooptu, Nandini. 'Caste and Labour: Untouchable Social Movements in Urban UP in the Early Twentieth Century.' In *Dalit Movement and the Meanings of Labour in India,* edited by Peter Robb, pp. 280–298. New Delhi: OUP, 1993.

Gorringe, Hugo. *Untouchable Citizens: Dalit Movements and Democratization in Tamil Nadu. Vol. 4.* New Delhi: Sage Publications, 2005.

Gupta, Smita. 'The Rise and Fall of Hindutva in Uttar Pradesh, 1989-2004'. In *Political Process in Uttar Pradesh: Identity, Economic Reforms and Governance,* edited by Sudha Pai, pp. 110–135. New Delhi: Pearson Longman, 2007.

Gupta, Surinder K. *The Scheduled Castes in Modern Indian Politics: Their Emergence as a Political Power.* New Delhi: Munshiram Manoharlal, 1985.

Herman, Edward S. and Noam Chomsky. *Manufacturing Consent: The Political Economy of the Mass Media*. New York: Pantheon,1988.

Hobsbawm, Eric, and Terence Ranger (eds). *The Invention of Tradition*. Cambridge: Cambridge University Press, 2012.

Jaoul, Nicolas. 'Political and Non-Political Means in the Dalit Movement.' In *Political Process in Uttar Pradesh: Identity, Economic Reform and Governance*, edited by Sudha Pai, pp. 191–220. New Delhi: Pearson Longman, 2007.

Jaoul, Nicolas. 'Casting the Sweepers: Local Politics of Sanskritization Caste and Labour.' In *Cultural Entrenchment of Hindutva: Local Mediations and Forms of Convergence*, edited by D. Bertie, N. Jaoul and Pralay Kanungo, pp. 273–306. New Delhi, Routledge, 2011.

Jayal, Niraja Gopal. *Re-forming India: The Nation Today*. New Delhi: Penguin Random House, 2019.

Jha, Prashant. *How the BJP Wins: Inside India's Greatest Election Machine*. New Delhi: Juggernaut Books, 2017.

Juergensmeyer, Mark. *Religious Rebels in the Punjab: The Social Vision of Untouchables*. New Delhi: ⬚janta Publication, 1988.

Kudaisya, Gyanesh. *Region, Nation, 'Heartland': Uttar Pradesh in India's Body Politic*. Vol. 10. New Delhi: Sage Publications India, 2006.

Kumar, Vivek. 'Bahujan Samaj Party: Some Issues of Democracy and Dominance.' In *Political Process in Uttar Pradesh: Identity, Economic Reforms and Governance*, edited by Sudha Pai, pp. 241–272. New Delhi: Pearson Longman, 2007.

Lee, Joel. *Deceptive Majority: Dalits, Hinduism and Underground Religion*. Cambridge: Cambridge University Press, 2021.

Lynch, Owen Martin. *The Politics of Untouchability: Social Structure and Social Change in a City of India.* Columbia: Columbia University Press, 1969

Mooij, Jos.(ed). *The Politics of Economic Reforms in India.* New Delhi: Sage Publications, 2005.

Mukhopadhyay, Nilanjan. *The RSS: Icons of the Indian Right.* New Delhi: Tranquebar, 2019.

Narayan, Badri. *Fascinating Hindutva: Saffron Politics and Dalit Mobilisation.* New Delhi: Sage Publications, 2009.

Narayan, Badri. *The Making of the Dalit Public in North India: Uttar Pradesh, 1950–Present.* New Delhi: Oxford University Press, 2011.

Narayan, Badri. *Republic of Hindutva: How the Sangh is Reshaping Indian Democracy.* New Delhi: Penguin Random House, 2021.

Neale, Walter C. *Economic change in rural India. Land tenure and reform in Uttar Pradesh, 1800-1955.* Yale University Press, 1962.

Pai, Sudha. *Dalit Assertion and the Unfinished Democratic Revolution: The Bahujan Samaj Party in Uttar Pradesh.* New Delhi: Sage Publications, 2002.

Pai, Sudha "Populism and Economic Reform: the BJP Experiment in Uttar Pradesh" in *Politics of Economic Reform in India,* edited by Jos Mooij, pp. 72–98. New Delhi: Sage Publications, 2005.

Pai, Sudha (ed.). *Political Process in Uttar Pradesh: Identity, Economic Reforms, and Governance.* New Delhi: Pearson Education India, 2007.

Pai, Sudha 'From Dalit to Savarna: The Search for a New Social Constituency by the Bahujan Samaj Party in Uttar Pradesh'. In *Political Process in Uttar Pradesh Identity, Economic*

Reforms and Governance, edited by Sudha Pai, pp. 192–121. New Delhi: Pearson Longman, 2007

Pai, Sudha. *Developmental State and the Dalit Question in Madhya Pradesh: Congress Response*. New Delhi: Routledge India, 2010.

Pai, Sudha. 'From Social Justice to Aspiration: Transformation of Lower Caste Politics in Uttar Pradesh in the 2000s.' In *Neoliberalism, Urbanisation and Aspirations in Contemporary India*, edited by Sujata Patel, pp. 212–232. New Delhi: OUP, 2021.

Pai, Sudha. 'New Phase in Dalit Politics: Crisis or Regeneration.' In *The Dalit Truth The Battles for Realizing Ambedkar's Vision*, edited by K. Raju, pp. 105-115. New Delhi: Penguin Random House, 2022.

Pai, Sudha and Avinash Kumar. 'Understanding the BJP's Victory in Uttar Pradesh.' In *India's 2014 Elections: A Modi-led Sweep*, edited byPaul Wallace, pp. 119–138.New Delhi: Sage Publication, 2015.

Pai, Sudha, and Sajjan Kumar. *Everyday Communalism*. New Delhi: Oxford University Press, 2018.

Pandey, Gyanendra. *The Ascendancy of the Congress in Uttar Pradesh*. New Delhi: Oxford University Press, 1978.

Patel, Sujata. *Neoliberalism, Urbanization and Aspirations in Contemporary India*. New Delhi: Oxford University Press, 2022.

Prasad, V. *Untouchable Freedom: A Social History of a Dalit Community*. New Delhi: Oxford University Press, 2000.

Raju, K. *The Dalit Truth (Rethinking India series): The Battles for Realizing Ambedkar's Vision*. New Delhi: Penguin Random House, 2022.

Ram, Kanshi. *Chamcha Yug* (The Era of Stooges). Aligarh: Anand Sahitya Sadan, 2016.

Ramakrishnan, Venkitesh (ed). *Uttar Pradesh–The Road Ahead.* New Delhi: Academic Foundation, 2009.

Ramakrishnan, Venkitesh 'The New Consensus Needs a Socio-political Ideology'. In *Uttar Pradesh: the Road Ahead,* edited by Venkitesh Ramakrishnan, pp. 61-65. New Delhi: Academic Foundation in collaboration with the Observer Research Foundation, 2009.

Rao, Vijayendra and Michael Walton (eds.). *Culture and Public Action.* Hyderabad: Orient Blackswan, 2004.

Robb, Peter (ed.). *Dalit Movements and the Meanings of Labour in India.* New Delhi: OUP, 1993.

Sardesai, Rajdeep. *The Election That Changed India.* New Delhi: Penguin, 2015.

Saxena, Gulshan Swarup. *Arya Samaj Movement in India, 1875–1947.* New Delhi: South Asia Books, 1990.

Shah, Ghanshyam (ed.). *Dalit Identity and Politics.* New Delhi: Sage Publications, 2001.

Sharma, Kanhaiya Lal (ed.). *Caste and Class in India.* Jaipur: Rawat Publications, 1994.

Shastri, Vijay S. *Hindu Charmakar Jati.* Delhi: Prabhat Prakashan, 2016.

Shastri, Vijay S. *Hindu Khatik Jati.* Delhi: Prabhat Prakashan, 2016.

Shastri, Vijay S. *Hindu Valmiki Jati.* Delhi: Prabhat Prakashan, 2016.

Shastri, Vijay S. *Dalit-Muslim Rajneetik Gathjod.* Delhi: Prabhat Prakashan, 2019.

Singh, Ajit K. 'The Economy of Uttar Pradesh since the 1990s.' In *Political Process in Uttar Pradesh Identity, Economic Reforms and Governance,* edited by Sudha Pai, pp. 273–294. New Delhi: Pearson Longman, 2007.

Singh, Mohinder. *The Depressed Classes: Their Economic and Social Condition*. New Delhi: Hind Kitabh, 1947

Srivastava, Gopinath. *When Congress Ruled 1937–38*. Lucknow: Upper India Book House, 1939.

Swaminathan, Siddharth, and Suhas Palshikar (eds). *Politics and Society between Elections: Public Opinion in the Indian States*, South Asia Edition. New Delhi: Routledge, 2021.

Swarup, Anand. 'Governance of Uttar Pradesh: A Case Study for Effective Restructuring'. In *Uttar Pradesh: The Road Ahead,* edited by Venkitesh Ramakrishnan, pp. 121-134. New Delhi: Academic Foundation, 2009.

Teltumbde, Anand. 'Onslaughts on Dalits in the Time of Hindtuva.' In *Re-Forming India: The Nation Today*, edited by Niraja Gopal Jayal, pp. 363–382. New Delhi: Penguin Random House, 2020.

Tyagi Hari Singh, 'New Social Consensus in UP: Problems and Possibilities'. In *Uttar Pradesh: the Road Ahead,* edited by Venkitesh Ramakrishnan, pp. 47–54. New Delhi: Academic Foundation, 2009.

Vaishnav, Milan. *Religious Nationalism and India's Future*. Carnegie Endowment for International Peace, 2019.

Wallace, Paul (ed.). *India's 2019 Elections: The Hindutva Wave and Indian Nationalism*. Sage Publications, 2020.

Wallace, Paul (ed.). *India's 2014 Elections: A Modi-led BJP Sweep*, Sage Publications India, 2015.

Articles

Atwal, Rajiv. 'Finding Balmikis.' *Economic and Political Weekly*, Vol. 54, No. 14 (12 October 2019): 43–50.

Bandhopadhyay, Sekhar. 'Transfer of Power and the Crisis of Dalit Politics in India, 1945–47.' *Modern Asian Studies*, Vol. 34, No. 4, (2000): 893–942.

Belli Melia. 'Monumental pride: Mayawati's memorials in Lucknow', *Ars Orientalis*, Vol. 44, 2014 https://quod.lib.umich.edu/a/ars/13441566.0044.006/--monumental-pride-mayawatis-memorials-in-lucknow?rgn=main;view=fulltext

Bhagat, R.B. and S.Mohanty. 'Emerging Pattern of Urbanziation and the Contribution of Migration in Urban Growth in India.' *Asian Population Studies*, Vol. 5, No.1 (2009): 5–20.

Chibber, Pradeep and Rahul Verma. 'The Rise of the Second Dominant Party System in India: BJP's New Social Coalition.' *Studies in Indian Politics*, Vol. 7, no. 2 (2019): 131–148.

Duncan, Ian. 'Dalits and politics in rural North India: Bahujan Samaj party in Uttar Pradesh'. *The Journal of Peasant Studies*, Vol. 27, No. 1 (1999): 35–60.

Gorringe, Hugo and Suryakant Waghmore. 'Go Write on the Walls that you are the Rulers of this Nation: Dalit Mobilization and the BJP.' *Indian Politics and Policy*, Vol. 2, No. 1 (April 2019): 31–52.

Gundameda, Sambiah. 'The Bahujan Samaj Party: Between Social Justice and Political Practice'. *Social Change*, Vol. 44, No.1 (2014): 21–38.

Gupta, Dipankar and Yogesh Kumar, 'When the Caste Calculus Fails: Analysing BSP's Victory in UP'. *Economic and Political Weekly*, Vol. 33, No.33 (18 August 2007): 3383-3396

Heath, Oliver and Sanjay Kumar. 'Why Did Dalits Desert the BSP in UP.' *Economic and Political Weekly*, Vol. 47, No. 28 (14 July 2012): 14-44

Jaffrelot, Christophe. 'Class and Caste in the 2019 Indian Election–Why Have So Many Poor Started Voting for Modi?' *Studies in Indian Politics*, Vol. 7, No. 2 (2019): 1–19.

Kumar, Pradeep. 'Dalits and the BSP in UP Issues and Challenges.' *Economic and Political Weekly*, Vol. 34, No. 14 (3 April 1999): 822–6.

Neale, Walter C. 'Economic Change in Rural India. Land Tenure and Reform in Uttar Pradesh, 1800–1955.' *The American Historical Review*, Vol. 70, No.1 (October 1964): 172–174.

Pai Sudha "Pradhanis in the New Panchayats: Field Notes From Meerut", *Economic and Political Weekly*, 33 no18, (May 2 1998):1009-1010.

Pai, Sudha. 'Changing Political Preferences Among Dalits in Uttar Pradesh in the 2000s: Shift from Social Justice to Aspiration.' *Journal of Social Inclusion*, Vol. 5, No. 1 (19 July 2019): 33–43.

Palshikar, Suhas. 'Towards Hegemony: BJP beyond Electoral Dominance.' *Economic and Political Weekly*, Vol. 53, No. 33 (18 August 2018): 36–42

Prasad V. 'The Killing of Bala Shah and the Birth of Valmiki: Hinduisation and the Politics of Religion.' *The Indian Economic and Social History Review*, Vol. 32, No. 3, (1995): 287–325.

Reeves, Peter. 'Changing Pattern of Political Alignments in the GEs to the UP Legislative Assembly, 1937 and 1946.' *Modern Asian Studies*, Vol. 5, N. 2, (1971): 111–142.

Singh, Shyam. 'Three years of BSP government in UP.' *Economic and Political Weekly*, Vol. 45, No. 38 (18 September 2010): 77–81.

Singh, Jagpal. 'Ambedkarisation and Assertion of Dalit identity: Socio-cultural Protest in Meerut District of Western Uttar

Pradesh.' *Economic and Political Weekly*, Vol. 43, No. 40, (3 October 1998): 2611–18.

Stone, Brewer. 'Institutionalized Decay and Traditionalization of Politics: The UP Congress Party.' *Asian Survey* Vol. 27, No. 10 (October 1998): 1018-30.

Verma C.S. 'Maternal health services in Uttar Pradesh: Has JSY delivered?' *International Journal of Social Science and Development Policy*, Vol. 2, No. 1 (January–June 2016): 49–61.

Teltumbde, Anand. 'A Mayawi revolution.' *Economic and Political Weekly*, Vol. 42, No. 23 (9 June 2007): 2147–49.

Main websites accessed

https://thewire.in
https://theprint.in
https://www.indiatoday.in
https://scroll.in
Rediff.com
https://frontline.thehindu.com
https://m.timesofindia.com
https://indianexpress.com
https://m.patrika.com
https://economictimes.indiatimes.com
https://www.hindustantimes.com
https://epaper.thehindu.com/
https://www.business-standard.com

Index

291

About the Authors

Sudha Pai became interested in Dalit politics in the mid-1990s with the emergence of Mayawati on the political landscape, reflected in her book *Dalit Assertion and the Unfinished Democratic Revolution: The BSP in Uttar Pradesh* (Sage, India, 2002). She is the author of several books, including *Developmental State and the Dalit Question in Madhya Pradesh* (Routledge India, 2011) and *Everyday Communalism* (Oxford University Press, 2018).

Sajjan Kumar is a researcher and a political scientist. Currently, he is a Fellow at Nehru Memorial Museum and Library, New Delhi. His writing has been published in *The Hindu*, *Indian Express*, *The New Indian Express* and *The Times of India*, among others. He is associated with PRACCIS, a Delhi research Institution specializing in fieldwork based political research.